A Changing International Division of Labor

International Political Economy Yearbook, Volume 2

W. Ladd Hollist and F. LaMond Tullis, Series Editors

A Changing International Division of Labor

edited by James A. Caporaso

Lynne Rienner Publishers • Boulder
Frances Pinter (Publishers) • London

Published in the United States of America in 1987 by
Lynne Rienner Publishers, Inc.
948 North Street, Boulder, Colorado 80302

Published in Great Britain by Frances Pinter (Publishers) Ltd
25 Floral Street, London WC2E 9DS England

Library of Congress Cataloging-in-Publication Data

A Changing international division of labor.

(International political economy yearbook; v. 2)
Bibliography: p.
Includes index.
1. International division of labor. 2. Comparative advantage (Commerce) I. Caporaso, James A., 1941- II. Series.
HF1410.I579 vol. 2 337′.05 s 86-20215
[HF1412] [382.1′042]
ISBN 0-931477-94-8 (lib. bdg.)

British Library Cataloguing in Publication Data

International political economy yearbook
Vol. 2: A changing international division of labor
1. International economic relations—political aspects
I. Caporaso, James A.
337 HF1411
ISBN 0-86187-679-2

Printed and bound in the United States of America

The paper used in this publication meets the new requirements of the American National Standard for Permanence of Paper for Printed Library Materials, Z39.48-1984.

Contents

Tables and Figures

Tables

Figures

Preface

The most revealing question that authors and editors can ask themselves is, "Why did I write (or edit) this book?" In this particular case, it was not to create a full-blown theory of the division of labor, nor a competitive empirical evaluation of rival hypotheses. Instead, what motivated this second volume of the International Political Economy Yearbook was the gap between a large number of crucial questions about the role of labor in politics, economics, and society on the one hand, and our ability to answer these questions from the existing stock of empirical and theoretical knowledge on the other.

An exemplary, but not exhaustive list of questions would include the following. What is the role of labor in the process of production, in the social relations surrounding the production process, and in what Burawoy has called "the politics of production"? What role does labor, considered both as an abstract process and a concrete political actor (e.g., unions), play in structuring the changing international division of labor? Arthur Lewis's frank question of why a peanut farmer in Nigeria earns one-tenth the income of a sheepherder in New Zealand struck me as a dramatically appropriate point of departure for trying to understand contemporary divisions among rich and poor in the global system. The question could be extended to inquire why factory workers in Hong Kong, Taiwan, India, Sri Lanka, the Ivory Coast, Algeria, Yugoslavia, Spain, West Germany, and the United States have such widely different wage levels, holding constant for differential productivities, varying capital-labor ratios, and differences among economic sectors. Finally, what are the major components of technological change and structural evolution of the work forces in the advanced capitalist countries, and what is the relationship between change in this arena and changes in less developed countries?

These questions are important ones that cry out for coherent answers. Yet, what sets them apart from many other questions is precisely the absence of adequate explanatory theories. Classical political economy did assign an important role to labor; Smith, Ricardo, Marx, and Mill all recognized labor as a class category that played a key role in production and distribution. However, as economics "progressed" as a discipline, the role of subjective utility and final demand came to predominate over earlier theoretical orientations, which were more firmly rooted in costs and conditions of production. As these intellectual changes occurred, the economy came to be thought of more and more as a distinct sphere of commodified relations, where goods and productive factors (including labor) were freely bought and sold in accordance with the laws of supply and demand. Along with this change, questions of static allocational efficiency gradually replaced the analysis of distributional consequences of production for different class groups.

If the transition from classical political economy to neoclassical economics was not conducive to an understanding of labor in production, modern political science was even more institutionally hostile to the challenge. Neoclassical economics relegated labor to the status of an abstract, homogeneous input into the production process; political science swerved between ignoring labor as a fundamental class category and treating it, in Burawoy's apt phrase, as "just one of a number of collective actors formed in the public sphere" (Burawoy 1985, 5). Labor became just another interest group and, in this regard, fit comfortably into the pluralist intellectual scheme. It occupied a position conceptually similar to the National Rifle Association, International Confederation of Sugarbeet Farmers, or an ecology pressure group. As such, while the organizational characteristics of labor were assessed (membership size, centralization, access to legislative and executive institutions), its role in the politics of the production process was ignored.

Although the contributions to this book do not answer all the unresolved issues identified above, they do attempt to place the discussion in the appropriate intellectual arena. Chapter 1 establishes the general context for the volume, suggesting some orienting questions, as well as a definition of labor, and locating labor within the process of production and within the larger society. The key theme of this chapter is that, although established traditions may have numerous defects from the standpoint of constructing and understanding of the international division of labor, it is better to search these bodies of knowledge than to attempt to construct a theoretical explanation *ex nihilo*. The three established traditions examined are classical and neoclassical economics, Marxian political economy, and segmented labor market theory. The second chapter, by Lynn Mytelka, is in some ways a logical extension of her earlier work on the role of technology in fostering patterns of dependency. Here she turns her attention to the source of technology, which is knowledge itself, and examines its role in the organization of production and in structuring the modern international division of labor. The central focus of the chapter is on the ways in which knowledge inputs (research and development, basic science, the cultivation of human skills) have become increasingly important to the process of competitive capital accumulation. In carrying out this central task, Mytelka examines different strategies of multinational corporations and how these strategies affect the growth of the firm, the nature of corporate competition, and the internationalization of production.

The starting point of Gerd Junne's chapter is the newly industrializing countries (or NICs, as they are often called), the movement of core capital to these countries, and their dramatic appearance in the global political economy during the past twenty years. Junne's goal is not to explain the rapid growth in the manufacturing sector of these countries, but rather to identify and assess the countervailing forces already at work in many advanced capitalist countries. Most important among these trends in core countries is the increasing automation of work, i.e., the displacement of living labor with the embodied labor of industrial robots. Machines are increasingly being used to make machines and to control the operation of machines as they produce goods.

From the standpoint of the firm engaged in the process of globally competitive production, the reasons for automation are readily apparent. The dramatic emergence of the NICs, the resulting export competition for firms in advanced capitalist countries, and the subsequent loss of jobs entailed by the migration of core capital to less developed countries all set the stage for economic adjustment among industries in the North (i.e., the advanced capitalist countries). Automation of the work process—the displacement of living labor with machinery and computer-controlled manufacturing—was one way to bring about the reduction of labor costs, increased competitiveness, and higher rates of profit.

The setting for John Kurt Jacobsen's chapter is Ireland, which itself reflects an interesting fact. Ireland is located within the advanced capitalist world but functions as an economic hinterland. As such, it faces many of the same choices that confront other less developed countries today. Should capital and technology be imported or locally generated? What are the merits of import-substitution as opposed to export-oriented policies? And what niche, defined either by a natural or created comparative advantage, is Ireland's industrial structure most suited for? In examining these questions,

Jacobsen relies on a political analysis of the economic choices confronting Ireland's leaders, as well as an assessment of the ideological factors involved.

Discussions of the international division of labor typically focus on the capitalist world economy and, in so doing, ignore the position of the socialist world. Of course, the socialist world, especially the Soviet Union, occupies center stage in the East-West conflict, but this is seen as qualitatively different and, for the most part, unrelated to questions of production, distribution, and development. Mette Skak shows in her chapter that the socialist countries of Eastern Europe are by no means insulated from the pushes and pulls of global economic and political forces. Whereas "high politics" may still set limits to the logic of production and distribution, these rules themselves are seen as entailing costs. During the 1970s, the decision by the Soviet Union to continue to supply its Eastern European allies with oil at artificially low prices, even in the face of greatly increased world market prices, entailed costs calculated in the billions of dollars (Marrese 1986).

The message of Skak's chapter is that the Soviet Union and Eastern Europe are part of the greater global division of labor, that they feel the logic of production and the pushes and pulls of the marketplace, and that intrabloc production decisions increasingly are made with an eye toward the world market. The focus of this chapter is on "East-South relations," i.e., Eastern Europe, the Soviet Union, and the less developed world. Skak's incisive comparisons of the role of the Eastern European members of the Council for Mutual Economic Assistance (CMEA) and the newly industrializing countries (NICs) demonstrates that the broad forces of cost-based production calculations, market competition, and comparative advantage operate with respect to the socialist states too.

Richard Higgott poses an interesting set of issues in Chapter 6. Australia is a large, thinly populated country rich in natural resources. Although a generous endowment of natural resources has generally been thought of as an advantage in development theory, this position has been the subject of some disagreement of late. The potential disadvantage could be put as a simple question: With Australia's economic structure determined in large measure by its relative factor endowments, will the country evolve in the direction of a raw material supplier for a dynamic and increasingly manufacturing-oriented Pacific region in the years ahead? If this occurs, in what ways will Australia's economic profile, national wealth, and economic well-being be different from many other LDC raw-material producers? These are questions that are central to Higgott's chapter as he systematically tries to unravel the dilemmas confronting an established member of the Organization for Economic Cooperation and Development (OECD) in a dynamic region dominated by Japan and the Asian NICs (South Korea, Taiwan, Singapore, and Hong Kong).

The final chapter of the book identifies the most salient trends relevant to labor and production in general. Five trends are singled out for close examination: the migration of capital from core to periphery, the rise of global production sharing, the peripheralization of labor in core countries, the growing reliance on female labor in both periphery and core, and the growing scope of use of industrial policy.

Colleagues have often asked why these trends have been chosen and not others. The answer comes in two parts: these are the trends that seemed to be the most important in pure descriptive terms, and they offered the potential of fitting together the pieces of the puzzle in some coherent ways. The important point was not just to identify and describe the trends in question, but also to construct an understanding of how the parts fit together. There were multitudes of fragments that one could observe at the many levels and locations in the global system. The challenge, as put by Burawoy, was to understand the "international recomposition of the industrial working class" (Burawoy 1985, 7). To this end, numerous feminist accounts of female labor in the periphery provided useful starting points. June Nash and Maria Patricia Fernandez-Kelly's edited volume, *Women, Men, and the International Division of Labor* (1983), proved to be a gold mine of ideas and research findings for assembling the different parts of the picture. Ross and Trachte's "Global Cities and Global Classes: The Peripheralization of Labor in New York City" (1983) argued with insight for the interconnections between core labor restructuring and broader political and economic forces. With studies such as these, it became possible to start to assemble the many disconnected fragments.

Numerous people have been instrumental in stimulating the ideas behind this volume and the movement from some vague conception of the importance of labor to actual research. Robert Cox, Ladd Hollist, and LaMond Tullis read the entire manuscript and gave penetrating and constructive suggestions for revisions. Two students at the Graduate School of International Studies of the University of Denver, Naeem Inayatullah and Alain Noël, were constant sources of friendly criticism and helpful suggestions. Two other graduate students, Robert Hazan and Chih-yu Shih, provided invaluable help with proofreading and manuscript preparation. Thanks are also due to Dianne H. Ewing, Gia Hamilton, and Lynne Rienner, all of Lynne Rienner Publishers, for encouragement and help in the production of this book. Finally, Diane De Rose Libero expertly typed several drafts of the entire manuscript and simultaneously attempted to keep track of authors, whose elusive travel habits covered scores of countries and several continents. To these people, and many others, the editor extends special thanks.

1

James A. Caporaso

The International Division of Labor: A Theoretical Overview

A book on the subject of the international division of labor resurrects an old topic with a very new face. Its subject matter reaches back hundreds of years, at least to Adam Smith, and spans several disciplines, most notably economics, politics, and sociology. It is very new in the intensification, indeed virtual outpouring, of books, articles, and monographs on this topic during the last ten years.[1] The words "new international division of labor" have formed a catch-phrase, a slogan of the seventies and eighties, and one likely to have more staying power than other fashionable terms, e.g., "interdependence."

Yet, there is a curious sense in which the old and new do not rest comfortably with one another. They coexist uneasily and in conflict, less explicit than waiting to be explored. The modern literature uses the classics frequently in an ad hoc and superficial way, often incautiously drawing conclusions not warranted by the sources used. One borrows something from Smith (perhaps the idea of division of labor itself), from Ricardo (most likely comparative advantage), or from Marx (the labor theory of value or the class conflicts embedded in capitalist development), but one rarely pursues the argument to its conclusion or carefully examines those critical arenas where alternative arguments intersect. As a result, modern interpretations of the international division of labor are extremely confused, a charge all the more serious since these interpretations include good portions of the literature on dependency, world systems analysis, and imperialism, as well as trade and investment-based theories of the division of labor, the latter almost exclusively a neo-classical sort.

A few examples will suffice. Emmanuel, in *Unequal Exchange,* attempts to derive a theory of international exchange from political and economic laws of domestic society. To his credit, he questions the assumptions of the classical economist—immobility of capital and labor internationally—and interests himself in the relevant case where capital is internationally mobile and labor much less so, or, as he puts it, sufficiently immobile to "ensure that local differences in wages . . . cannot be eliminated . . ." (Emmanuel 1972, xxxiv). These differential wages lead to differential costs, which, on a cost-based theory of prices, lead to higher prices. The prices of goods then traded internationally reflect the superior organizational and bargaining capabilities of workers in the core countries and not the relative number of labor hours embodied in traded products.

Emmanuel's intention of deriving unequal exchange relations, not from the realm of exchange itself but from the realm of production, is admirable. The difficulty is that the argument is not pursued to its fullest and assumptions fully needed to make the theory work are not uncovered. For the theory to work there must be a monopoly in product markets on the part of the exploiting (i.e., strong labor) country. Otherwise, the higher price of goods exported by the country where labor is organizationally strong would soon be undercut by a competitor who, with an equal technology and lower labor costs, is able to sell more cheaply on world markets. In addition, there is the questionable assumption that, with respect to the issue of mobility-immobility, capital and labor do not interact. To put this more precisely, Emmanuel must assume that the price of labor (i.e., wages) is not conditioned in a downward direction by the free movement of capital across national borders. But if we ask if this is so, we are not likely to find an easy answer. Indeed, there seem to be good theoretical reasons for concluding that exit of capital from a country will exert downward pressure on wages, on the grounds that the demand for labor decreases and the bargaining power of capital increases. Thus, it is not at all clear, if one pushes the classical theory (including Marxian theory) far enough, that Emmanuel's theoretical results will hold, and, if they do, it seems fair to say that they will have a very restrictive relevance.

Unequal Exchange is only one of the more recent efforts to locate the sources of international inequality. This same project is shared by many others, among them, most notably, Immanuel Wallerstein and Raul Prebisch. Wallerstein's *The Modern World System* is justly considered a monumental work on the origins of the contemporary world. It is a massive effort, at once encyclopedic and abstract, which attempts to trace and interpret the paths that led to our present world, a world of nation-states, capitalist economies (or rather *economy,* stressing the unity of the global system), and different forms of labor control. The sociological insights offered and the historical evidence presented are invaluable. But what about its core argument of how the modern world system came to be so unequal? The argument, insofar as this can be reconstructed, concerns different forms of labor control and the ways in which these forms led to differential wealth and power capabilities among countries, or what were, at an early stage, simply differentiated zones of an emerging system of states.

Without elaboration, let me simply assert that zones of the world political economy become richer or poorer, à la Wallerstein, as a result of two broad sets of factors: the mode of production and labor control employed, on the one hand, and, on the other, the predominant type of exchange relations among zones. But, to the degree that Wallerstein tries to explain global differentiation (principally what we now call the North-South cleavage), he runs into the same problem facing Emmanuel, namely how to conceptually identify, let alone to observe and measure, the transfer of greater value in one direction versus another. Wallerstein fails to dig deeply into Marxian value theory for guidance and, despite brief flirtations with classical and neo-classical formulations (supply and demand, contrived scarcities, differential elasticities of demand for primary and manufactured goods), he does not fully pursue these ideas either. The result is an undifferentiated, eclectic mix of theories, both neo-Smithian and Marxian, as suggested in Brenner's important article (Brenner 1977), in which two theoretical traditions with quite different implications for understanding global inequality become impossible to disentangle. This unclear admixture allows Wallerstein to draw, in ad hoc fashion, from different theories as the occasion arises; he shifts languages according to circumstance, talking now of labor control and surplus transfer, and at other times, specialization, division of labor, and efficiency. But the final result is the same—a kind of theoretical indeterminacy about his system and a profound sense in which the facts of the modern world system are not clearly assignable to, and hence explainable by, a body of theory.[2]

The range of examples could be extended to include Prebisch, whose analysis of long-run adverse terms of trade for primary producers must be questioned because it is based on market factors (both classical and neo-classical economics are agnostic about long-term movements in supply and demand), as well as (and one could argue about this) secular trends in consumption profiles. Similarly, modern neo-classical economists are likely to explain global differentiation of wealth and production as a branch of location theory and applied analysis of comparative cost (e.g., Johnson 1981). Having rejected much of what Ricardo offered, they hold firmly to his principle of comparative costs and interpret much of the movement in the contemporary world economy in terms of "shifting comparative advantage" in both product and factor markets (Balassa 1979; Chenery and Keesing 1979).

Unlike many others, these neo-classical economists at least offer the advantage of consistency and firmly root their analysis in a distinctive theoretical tradition running from Smith (the efficiency gains due to specialization), Ricardo (comparative cost theory), Jevons (marginal analysis), Heckshher and Ohlin (factor-proportion theory), and Samuelson (factor-price equalization). Here the critique cannot be based on conflating different arguments or failing to ground them in clear theoretical traditions. Instead, one is more likely to ask what has been left out, how these omissions affect the explanatory status of the theory, and how far the restrictive assumptions limit the theory's scope of application.

All of the above is not meant to be a preface to a call for a "dialog" between different theoretical traditions, a discussion of alternative world views, or even our periodically heard pleas for tolerance concerning different approaches. There is no doubt that all of these things are sometimes needed, but it is even more pressing to state distinctive theoretical positions clearly and to boldly deduce the implications contained in them. Before cross-discussion can occur and competing paradigms can be brought into mutually intelligible discussion, separate paradigms must exist. Before bridge-building, the shores must be firmly in place.

The remainder of this introduction will attempt to do two things: (1) conceptualize what is meant by the international division of labor, trace broadly the meaning of the term labor, and locate this term within the modern political economy discussion; and (2) present at least the foundations (perhaps theory-sketches is a better term) of several different bodies of theory that are relevant to the theme of this volume.

THE INTERNATIONAL DIVISION OF LABOR: PROBLEMS OF DEFINITION AND CONCEPTUALIZATION

The separate efforts of the academic specialities—political science, sociology and economics—do not naturally add up to a comprehensive understanding of labor. In a sense, the intellectual division of labor is not so arranged as to give us a satisfactory account of the international division of labor, a division which itself includes an intellectual component. In political science, labor is not treated at all as a process, as an activity directed toward the creation of wealth, or as part of more comprehensive economic processes, such as the accumulation of capital. Instead, labor is treated as a group—an interest group, to be exact—one among many such groups to engage in the political process. This accords with pluralist philosophy, which places organized group life at the center of political phenomena. In economics, by contrast, labor is treated as a productive factor: one of three (or four, if technology is treated separately) that enters the productive process. The general framework for analyzing labor is supply and demand—hence labor market theory; labor markets, like other factor markets and product markets, are subject to equilibrium conditions. The importance of labor (and its rewards) is not a topic for general philosophical discussion, but is, instead, evaluated in terms of its marginal contribution to the total product or, alternatively, as the diminished product due to a certain quantity of foregone labor, i.e., by its opportunity cost.

The contributions of sociologists are more difficult to summarize neatly, perhaps because this discipline is more heterodox than political science and economics in regard to labor. Although significant differences within sociology will be explored later, the striking aspect about this literature is that it is more inclined to examine the social relations surrounding the production process. These relations may include the distribution of work roles by gender, race, religion, and ethnic group; the impact of work on the family; relations between manual workers and supervisors, and between those who directly produce the product and those who consume it. *Divisions of Labour* by R. E. Pahl may be taken as exemplary of this tradition.

These three traditions, though valuable, are most often disparate, and have very little direct theoretical relevance to the international dimension. The worlds of efficiency, power, and social relations of production lie strangely distant from one another. Economists, by limiting their scope to questions of allocative efficiency, cut themselves off from asking about the importance of power and institutions. Before the writings of economists and political scientists such as Berger and Piore, we knew very little about fundamental phenomena, such as the bargaining power of labor, segmentation of labor markets, and the role of the state in structuring and using these segmented markets. Similarly, until Mancur Olson's seminal book, *The Logic of Collective Action* (1965), we knew almost nothing about the kind of group world that would exist if neo-classical economic assumptions about human behavior were true. The linkages among studies of labor by political scientists and sociologists are similarly weak; many of the sociological studies are micro in focus and almost anthropological and clinical in their methods of observation and interpretation. Pahl's previously mentioned book is based on a case study of the peoples of the Isle of Sheppey, while Paul Willis's *Learning to Labour* is really an ethnographic account of twelve working-class youths from a fictional Hammertown, England. These studies are difficult but not impossible to integrate with the more encompassing focus of the political scientist on "organized group life." Political science's persistent avoidance of the relationship among organized groups, classes, and status orderings—not to mention capital-labor relationships—rounds out the three-way series of lost opportunities.

Definition of Labor: Biography of Concept

I will start by equating labor to work, and set both terms equal to *activity of a physical or mental sort intended to produce wealth,* that is, some object or service that contains something of value to people. This definition includes a variety of activities, which are perhaps too heterogeneous in both content and functional significance to be of much use: combing one's hair and brushing one's teeth, tilling a field, working in an assembly line, and inventing an atom smasher would all qualify. Clearly this definition of labor is not equivalent with the expressions "employment" or "job," although, clearly, all three terms overlap.

The terms labor and work, used almost interchangeably in modern language, have a long natural history and biography of their own. Perhaps a brief tracing of the evolution of these terms can illuminate the worlds of labor and work that they try to describe. The first thing to note is that the modern understandings of labor and work that prevail among upper classes of the advanced capitalist countries, with their connotations of enrichment, individual fulfillment, and personal growth, as well as emphasis on work as an end rather than a means, are not likely to provide a fruitful starting point for analysis. Conceptions of work have varied significantly from classical times to the present.

What strikes one most forcefully in reading the ancient Greeks is that they placed labor in such a subsidiary, one might say demeaning, role by modern standards. According to Anthony,

> Work, as Aristotle sees it, gets in the way of the more proper pursuits of a citizen, not only wasting his time in inferior activities but corrupting him and making his pursuit of virtue more difficult. (Anthony 1977, 17)

Hannah Arendt, in *The Human Condition,* agrees, although she spoke of labor rather than work. She makes a strong case for separating the terms labor and work, the former having to do with exertions performed to satisfy subsistence needs, while the latter is reserved for activities in excess of these necessary exertions. Since labor was tied to the realm of the necessary, it referred, by extension, to what was common between man and animal. This distinction lay at the base of the Greek idea of slavery. Aristotle's discussion of slavery in *Politics* begins with the comment that "without the necessities life as well as good life is impossible" (Arendt 1958, 83). Slaves were not thought to be human; it was their function to produce life's necessities (what were later called subsistence needs or necessary product) for both themselves and their masters. True citizens had the necessary labor performed for them by others so that they could go on to do what was human. However, not all that we today would include in the term labor was considered demeaning. Those activities not tied to what was necessary to man's reproduction belonged in a different realm, presumably a realm more linked to freedom and creativity. This distinction, between labor and work, so neglected in our theory, "yet so obstinately preserved in our languages," is an important one (Arendt 1958, 94). In Latin we have *laborare* and *facere,* in German *arbeiten* and *werken,* and in French *travailler* and *ouvrer,* the former term in each pair tied to necessary exertions and the latter to the more human and creative activities of man. Indeed, the connotation of necessary exertion is perhaps not putting it quite strongly enough. According to Lucien Febre, in his *Travail: Evolution d'un mot et d'une ideé,* the word *travailler* entered the French vocabulary in the sixteenth century, its meaning derived from the Latin *tripalium,* an instrument of torture made of three stakes. In the twelfth century *ouvrier* (worker) appeared, which, in turn, derived from the Latin *operarius,* meaning man of pain and affliction (cited in Pahl 1984, 18). Also interesting is the fact that the German noun *Arbeit* was originally restricted to farm labor carried out by serfs, while *Werk* was used for the craftsman's exertions.

We can see that labor is not only tied to necessary exertions; it is also distinctly linked to what is unpleasant, painful, and is due to man's sinful nature. According to Arendt (1958, 83), labor and work are distinguished between by Hesiod, where work is due to Eris, while labor comes out of Pandora's box and is a punishment by Zeus (Arendt 1958, 83). Similarly, the Bible contains references to labor as unpleasant, difficult, and connected to man's fall from grace. While an etymological discussion of labor can be illuminating, we can also ask about the "ideology of work," i.e., the more or less conscious ideas, attitudes, and even philosophies of work characteristic of different historical periods. Between the Classical Period and the end of the Middle Ages there is, according to one authority, little in the way of a conscious philosophy of work (Anthony 1977, 37-38). Huizinga, for example, in *The Waning of the Middle Ages* does not include a single chapter on labor or work, nor does the index to his book contain either of these two terms; similarly, Laslett, in *The World We Have Lost* does not single out labor for special treatment. This does not mean that these authors think labor is unimportant; there are sometimes detailed treatments of the art of baking bread, toiling in the vineyards, or the daily life of the serf who plows the fields. What is lacking, to be clear, is not work or descriptions of the content of work life, but a more or less explicit philosophy or conception of work, apart from the most general meaning imparted to work by religious doctrine.

Why did this gap exist? One clue is provided by just that which is left out in many scholarly treatments of the Middle Ages by economic and social historians. In chapter after chapter, Laslett seems to return to the family and to use the family structure as a touchstone for analyzing many different parts of medieval society. What is striking is the lack of differentiation between labor specifically and social and familial life in general. In one sense, life in the Middle Ages was not very specialized, at least not by comparison with the modern world. Feudal manors, although differentiated into occupational groups, were, for the most part, self-sufficient communities within which there was a closer tie between work and life as a whole than exists today. Weber's powerful triad of social forces—class, status, and power—much debated (particularly as to the congruity or incongruity of them) in the nineteenth and twentieth centuries—probably had little meaning in the feudal manor, where all three blended together.

Another reason for the lack of an explicit philosophy of work perhaps lay in the extremely hierarchic form of medieval society. A chronicler of the fifteenth century, Chastellain, had this to say:

> God . . . created the common people to till the earth and to procure by trade the commodities necessary for life; he created the clergy for the works of religion; the nobles that they should cultivate virtue and maintain justice, so that the deeds and the morals of these fine personages might be a pattern to others (In Huizinga 1954, 59).

Hierarchy, order, permanence! These were the fundamental qualities of the ideology of medieval society, qualities all the more influential since they were reinforced by the view of history that was cyclical rather than progressive. These were not qualities designed to foster upward mobility, the nourishment of achievement motivations, or even the questioning of one's place in society. The Thomistic doctrine of "the harmony of the Christian commonwealth in which every class did its own 'proper work'" (Anthony 1977, 37) played an important role not only in legitimizing a hierarchically structured society, but also in discouraging a deep curiosity of the labor process.

The third and final phase of the evolution of the concept of work is the modern period. Here we can discern two separate movements. The first movement is initially of an almost totally religious nature and centers on the Protestant Reformation; the second begins later, perhaps in the middle of the seventeenth century, and centers around the views of labor and property spawned by Locke, Smith, Ricardo, and Marx. I will discuss each of these two strands of thinking in turn.

Long before labor theories of value assumed their mature form in Smith, Ricardo, and Marx, ideas were taking shape in parts of Europe that would alter the ideology of work in everyday life. Medieval theology held several things that hindered not only the development of capitalism, but also the development of the concept of labor as we know it today. In this category one could include the hostility to usury, to "buying cheap and selling dear," and to the prevailing belief that the pursuit of material gain beyond subsistence was a sign of the absence of grace. The Protestant Reformation was to change all this.

Catholic theologians had the quaint idea that "the aim of worldly success was the enjoyment of a life of ease and luxury" (Heilbroner 1980, 55), while, according to Weber, "English, Dutch, and American Puritans were characterized by the exact opposite of the joy of living . . ." (Weber 1958, 41). In contrast to Catholic disdain for the affairs of the world (Augustine's *City of Man*), Calvinist teachings stressed earthly success as a sign of salvation. Calvinism's original core, in which a harsh doctrine of predestination was propounded, gradually softened to allow the hint, and hence the hope, of worldly activity containing some indication of the afterlife. The link between predestination (which suggests acceptance and passivity) and the acquisitive spirit associated with the Calvinist roots of the Protestant ethic, is provided by the concept of a calling, or what Weber called *Beruf.* The term signals something much more compelling than employment or occupation. Indeed, Weber, who devotes an entire chapter to "Luther's Conception of the Calling," goes to great pains to tell us about the distinctly religious flavor of the German *Beruf* and informs us further of the absence of a similar term among "predominantly Catholic peoples [and] those of classical antiquity" (Weber 1958, 79). The concept of a calling, with its suggestiveness of the afterlife, became important in structuring attitudes toward work, and work itself. Calvinism shared with Catholicism the idea that work was instrumental, but at this broad level the similarities ended.

One might ask, instrumental for what? In Catholic theology, work played a necessary role in extracting a "living" from nature (Marx was later to define labor as "man's metabolism with nature"); for Calvinism, work was instrumental in a more spiritual sense. Hard work, diligence, frugality, and abstinence became important, and the acquisition of material gain (Marx's nonconsumed product) took on an utterly different image as the visible embodiment of one's spiritual standing, of being among the *elect.* In short, what one sees in the sixteenth century is the birth, at the ideational level, of the surplus as a quantity to be used distinctively for purposes of accumulation—an idea that was to form a, if not *the* centerpiece of political economy for hundreds of years.

While the Reformation had an effect on attitudes toward labor and its material consequences, it wasn't until the seventeenth century that significant developments in the philosophy of labor took place. Locke's *Two Treatises of Government* constituted a major turning point and had a revolutionary impact on our modern conceptions of labor. As Arendt put it, "The sudden, spectacular rise of labor from the lowest, most despised position to the highest rank, as the most esteemed of all human activities, began when Locke discovered that labor is the source of all property" (Arendt 1958, 101). This conception of labor runs from Locke to Adam Smith, who developed the argument that labor was the source of wealth, and found its fullest expression in Marx's elaborate labor theory of value.

Locke's insight was very simple and he spent only a short chapter in the *Second Treatise* to develop it. He argued that things become private property by the mixing of an individual's labor with them; by this simple activity, those things that are part of the common ownership of mankind pass into the realm of private ownership:

> Though the Earth, and all inferior creatures be common to all Men, yet every man has a Property in his own Person. This no body has any Right to but himself. The Labour of his Body, and the Work of his Hands, we may

> say, are properly his. Whatsoever then he removes out of the state that Nature hath provided, and left it in, he hath mixed his *labour* with, and joined to it something that is his own, and thereby makes it his *Property* (Locke 1965, 328-29).

Although Locke was specifically interested in property, and not value in general, one can see how his labor theory of property might be generalized, or perhaps transmuted, to play a role in labor theories of value. Indeed, Locke's thoughts on labor are not lost on Marx, who quotes him approvingly in *Theories of Surplus Value:*

> It is labor indeed that put the difference of value on everything. . . . Of the products of the earth useful to the life of man . . . ninety-nine hundredths are wholly to be put on the account of labour (Marx 1963, 366, quoting from John Locke, *Of Civil Government,* book 11, chapter 5).

Both Adam Smith and David Ricardo had important things to say about labor in general and division of labor in particular. Indeed, in the modern world Smith is rememberd most for his thoughts on the salutory effects of the division of labor; Ricardo, among trade and development theorists at least, is recalled for his contributions on comparative advantage. Their important contributions on the value of labor notwithstanding, it remained for Marx to develop the labor theory of value to its fullest.

For Marx, all value comes from labor, and what appears as an independent return to capital is a fiction resulting from the failure to see capital as embodiment of past labor, of "dead" as opposed to "living" labor. "All commodities," therefore, including commodities used to produce commodities, "are only definite masses of congealed labor time" (Marx 1906, vol. 1, 46). If one accepts this, it does not make sense to assess the value of capital according to its opportunity cost, that is, according to the foregone product resulting from withdrawing a certain quantity of capital from the production mix, or what is the mirror image of the same process, the marginal contribution of capital to total product.

For Marx, then, labor comes to occupy center stage in life in general, and productive life in particular. Indeed, "productive activity, if we leave out of sight its special form, viz., the useful character of the labour, is nothing but the expenditure of human labour-power" (Marx 1906, 51). This transformation of the conception of labor was profound and, of course, did not happen in one stroke, but rather was the culmination of the work of Hobbes, Locke, Petty, Hodgkins, Smith, and Ricardo. This transformation had many implications, among them the following.

The first implication of the Marxian labor theory of value was a shift of attention from exchange to production. Instead of looking upon the value of a commodity in terms of what one is willing to pay (i.e., to give up) for it, or in more impersonal terms, what the market, with its law of supply and demand, is willing to fetch for it, Marx tried to anchor value firmly in the laws of production. In his critique of Proudhon, Marx argued that "in principle there is not an exchange of products, but exchange of labours which compete in production. It is on the mode of exchange of productive forces that the mode of exchange of products depends" (Marx, *The Poverty of Philosophy,* quoted in Dobb 1973, 32). How strikingly different this is from the economics spawned by the Jevonian revolution, in which value becomes a purely subjective affair, a psychological propensity, a kind of "feeling thermometer" or temperature gauge inside every person, the determinants of which were unknown and not even considered part of economic theory.

A second implication of the Marxian world view is that labor, first glorified as the source of all wealth, is then itself made a commodity, something to be bought and sold. If the value of anything is the number of labor hours required to produce it, then the value of labor is equal to the number of labor hours needed to reproduce labor; in exchange terms, this quantity is of course equal to the subsistence wage. More important, the productivity of labor is now measured against a new baseline, namely its own ability to produce more than the requirements for its own reproduction.

The production by labor of more than is needed for its own reproduction leads us naturally to the final point, the link between the Marxian theory of labor and the processes of surplus production and capital accumulation. Once the subsistence requirements of workers are met, and once capital is reproduced, any remaining product can be looked on as a surplus. The existence of this surplus, who has access to it, what kinds of property rights a society institutes for its disposal, and the struggles among class and state forces for control over it are very much the subjects of political science, sociology, and political economy. But, for Marx, the existence of a surplus, conceived at bottom as surplus labor time rather than surplus product, opened the way for two things: the possibility of some classes living off the labor of others; and the possibility of different modes of capital accumulation, i.e., different ways of investing surplus to advance the productive forces. Although this is a theme I cannot pursue here, several papers in the volume speak about it in some detail.

THEORETICAL FOUNDATIONS OF GLOBAL POLITICAL ECONOMY

Labor and the Division of Labor: Conceptual Foundations

Since the concepts of labor and division of labor are not familiar, at least not in a precise way, the first order of business is to attempt some elementary conceptualization of these terms; references to "labor" and "division of labor" abound in the literature on domestic and global political economy. For example, Fröbel, Heinrich, and Kreye, in their important book, *The New International Division of Labour* (1980), break new ground. For the most part, however, their contributions lie in the empirical realm. They examine in great detail the ongoing transformations in industrial production, the flight of capital from core to periphery, the rise of an industrializing semiperiphery, and the limitations of this style of industrial growth for the broader processes of economic, political and social development. What is missing is a sense of how these terms might be conceptually developed and located within a theoretical structure. Of course, classical political economy, including the works of Smith and Marx, attempted to do precisely this, arguably with considerable success. But the classics were also not without profound ambiguities regarding the conceptual meaning and theoretical utility of these concepts (see Inayatullah 1985). These ambiguities, plus the historical and theoretical hiatus between classical and contemporary political economy, have made it difficult for modern political economy to build upon or to be grafted onto its intellectual ancestors.

The first task, then, is to explore the meaning of labor. Labor may be defined simply as an activity or expenditure of energy (physical or mental) with the purpose of producing something of value. This definition highlights three things: labor refers to an activity that involves an exchange of energy with its environment; it is conscious and purposeful; and, it has as its end the production of something of value. Whether the labor process produces only a use-value or an exchange-value also, whether the activity occurs within or outside the wage nexus, and whether the labor was productive of surplus or produced only its own subsistence are matters that lie outside the definition. Marx argued that one has to consider "the labour-process independently of the particular form it assumes under given social conditions" (Marx 1906, 197). Without abstracting from the particular conditions in which labor is performed, one does not have a concept general enough to serve as a useful historical or comparative device.

Considered purely as an activity, however, labor by itself, i.e., without objects of nature (raw materials) and tools, can produce very little besides the simplest of services. To produce the great majority of goods to which we are accustomed today requires large inputs of materials and, often, very sophisticated tools and machinery. Logically, then, the labor process requires three things: labor itself (the work or energy involved); objects of work; and, instruments of work (Marx 1906, 198). It is these three things recognized by Marx and the classical economists, later to become the famous labor, land, and capital of neo-classical theory, that are responsible for the greater part of what is produced.[3]

With this simple definition of labor in place, we can now turn to the division of labor. If labor is activity whose purpose is to produce use-values, then the division of labor simply refers to the way this labor is distributed, or to the primary cleavages that the labor process assumes. This definition, while highly general, invites more specific applications. One important aspect of the division of labor concerns how labor is divided within a particular industry. This is the case dealt with by Adam Smith in his famous example of the pin factory. If all tasks involved in manufacturing pins are performed by one person, the production of pins will be much less efficient if compared to a highly differentiated production process where many workers are individually responsible for only one aspect of production. This type of division of labor, involving increasing refinements and partitions in the labor process, is what Marx called the detailed division of labor or the division of labor in manufactures. It was distinguished from the social division of labor, in which whole occupations were set off from one another in society. The detailed division of labor involves the increasing subdivision of tasks within an industry, but the social division of labor involves the differentiation of occupational categories themselves. The significance of this distinction for Marx lay in his argument that the products of the social division of labor are commodities (Marx 1906, 390).

In addition to the detailed and social division of labor, there is the territorial division of labor. This term simply refers to the ways in which different types of labor (marked by differences in skill, wages, products made, etc.) are distributed over space. The location of industries is a subject treated by both neo-classical economics (location theory, regional economics) and radical theories. One popular version of the spatial, or territorial, division of labor is the center-periphery scheme, in which the world is divided into core areas of high wealth, skilled labor, technologically advanced industries, and peripheral areas marked by poverty, low wages and low-skilled labor, and technologically backward industries. The theories attempting to explain the contemporary global division of labor are themselves not very developed, but some important beginnings have been made (Baran 1957; Lewis 1978). In any case, quite apart from the inadequacy of theoretical explanations, the inequality in the distribution of different types of labor worldwide and the concentration of specific industries in definite places is so marked as to cry out for explanation. The center-periphery scheme, primitive and blunt as it is for analytic purposes, nevertheless recognizes—if only through labelling—this important descriptive fact.

Just as the division of labor may take place across regions of the world, so it may occur among classes. Indeed, many would argue that the division of labor among classes is a much more fundamental type of division than the others (e.g., Brenner 1977). A simple division occurs when capital is owned by a distinctive class of persons (capitalists) and labor power is owned by another class (workers). For Brenner, this simple division lies at the root of capitalist expansion and is an important component in explaining the modern territorial division of labor. Class divisions can, of course, be multipled. The separation between town and country, between producers and sellers of goods, between financiers and those investing in directly productive assets all gave rise to specialized class positions (merchant, financial, and industrial capital). Each type of capital has implications for the associated labor process.

Finally, we note that the division of labor can be associated with any number of social, political, and economic properties. There is a gender division of labor, according to which household, low-skilled and seasonal work are performed mostly by women, and high-skilled, unionized, high-wage, and "permanent" jobs go to men. There is also a racial division of labor, and one that may occur by ethnic group, religion, culture, and other properties. It is the task of theories of labor to try to comprehend these various divisions.

There are several leading contemporary approaches to understanding global political economy, among which are included dependency theory, world systems theory, and long-cycle analysis, as well as a variety of extensions of neo-classical economic theory (e.g., see Balassa 1979; Chenery and Kessing 1979). Although each of these approaches has something to tell us, I chose not to follow the route of surveying contemporary theories, because, quite simply, my belief is that none of these bodies of thought rests on firm, or even clear, theoretical foundations. Each, with the exception of neo-classical economics, is an admixture of different theoretical strands, which either has not, or perhaps cannot, be integrated into a coherent whole. To take one example, dependency theory, a body of thought concerned with the integration of less developed societies into the global capitalist economy and the effects of such integration on both peripheral capitalism and its social formations, does not build on a solid theoretical base. That dependency theory has been vigorously criticized from both the left and the right reflects the fact that it is neither classical Marxian nor classical liberal in theoretical structure. Despite dependency theory's emphasis on external reliance, and constrained, concentrated reliance at that, it has failed to ground its analysis within an opportunity cost framework (e.g., see Harsanyi 1965; Coase 1960; Buchanan 1969; Knight 1924), or to build upon the theoretical achievements in the constrained choice literature.[4] Similarly, despite affinities with theories of capital accumulation and imperialism, dependency theory writers have usually not pursued this line to its conclusion.

Instead of focusing on contemporary theories, a different approach was taken, namely, to start with the clearest, most solidly based theoretical traditions, and to ask what their extensions onto our contemporary terrain would look like. Only three bodies of thought seemed to clearly qualify for this exercise: classical and neo-classical political economy, Marxian political economy, and segmented labor market theories.

Before entering our discussion of each of these bodies of thought, one caveat is in order. Clearly segmented labor market theories are not in the same category as classical political economy, neo-classical economics and Marxian political economy. These latter three bodies of literature span hundreds of years, include thousands of contributions, and have made a substantial impact on both the scholarly and practical worlds. In addition, despite all the internal variants that exist within these three intellectual traditions, there is a core statement within each about the fundamental principles according to which the economy functions. While these core statements may not (indeed, they probably do not) contain a systematic theoretical treatment of the principles governing the political system, they do at least tell us how economic behavior would transpire in the absence of disturbing political influences. Segmented labor market theories are different in that they do not have well-developed theoretical cores, are of much shorter duration than the other theories considered, are eclectic in nature, and indeed, they draw upon classical, neo-classical, and Marxian economics for insight and theoretical nourishment.[5]

1. Classical and neo-classical political economy. Although classical and neo-classical political economy are different from one another in important ways (e.g., the classical effort to ground value in a cost theory of production versus the shift to a value theory determined by subjective utilities in neo-classical economics), there are enough continuities for them to be treated together here. In any case, it is hard to pinpoint a historical divide that makes perfect sense from our standpoint. The published work of Jevons, Walras, and Menger, in the first half of the 1870s, generally marks the transition to both marginalism and subjective utility theory, but, from our standpoint, it would not do to take this too seriously—everything before the 1870s being classical, everything after, neo-classical. Some theoretical developments that come quite later—the Hecksher-Ohlin theorem of the 1930s (Hecksher's contribution actually went back to a 1919 article), and Samuelson's contribution on factor-price equalization (1948)—seem best understood as extensions of the Ricardian model of comparative cost differences. On the other hand, Hirschman's opportunity cost analysis of foreign trade and power (1945) can be more appropriately viewed as an extension of Marshall's earlier work, which Hirschman specifically recognizes.

The important point can be succinctly summarized. Modern neo-classical economics is a blend of classical and postclassical thought; it is, in some sense, an integration of ideas, although it would be a mistake to miss the sense in which this integration involves a unity based on conquest and neglect of certain ideas at the expense of others.

Among the contributions of classical political economy, two stand out as especially important: the idea of division of labor and the doctrine of comparative cost advantage. The division of labor is the subject of the first three chapters of Adam Smith's *The Wealth of Nations.* In them, he outlines the concept, ties it to the productive powers of labor and, in turn, shows how the latter is responsible for the total wealth that any country may produce. The first thing to note is that Smith located the wealth of nations in the way countries utilize the labor at their disposal:

> The annual labour of every nation is the fund which originally supplies it with all the necessaries and conveniences of life which it annually consumes, and which consists always either in the immediate produce of that labour, or in what is purchased with that produce from other nations (Smith 1970, 104).

With labor now at the center of his analysis, Smith went on to ask on what factors the productivity of labor depended. To this broad question, he gave two answers. The first had to do with the number of people a society usefully employed, or rather the proportion of those usefully employed to all members of society. This category of "useful employment" was part of a long discussion, both before and after Smith, concerning the nature of productive and nonproductive labor.[6] The second part of Smith's answer had to do with the way in which productive labor was organized. It is here that his discussion of the division of labor becomes relevant.

If a country's wealth is a function of the amount of labor it usefully employs and of the way in which productive labor is organized, the task is then to identify those aspects of labor that are associated with its productivity. Smith does not take long to answer this question; in the first sentence of chapter one, book one, he says:

> The greatest improvement in the productive powers of labour, and the greatest part of the skill, dexterity, and judgment with which it is anywhere directed, or applied seem to have been the effects of the division of labour (Smith 1970, 109).

Why is the division of labor so critical for productivity? After centuries of specialization, one may take the answer to this question for granted; Smith did not. He argued that the underlying reasons were three: improvements in job skills and dexterity; efficiency gains resulting from rationalizing the flow of work in factory settings (as opposed to the time lapses involved in one individual moving across different work tasks); and, the introduction of machinery, which was facilitated by the division of labor (Smith 1970, 112-14).

One further point needs to be mentioned. If the division of labor was seen as the primary determinant of the productivity of labor in a country, it was not itself a *primum mobile,* but, in turn, the result of what Smith termed, somewhat ambiguously, "extent of the market." Although his discussion of this important factor made clear that he had geographic extent in his mind,

it may make more sense, following Berger and Piore (1980), to interpret market extent in terms of income levels, since this formulation is more in tune with modern demand theories.

Smith's contribution to modern understanding of economic theory is incontestable. His insights into the division of labor as a motor of economic development and as a way of linking differentiated social production, on the one hand, with market controlled processes, on the other, constituted a major advance. To put it in somewhat Rawlsian terms, the initial gains resulting from the social contract (the social division of labor) were great, a point that is often ignored by theorists concerned only with distribution of the surplus. Smith, by focusing on the elaborate contractual system that was the division of labor, helped us to understand these processes more adequately. At the same time, unequal exchange theorists, such as Emmanuel and Prebisch, are correct when they say that research in the Smithian tradition has a blind spot when it comes to the distribution of the product; its greatest advances are in the area of "general welfare improvements," resulting from technically new combinations of productive factors and/or changes in the scope of the market.

This leads us to an important, and often unrecognized, point. Simply put, one can say that all of Smith's reasons for improvement in the productivity of labor lie at a technical/organizational level (skill, work, organization, machinery); on the matter of the social relations of production of capitalism Smith has nothing to say. To be sure, people who specialize acquire new dexterities, and machinery may indeed have an affinity with socially organized production; but, these things are true, to the extent that they are true at all, across a number of different types of productive relations. To take just the most obvious examples, what Smith says is likely to be true (or false) under capitalist, socialist, and perhaps even feudal modes of productive organization, at least to the extent that these economic systems are tolerant of different forms of market organization. Yet capitalist social relations, in particular the relations of wage earner to capitalist, surely make a difference in how productive a purely technical division of labor is. This point is specifically addressed by Marxian theory, to which we shall turn shortly.

The second great contribution of classical political economy is the comparative costs doctrine. The central idea is, of course, familiar to all students of international political economy. Actors in different countries, being able to produce commodities at different relative costs, have much to gain specializing in what they do relatively better and by exchanging goods in which they have a relative advantage for goods in which they have a relative disadvantage. Ricardo's famous chapter 7 on foreign trade firmly established this proposition. It demonstrated that the beneficial effects of trade were quite independent of the absolute advantage held by a country in the number of labor hours invested in a product, the classical example being that Portugal would do well to export wine and import cloth even though she could produce both with less labor hours than Britain.

Specialization and trade, according to comparative costs principles, bring a number of advantages. First, and perhaps least important, countries are able to consume commodities not available domestically, i.e., goods for which there are no import-competing industries. Second, specialization and trade allow a country to "escape from the confines of its own resource endowments and consume commodities that lie outside its production possibility frontiers" (Todaro 1977, 344). In short, people can consume bundles of commodities that are both qualitatively and quantitatively distinct from the ones available domestically, and can do so with production processes that are more efficient. A third benefit (one that is not always recognized) is that trade can foster the accumulation of capital. By allowing countries to import goods that cost less—relatively or absolutely—they may be able to lower the cost of the commodity basket of labor and, in so doing, cheapen wages, hence opening the way to increasing profit levels. Ricardo was clear on this point, arguing "that the rate of profits can never be increased but by a fall in wages, and that there can be no permanent fall in wages but in consequence of a fall of the necessaries on which wages are expended" (Ricardo 1973, 80). This is a point well recognized by political leaders today. Imports are seen as deflationary; and, especially when coupled with the fact that in advanced capitalist countries they tend to be disproportionately consumed by working-class people, they are a damper on wage increases.

The doctrine of comparative cost advantage has proved to be a powerful one. Ricardo's trumpeting of its merits, in the early nineteenth century, no doubt signalled that it was already a conquering idea. It has proved to be a durable one, and has continued to energize the modern world, both intellectually and politically. It has been used as a guide to policy making and a justification for outward-looking policies; it has been refined, deductively elaborated and, to some arguable extent, inductively confirmed. The idea is not without its critics, particularly those associated with the transitional need for some measure of autarky (as in infant industry arguments) or, more strongly, proponents of self-reliance. My point here is not to defend the idea from all critics, but only to affirm what most would concede in principle (even if they tend to neglect it in practice), namely, that comparative cost theory has been enormously influential at the intellectual and practical levels.

Powerful enough at the general level, the comparative cost doctrine has certain important corollaries. These corollaries may be most usefully illustrated by accepting a counterfactual example as a baseline. Suppose, for the sake of argument, that two countries produce exactly the same bundle of goods at exactly the same relative costs. Under this improbable condition, no trade would occur and no welfare improvements would accrue to the citizens of these respective countries; but, by relaxing these assumptions and introducing modest differentiations in relative costs, trade becomes profitable. Carrying this logic further, one can see the first corollary: trade among countries will be more profitable if the comparative cost differences among them are larger. The second corollary appears contradictory, but can easily be reconciled with the first: the greater the redundancy (of things produced) among countries, the greater the gains from trade. The greater the redundancy, the greater the domestic reallocation of productive factors, when exchange takes place. These corollaries have become important in guiding trade theory in general, and customs union theory in particular.

If classical and neo-classical political economics are to provide an adequate account of the modern global system, they must have a political, as well as an economic, theory. So far, I have talked exclusively of economic factors, as if the world were composed solely of wealth-maximizing (not power-maximizing) individuals operating within well-functioning markets. What kinds of political extensions of classical and neo-classical economics are possible? What would the political world look like if it operated strictly in accordance with neo-classical principles?

The simplest answer to these questions is that it would be a world of minimal political institutions and policies; they would be limited to those necessary to facilitate production and distribution of such commodities that would not otherwise be produced. Governments would provide what is clearly necessary to allow markets to function well—defense from predators, domestic law and order, money, and infrastructure. Ownership of capital and political restraints on markets would be kept to a minimum; the boundary between what is in the domain of markets and the domain of rights would generally be decided in favor of markets. In brief, this is the neo-classical political world, a world of political institutions designed to make markets function better and to provide a set of well-defined, limited rights.

What if markets do not work? The neo-classical model recognizes the importance of this question and attempts to respond to it. Indeed, the concept of "market failure" provides an entering wedge for politicized notions of the economy. Conceptions of the political system enter in a very definite way, not as a predatory animal preying upon different parts of society, nor as a defender of class interests but, instead, as a conduit for achieving goods not individually achievable. While this literature is general (e.g., Buchanan 1975; Buchanan and Tullock 1965; Mueller 1979), and applies to broad reaches of individual and social behavior, it has a specific international political economy extension, perhaps best discussed under the "international regimes" heading.

Let me start by asking a question posed most sharply, and provocatively, by Keohane (1982, 1984). The question, which arises from the economist's maximizing perspective, asks naively why the advantages of cooperation at the international level are vastly underutilized, and why the potential welfare benefits usually far exceed those actually reaped. Are individuals irrational, perverse, myopic, or xenophobic? Or are they simply ignorant of the benefits out there? All of these factors may play a role. Yet, from a regime theorist's viewpoint, the central defect is an institutional one, or rather the defect is the absence of international institutions appropriate to maximizing behavior. It is in this context of institutional weakness at the international level that regimes enter the economic discussion. Regimes, defined by Krasner as "sets of explicit or implicit principles, norms, rules and decision-making procedures around which actors' expectations converge . . ." (Krasner 1982, 186), are emergent international institutions that can facilitate cooperation by mitigating some of the structural obstacles to the rational pursuit of cooperative interests embedded in the interstate system. According to Keohane:

> These regimes create a more favorable institutional environment for cooperation than would otherwise exist; it is easier to maintain them than it would be to create new ones. Such regimes are important not because they constitute centralized quasi-governments but because they can facilitate agreements, and decentralized enforcement of agreements, among governments. They enhance the likelihood of cooperation by reducing the costs of making transactions that are consistent with the principles of the regime: they create the conditions for orderly multilateral negotiations, legitimate and delegitimate different types of state action, and facilitate linkages among issues within regimes, and between regimes. They increase the symmetry and improve the quality of the information that governments receive. By clustering issues together in the same forums over long periods of time, they help to bring governments into continuing interaction with one another, reducing incentives to cheat and enhancing the value of reputation (Keohane 1984).

The value of studying regimes, then, is that they provide an institutional basis for cooperation. They contribute to the reduction of ignorance, suspicion, and fear of being exploited when one behaves cooperatively (characteristic of the prisoner's dilemma situations that often face nation states). But how do regimes emerge? Under which conditions, among which countries, and at what periods of time do regimes come about and develop? I will briefly explore two theories that attempt to respond to these questions.

The first theory focuses on the presence of absence of a hegemonic power in the global system. According to this approach (Avery and Rapkin 1982, 9), only a hegemonic power has enough resources and capabilities to invest in public goods (such as military order, free trade, and a stable currency). Keohane also argues convincingly that there is a disproportionate incentive for large powers to provide public goods, on the same theoretical grounds that large members of an alliance pay a disproportionate share of the costs of an alliance. The reasoning is that failure of a large country to support the production of public goods carries a high probability that they will not be produced, and thus, unlike the situation for a small country, provides little temptation for the free rider.

If we apply the public goods argument to the international system, we arrive at the following counterintuitive conclusion, namely that the more unequal the relations among countries, the greater the likelihood that the largest and most powerful will play a leadership role in providing public goods. Without judging the empirical results, this hypothesis might apply to cleaning up international bodies of water, coordinating interest rate policies, and allowing the larger country to play a pioneering role in developing new technologies. International institutions playing a supporting role in providing public goods would have the characteristics of regimes.

A second body of theory relating to regimes is that of market failure, a theory that studies the ways in which market processes systematically fail to provide (or underproduce) certain goods.

> In situations of market failure, economic activities uncoordinated by hierarchical authority lead to inefficient results, rather than to the efficient outcomes expected under conditions of perfect competition. In the theory of market failure, the problems are attributed not to the inadequacies of the actors themselves (who are presumed to be rational utility maximizers) but rather to the structure of the system and the institutions, or lack thereof, that characterize it (Keohane 1982, 35).

To the extent that markets fail, the demand for regimes will be greater. Keohane then goes on to argue that there are three explanatory variables related to market failure. These three variables are the presence or absence of a framework establishing legal liability for individual actions, scarcity of information needed to make intelligent international decisions, and positive transaction costs. The presence of any one of these variables suggests a demand for international regimes, and increases in all three should create a strong pressure for regime formation. If well-defined norms of legal liability do not exist, there will be strong temptation for countries not to cooperate with one another, especially in prisoners' dilemma situations. If adequate information does not exist for taking coordinated actions, the benefits of cooperative behavior may again be missed. If the costs of making an agreement in the absence of a regime are too high, cooperation will not occur. In all cases, the pressures to form an international regime to facilitate the exchange of information, lubricate transactions, and provide the infrastructure for meeting and cooperation will be great.

In this section I have tried to provide the broad outlines of the international political economy addressed by classical and neo-classical economics. It is a perspective that sees the global system as open, cosmopolitan and marked by an extensive and ever deepening division of labor. With division of labor and comparative advantages as centerpieces, this body of theory stresses the sources of movement in the international system and the possibilities such movement entails for developing countries. Whether one focuses on capital costs or labor costs, labor productivity, proximity to markets or other factors, the emphasis is on the ceaseless change among them. Singapore may have had cheap labor ten years ago, but this is not the case today—at least relative to other less developed countries (LDCs). South Korea's wages have gone up several hundred percent in the past fifteen years, making other LDCs more competitive in labor-intensive goods. The "shifting nature of comparative advantage" (Balassa 1979) provides numerous opportunities for LDCs, multiple access points for entering *the* developmental path, and an ever changing but always present strong card to play (relative advantage). The role of the state is minimal, generally neutral, and instrumental in allowing private-regarding, self-interested individuals to achieve collectively what they cannot attain as individuals. Finally, and this is a point I have not mentioned, classical and neo-classical economics see the global political economy as consisting of a complex network of self-correcting forces. The basic structuring principles that govern the global economy are of a general equilibrium type, constantly balancing the flows of capital, commodities, differential demands for labor and so on. The "final" result of such a world should be an elaborate, global division of labor with wealth for all and factor prices gradually converging toward equilibrium among countries and across sectors (Samuelson 1948).

2. *The Marxian approach to the international division of labor.* One difficulty in developing the Marxian perspective on the international division of labor is that much disparate material is included (or includes itself) under this label. In loose usage, Marxism has become synonymous with those studies that use terms like surplus-extraction, capital accumulation, exploitation, unequal exchange, and underdevelopment. Others see Marxism less as a question of analytic method than of adopting the correct political positions—inequality is bad, less developed countries have been exploited, redistribution (presumably, of product and wealth-producing assets) is a good thing. Marxism, as method and substantive theory, is reduced to a psychological valence, a sentiment. A third group has blended, some might say "submerged," Marxist analysis into an overall power-bargaining critique of international political economy (Resnick et al., 1985, 88). According to this synthesis, large, powerful nations exploit smaller, weaker ones with the result that both the power and wealth of the advanced countries are systematically reinforced. The resulting mirror-image conditions of development and underdevelopment are produced, but the theoretical

machinery producing them is composed of bargaining variables: relative power position, monopolies in product and factor markets, and superior scientific and technical know-how. Nothing concerning class and social relations of production appears in the analysis. This leads, as Resnick et al. have argued, to a paradoxical situation in which "the literature on international capitalism constantly uses Marx as a touchstone, various writers dutifully claiming to refute or vindicate Marx's vision of capitalist development. Yet, on the other hand, the specific focus and insight of Marx's monumental study of capitalism, the role of class processes in history, has dropped from sight in both the orthodox and radical literatures" (Resnick 1985, 88). In what follows, I will try to show (relying heavily on the work of Steve Resnick and his coauthors) that Marxism does have a distinctive statement to make about the international division of labor and international political economy in general.

There are three major theoretical entry points for a Marxian analysis of the international division of labor: the labor theory of value, Marxist theories of imperialism, and concepts centering around the social relations of production. The advantage of the first approach is that it develops the philosophical and logical foundations of value, thus placing labor right at the center. The second approach stresses the ways in which capitalism, operating first on a small scale, gradually transforms itself into national and then international capitalism. The third approach, the one chosen here, focuses on the social relations of production and highlights the class relationships on which capitalism rests.

It is perhaps best to begin Marx's analysis of the social relations of production, once again via Marx's reaction to Adam Smith. In this, it is ironic to note the beginnings of Smith's and Marx's major works, beginnings that might well have substituted for one another. Smith opened the introduction to *The Wealth of Nations* with a praise of labor: "The annual labour of every nation is the fund which originally supplies it with all the necessaries and conveniences of life" (Smith 1970, 104), while Marx started the first volume of *Capital* with an analysis of commodities: "The wealth of those societies in which the capitalist mode of production prevails, presents itself as 'an immense accumulation of Commodities'" (Marx 1906, 41). Despite this, Marx was to provide the more profound analysis of labor. In part, this was due to the fact that Marx already had Smith to build upon and, in part, to his extending beyond Smith's work, incorporating factors tied to the relations of production in his analyses. Smith's analysis of the division of labor was superb, but, as stated before, it was limited to a set of concerns one might label technical and organizational. These factors are important in their own right but, for Marx, they failed to isolate what was central to the process of economic change—division of labor and accumulation of wealth. For Marx, commodities were so important because, in addition to being objects embodying use values, they also embodied labor, indeed more labor than necessary to replenish itself. From this fact that labor was able to produce more exchange value than needed to replenish itself arose the possibility of accumulation. But, to understand just how this additional value was appropriated and used, we must understand the concept of social relations of production.

Marx wanted to ground the laws of exchange in the laws of production. To do this convincingly, he had to accomplish two major, interrelated feats. First of all, he had to demonstrate that the realm of exchange was not a fundamentally independent realm; this he took up directly in his critique of Proudhon (Marx 1955). Second, it was his task to reject subjective theories of value that had made substantial progress in the two decades following Ricardo's death in 1823 (Meek 1956, 121). In carrying out these tasks, Marx developed his analysis based on the central role of labor in the productive process, which had distinctive class elements. He started with a definition of the *labor process,* which he viewed as "human action with a view to the production of use-values, appropriation of natural substances to human requirements" (Marx 1906, 204-5). Labor was truly a "metabolism with nature" because, without it, man's bodily processes would come to a halt. Labor might be conceived in its different forms: weaver, breadbaker, medical doctor, or, in a more abstract, homogeneous way, as so much *"muscles and brains at work with a purpose"* (Inayatullah 1985, 11).

From there, Marx went on to set the value of labor as equal to the socially necessary abstract labor time needed to reproduce labor. By extension, then, any value produced by labor in excess of its own reproduction needs was surplus labor. Thus, the total product of labor could be divided into two parts: necessary labor (i.e., required for reproducing the conditions of labor's existence) and surplus labor (the excess). In turn, necessary labor, as a category, was partitioned into labor needed to reproduce living workers themselves and that needed to reproduce the machinery with which they worked. These categories now easily translate into the famous c (constant capital), v (variable capital), and s (surplus) scheme. It is a short, algebraic hop from there to the related expression of exploitation (s/v), organic compositions of capital (c/v), and rate of profit [$s/(c + v)$].

These terms form part of the analytic foundations of the Marxian system; they are purely accounting expressions, in so far as they have been elaborated here. To bring them to life, they have to be embedded within a historical framework. The institutional datum missing is the social relations of production, in particular, the existence of a capitalist class (which "lives" purely by virtue of its ownership of capital) that joins its physical capital to the labor power of workers. From the chemistry of the combination of privately owned capital and wage labor, in tandem with, or perhaps disciplined by, a competitive market, results a quantity of value sufficient to replace labor and the original capital furnished, plus an additional amount (surplus). The existence of this surplus, the struggle for access to it, its distribution among various class groups, and the degree to which it is reinvested (capital accumulation) versus consumed are central topics of Marxian analysis. For now, I simply want to emphasize that a surplus exists, that it was *produced* rather than *acquired through exchange,* and that its production transpired within a matrix of social relations, and not as a result of a disembodied technical process.

Capitalism did not invent the surplus, nor was it the first economic system to produce exchange values and to accumulate capital. Capitalism was more of a social invention, a new way of organizing relations among people within the productive process and, above all, a new way of producing and extracting the surplus. For Marx, the critical first question was how it happened that labor and capital "come to confront one another as two persons . . .?" (Meek 1965, 138). Indeed, this question provides a good starting point for the analysis of capitalism as a social relationship. As a social relationship, capitalism required private property rights to productive capital, a free wage-labor class (i.e., without its own means of production) and a contractual system (backed by the state, if necessary) joining the two together. The institutional novelty of capitalism lay in the way the surplus was produced and extracted voluntarily, through agreement between owner of capital and owner of labor power, however asymmetrical their respective positions. Marx concisely summarizes the social relations accompanying the capitalist production process:

> The labour-process, turned into the process by which the capitalist consumes labour-power, exhibits two characteristic phenomena. First, the labourer works under the control of the capitalist to whom his labour belongs; . . . Secondly, the product is the property of the capitalist and not that of the labourer, its immediate producer. (Marx 1906, 206)

In Marxian analysis, the rise of the modern division of labor is not primarily a technical fact, nor is it primarily due to the acquisition of new skills or to the introduction of machinery into the work place. These things are important, but they flow from the social fact that the surplus is produced in a wage-private capital nexus and that the competitive pressures of the market foster—indeed require—continual accumulation. For economic units to survive in a competitive marketplace, they must accumulate capital; to do this, they must constantly improve this productivity, and, to grow, they have to introduce ever finer specializations. The detailed or technical division of labor, in short, grew out of the social relations of production of capitalism.

3. Marxian class analysis of international division of labor and international political economy. A Marxian approach to the international division of labor asks many questions, some of which are similar and some different from those conventionally posed. Why are some countries and some classes rich and others poor? How did it happen that certain classes in certain countries specialized in commercial capital, while others specialized in industrial capital? What about the earlier specialization between landed and industrial capital, or the later differentiation between industrial and financial capital? Why do some countries (classes within countries) seem to specialize in agricultural production, raw materials, or simple finished goods, while others concentrate their energies on capital-intensive industries?

Most of these questions can be posed by any theorist of the international division of labor. But in answering them, the Marxian approach insists that one start from the realm of production and try to understand exchange relations as an outgrowth of production, rather than the other way around. This enables one to develop a class analysis of international political economy and to distinguish clearly the role of states and class in the international system. I will try to do this once again, relying heavily on an article by Resnick, Sinisi, and Wolff (1985).

Resnick et al. start by making a distinction between *fundamental* and *subsumed* class positions. A fundamental class position is one in which the capitalist directly receives a surplus value generated by the labor process. A subsumed class position is one in which surplus value is distributed to classes that "secure the conditions of existence of capitalist exploitation . . ." (Resnick et al., 1985, 100). The authors add that Marx "carefully and explicitly defined 'exploitation' to refer to the presence of the capitalist fundamental class process within any social relationship" (Resnick et al., 1985, 99). Given this definitional scheme, what can and cannot be said about international exploitation?

The most important consequence of this formulation is that exploitation is rooted in production rather than exchange. Thus it becomes definitionally impossible for exploitation to occur purely at the level of exchange, e.g., in terms of trade phenomena. This was the crux of Marx's criticism of Proudhon:

> In principle, there is no exchange of products—but there is the exchange of labour which cooperated in production. The mode of exchange of products depends upon the mode of exchange of the productive forces (Marx 1955, 67).

Although the Marxian scheme turns our attention toward production relations, it still enables us to discuss a wide range of intra- and international phenomena. Resnick et al. shows how the approach can be used to discuss foreign exploitation, profit transfers where no foreign exploitation is involved, and distributions of the surplus involving class and nonclass processes in several countries. Briefly, foreign exploitation takes place when foreign direct investment occurs that joins foreign capital to domestic labor, creating a surplus that is directly appropriated by a foreign capitalist class. This is a fundamental class process. Foreign exploitation does not occur when trade among nations takes place, no matter how unequal that trade may be. Indeed, it is not even clear what, if anything, the term "unequal trade" could mean in this context. Finally, what do we do with the many examples of situations in which a foreign class facilitates the extraction of surplus value in a foreign country and receives, in return, a "profit" for it? Subcontracting, loans, leasing of technology, and consulting all fit into this category. Although direct appropriation of surplus value by a foreign class does not take place, wealth is being transferred from groups in one country to groups in another. Resnick et al. place these examples under the category of subsumed class processes, since they involve nationals from one country making it possible for others to create and appropriate surplus value (1985, 104).

Let me attempt to summarize the preceding section. In the first place, Marxism clearly has a distinctive message concerning the division of labor. By grounding its analysis in class categories generated by the social relations of production, it creates a language that makes it possible to discuss production and exchange in class terms; while, ultimately, neither sphere may be reducible to the other, it is clear that production is primary, since it is here where the fundamental class processes occur (by definition).

What kind of global political economy is envisioned by the Marxian approach? In some ways, it is surprisingly similar to the one projected by classical political economy. It is open (even if coercively), integrated (even if hierarchically), and cosmopolitan. The driving forces of competitive capital accumulation act as homogenizing influences, much as the more neutral "spread of commerce and market" would for Smithians, eliminating or incorporating, in hybrid form, precapitalist and noncapitalist forms of labor control, and churning everything into the capital-wage-labor vortex.

Although these similarities exist, there are important differences too. First is a difference of analysis. Smithians see the global political economy and its division of labor as primarily a result of a technical differentiation flowing out of man's propensity to "truck, barter, and exchange." Marx, on the other hand, sees the division of labor as a more historical phenomenon, not part of any intrinsic bartering instincts, but instead encouraged—one might say demanded—by a particular historical configuration of capital and labor. That Marx saw and understood the great technical (productive) advantage of what he called "social" or "cooperative labor" is obvious; he spends most of chapters 13 and 14 of *Capital* setting out these advantages in some detail. The great difference between Marx and his predecessors is that, for him, the development of the division of labor is neither theoretically exogenous nor ascribed to intrinsic human propensities, but, instead, is considered part and parcel of the private capital-free labor relation.

A second, and for now final, difference between the classical and Marxian pictures of the global political economy is that the latter does not adopt the equilibrium assumptions of the former. By now, the reasons are clear; inequality is built into class relationships and these inequalities are of a sustained, self-reproducing type. And, insofar as these inequalities can be reproduced and transmitted internationally, they can also function as explanations for the hierarchical nature of the global political economy.

4. Segmented labor markets approach. In a sense, segmented labor market theories (Doeringer and Piore 1971; Edwards, Reich, and Gordon 1973; Berger and Piore 1980; and Gordon, Edwards, and Reich 1982) differ significantly from both neo-classical and Marxian theories. Both of these traditions predict a homogenized labor force: the neo-classical paradigm relying on general equilibrium principles to get there, where Marxian arguments stress the process of accumulation. To be sure, Marx recognized different forms of labor control, as well as different "capitals," but it is fair to say that as capital and accumulation proceeds, from simple reproduction to simple and then complex accumulation, labor becomes less skillful, less marked by regional and cultural variety—in short, less heterogeneous. Labor becomes abstract, and homogeneous under the laws of motion of capitalism. Beyond these views about labor, the neo-classical and Marxian paradigms share an overriding image of "industrial society" in which the broad forces of industrialism triumph. Rationalization, mechanization, commercialization, bureaucratization, the introduction and spread of scientific knowledge into human affairs were all seen as components of this new age. In this respect, the economists, from whatever tradition, had much in common with nineteenth-century sociologists (Comte, Spencer, Toennies, Maine) and, later in the twentieth century, the modernization theorists.

As Berger and Piore (1980, 133) point out, the mechanisms propelling these processes for Marxian and neo-classical theories are surprisingly similar. Industrial capitalism spread outward from core areas and the primary mechanism used is the market, since it is the market, in the last analysis, which places the products resulting from different forms of production in the arena as alternatives to the consumer. A single, homogeneous market soon leads to a homogeneous set of production relations. The attraction of cities, the spread of highways, improved communication, etc.—in addition to the spread of the market—result in migration from countryside to urban areas, further homogenizing the population. The result is an increasingly unified industrial society with traditional groups marginalized and confined to the fighting of historical skirmishes they are bound to lose.

One antecedent of the segmented labor market theories is the dual economy concept, first set forth to my knowledge by Boeke in a lecture given in 1930 and later published (1961). The basic idea is simple: most less developed countries are composed of not one economy, but two. First, there is a modern economy marked by capital-intensive production, mechanization, and a disciplined urban-industrial labor force. Second, there is an economy variously termed "backward" or "traditional," and characterized by small-scale and labor-intensive production, informal work patterns and the absence of mechanized forms of production.

A variant of the dual economy model is elaborated by some dependency theorists, who see, first of all, the modern economy arising from a fusion between local and foreign capitalists, an alliance that is, in reality, against the nonmodern sector (periphery) of the host country. This enclave model is then generalized to one characterizing society as a whole. Sunkel's "structural heterogeneity" (n.d.) and Brewster's "disarticulated economy" (1973) are representations of this basic idea of nonuniform, even unconnected economic processes. Clearly, these internal social and economic divisions are understood as long-term, structural forces, hence not to be undone by the self-eroding effects of modernization.

Segmented labor market (SLM) theories are extensions of the above approaches, as well as genuinely innovative departures from them. Since SLM theories have been set out in detail elsewhere (Berger and Piore 1980; Gordon, Edwards, and Reich 1982), I will attempt only a brief summary here. The major argument is that modern economies, including advanced and less developed, are integrated ensembles of numerous differentiated labor markets, each operating with a distinctive logic and maintaining its own boundaries while, at the same time, connected to the whole.

SLM theories explicitly reject the idea of one, overarching labor market, operating within the mechanized, capital-intensive sector and incrementally absorbing other forms of labor. First, theorists of this school posit primary and secondary segments. They are distinguished by the kinds of characteristics required to work in them: primary jobs require stable work habits, skills are acquired on the job, wages are high, and a job ladder exists (Edwards, Reich, and Gordon 1973, 359); secondary jobs do not require these characteristics. Indeed, the demand for work is unstable, turnover is high, and job ladders seldom exist. Frequently, secondary jobs are filled by minorities, migrants, youth, and women (Edwards, Reich, and Gordon 1973, 359-60). In addition, within the primary sector there is a distinction between subordinate and independent jobs; the former are more routinized and encourage discipline, reliability, and the ability (and willingness) to execute orders, whereas the latter require creativity and the ability to make broad decisions.

This is the basic form of the model. It could be extended (and has been) to include additional segments, but the basic point is the same: a society is a collection of work forms that are not moving in any standard direction. The divisions are many, real and enduring. If this model of the "economy" is accurate, it has some troubling implications. The first is that much neo-classical theorizing and elegant model building in the dual economy tradition is misconceived from the start (see, e.g., Fields 1980). In addition, much macrosociology, in both its modernization theory and world systems theory variants, simply misses the point that there are many labor forms that are small-scale, durable, and resilient. They are not simply "pulled along by" or "integrated into" (to use two very different metaphors), or even resistant to a single logic of global capitalism. Nor is it correct to see world labor as becoming proletarianized in some irreversible sense. In some ways, particularly in the advanced capitalist world, labor has become decommodified, particularly in those arenas where "rights" and "entitlements" have displaced activities previously regulated by markets (Offe 1984; Bowles and Gintis 1982; Levine, forthcoming). Finally, these forms of labor are often different not only in technical terms (scale, skill level, etc.), but also in terms of the social relations of production in which they are embedded. The SLM model is not presented merely as a "survival," an atavism, or as due to the recalcitrance of cultural groups opposed to the inexorable forces of modernity. Some of these forces may be at work, but the primary reason for the durable variety of labor forms lies within the capitalist political economy itself.

There are three major ways that segmented labor markets help the capitalist economy and political forces supportive of accumulation. The first is by providing an enormous flexibility with respect to utilization of productive capacity and labor employment. Where the primary economy has become rigid, particularly in countries like France and Italy (much less so in the United States), because of large sunk costs (initial capital investments) and restrictions against laying off workers, the secondary economy remains fluid and able to move with the ebb and flow of the economy as a whole. In a sense, the existence of different labor markets provides some structural opportunity for heating up and cooling down the economy. It is a countercyclical device that, once in place, does not have to be consciously manipulated by policy markets. Berger and Piore put it well when they say:

> The relative ease with which the traditional sector expands and contracts and its greater sensitivity to the economic cycle all help compensate for a loss of responsiveness in the system as a whole. The flexibility that the traditional sector provides to the economy results from particular kinds of producers, particular kinds of firms, and the relationship that these workers and firms enter into with the modern sector. (Berger and Piore 1980, 103-4)

A second way in which employment outside of the large, organized, capital-intensive firm aids some groups in society is by placing various fractions of labor and capital outside the extractive reach of the state. A migrant working illegally does not have to pay taxes, and his employer evades social security payments; a cab driver or waiter claims less than his actual earnings in tips. Similarly, as Berger and Piore point out (1980, 105), small, independent businesses in France and Italy are less likely to invest in new capital equipment on the basis of outside financing since, if they do so, the state acquires access to the accounting books. And, if workers outside the family are employed, the informality of family business and lack of state control make it easier for these small firms to take on and lay off workers. The economy retains an element of flexibility, the worker must adapt to greater uncertainty and insecurity.

The third and final way that different labor markets survive is by benefiting (and being benefited by) elements of the political system. These markets perpetuate themselves not only because they are functional for the economy, but also because of their role in the political order. But here we start with a puzzle. Most governments in the advanced capitalist world openly proclaim their commitment to modernization, and policies pursued seem to support this commitment. The common agricultural policy in the European Economic Community (EEC) seems to bear this out, emphasizing as it does increases in scale, elimination of small farms, and mechanization. Similarly, the efforts of the European Commission in the arena of industrial policy, which stresses mergers and concentrations of industrial capital, carry the same message, particularly during the period when Colonna Di Paliano was EEC commissioner for industrial policy. In spite of these modernist tendencies, in some European countries other policies adopted have "protected small shops against supermarkets, sheltered small business from the full impact of social security and fiscal legislation, and doled out subsidies and exemptions to the very traditional firms whose existence blocked the expansion of the modern sector" (Berger and Piore 1980, 110).

Why do these contradictory policies survive? How does one account for the anomalous situation in which support for big capital and small capital coexist? One approach is to see these contradictory forces as a result of the countervailing pushes and pulls on the political system. The discordance of goals at the constituent level is then projected as a collective irrationality at the level of public policy. Such a result, where divergent interests work at cross-purposes, is not all that rare in politics.

A second approach sees these policies not as contradictory, but as effectively integrated into an overall pattern that is functional for the interests of large and small capital, and to some extent, for the worker too. Alessandro Pizzorno, for example, sees these apparent contradictions as the social price paid by the modern capitalist sector for aligning itself with the petty bourgeoisie (Berger and Piore 1980, 110). Berger and Piore, adding their own interpretation, argue that the informal, small-scale, traditional labor market acts as an effective bulwark against social unrest and mobilization by parties of the left. It does this by providing temporary employment and by locating jobs within a sector that is small, competitive, and dispersed, thus making collective action difficult for the workers. The structural characteristics of the traditional sector make for high transaction costs among workers, ease of free riding, and difficulty in capturing any gains resulting from individual-level cooperative behavior. In short, all the Olsonian conditions unfavorable to collective action exist in this sector, with the predictable final result of a failure of classwide politics.

To my mind, the SLM approach has many advantages, chief of which are three. First, it is capable of recognizing and theoretically accomodating many different forms of labor that populate our contemporary world, and it does so without treating them as "backward cultures," "victims of modernization," or "survivals" from a premodern era. The chief strength of this approach is that its recognition of labor variety is not ad hoc, but flows naturally from its central theoretical premises. Thus, the modern corporation, the household economy, the petty commodity producer, the petty trader, thief, loan shark, the "bullock capitalist" in India, and family enterprise all have a place in this approach.

A second advantage is that the SLM approach "naturalizes" the study of an otherwise unrelated set of economic tactics; it makes a variety of economic tactics, employed by economic, as well as political, actors interpretable by reference to a single theoretical system. Thus, subcontracting (from a primary to a secondary labor market firm), divide and rule (among workers in organized versus unorganized markets), parallel production strategies (subsidiaries in different countries or different parts of the same country), sweatshop labor, utilization of migrant workers, and the putting-out system of household labor (farmed out by factories) are all understandable by reference to a theory that stresses the behavior of forces counteracting economic rigidities that, looked at in a different light, were historical achievements won by labor in the workplace and in the political system itself.[7]

Third, the SLM approach facilitates a comprehension of other societal groups, legal, ethnic, racial or gender groups—and the differential place of these groups in the economy. In many countries, women, the young, blacks, and minorities play an important role as part of the secondary labor market. In the United States, the average proportion of women in the twenty sectors of the economy most damaged by international competition is 57 percent, while the corresponding percentage for the twenty most positively affected sectors is 20 percent (Aho and Rousslang 1979). Data suggestive of a similar status for women exist in France, where, in the rural sector, "female unemployment rates . . . show a paradoxical tendency to rise with industrial employment" (Berger and Piore 1980, 50) and in England where, although 40 percent of the workforce are females, "40 percent of all female employees are part-time workers . . ." (Pahl 1984, 79).

One could also enumerate disadvantages of the SLM approach, and, indeed, it has been subject to criticism in economic and political journals (Cain 1975; Cain 1976; and Lever-Tracy 1984). My aim here is not to draw up a balance sheet, but to note its strengths and to identify the weaknesses that are most significant for my purposes. From this standpoint, the central weakness is that the extension to the international arena is not made by either economists of the SLM school or by what I call "microsociologists" working on various parts of the labor market. While the extension of segmented labor market theory to the global level is beyond the scope of this paper, I will make a few suggestions along these lines.

In one sense, a global SLM theory is a straightforward extension of its domestic counterpart; it is merely the sum total of labor markets and forms of labor found domestically. The problem with its additive formulation is that it does not make endogenous the interconnections among countries and diverse forms of labor and, consequently, does not recognize the implications of these links for internal labor activities.

To elaborate on this idea, one can ask what impact a large but unemployed, seasonally employed, or lowly paid, potential labor force might have on any number of international activities. The answers could include the attraction of foreign capital, the incentives for foreign technology to locate in the country, incentives for domestic labor to emigrate, and the disposition of the state toward the labor resource. The point I am trying to make is that understanding the principles of SLM theory at the global level is not a simple process. Complications are introduced in terms of scale factors, increased complexity, structural-functional variety, cultural variety, and the introduction of state boundaries and interstate behavior. To understand segmented labor market theory at the global level, therefore, requires a sophisticated understanding of how all these factors interact.

A global SLM approach might be developed along the following lines. It might recognize the driving force of the process of competitive capital accumulation and try to interpret domestic activities in relation to this governing process. The interconnections among countries in the form of trade links, direct investments, financial flows and other forms of contact could be explicitly recognized, and their effects on the primary and secondary markets assessed. Aho and Rousslang (1979) have begun to make these assessments for trade-impacted industries in the United States, and Fröbel, Heinrich, and Kreye (1977) have carried out an impressive, comprehensive study of the effects of the global division of labor on the German economy and the economies of many LDCs.

In making the extension to the global level, one point should be kept in mind, namely, that the processes of capital accumulation require not only "global space" but "local space" also. Just as capital sometimes expands in order to find new markets or sources of labor, it sometimes contracts, that is, to cut labor or other production costs in times of adversity. With a conception of the economy that is at once global and local, and simultaneously allows a variety of forms of labor that can move in time with the ebb and flow of the economy, a powerful if sometimes cumbersome tool of analysis is provided. Examples of studies that could and sometimes have fit into this framework abound. Pahl's account of the Isle of Sheppey (1984), Hart's study of the informal work market in Accra, Ghana (1981), Ross and Trachte's insightful account of the peripheralization and specialization of labor in New York City (1983), Cornelisen's fascinating vignettes of five Southern Italian women and their work (1976), and Banfield's memorable *Moral Basis of a Backward Society* (1958) might all be reinterpreted within this promising framework. It is a monumental task, but one that promises great rewards.

CONCLUSION

The central focus of this chapter is the evolving division of labor both within and among countries. My chief aim has been to explore various theoretical contexts for understanding current discussions concerning the division of labor. After examining the meaning (or meanings) of labor, the labor process, and the division of labor, I surveyed three bodies of theory that attempt to provide some theoretical leverage for comprehending a remarkably broad, disparate, and difficult to integrate set of processes: the fragmentation of tasks, the routinization of production, the physical (spatial) decentralization of work and the reintegration of physically decentralized, part-processing operations for final assembly and marketing. The divisions of work by gender, class, ethnic group, and type of capital were also considered important to the broader questions dealing with the division—or rather divisions—of labor. Whatever else, no one will call my aims in this chapter (or our aims in this book) excessively modest.

One is grateful that the authors of this volume did not have to start from an empty slate. The concept of division of labor is an important one in Smith's *The Wealth of Nations,* Ricardo's *Principles of Political Economy and Taxation,* and Marx's *Capital.* Weber's essays on bureaucracy (with his wider work on economic and political organization) and Durkheim's *Division of Labor in Society* are also potentially valuable sources, not directly used here. Despite the immense contribution of these works, they demonstrate how little we know when it comes to asking specific questions about our own modern global political economy. Indeed, one can say without exaggeration that one of the chief benefits of reading the classics is that they point to a huge discrepancy between the kinds of knowledge we have about the division of labor and the kinds required to provide a foundation for understanding our modern world.

What kinds of knowledge do we have? First, we have a theoretical representation of the well-functioning, competitive market economy. This theory will tell us how the economy behaves, given a very restrictive set of conditions—e.g., perfect competition, ease of entry into the market, and widespread availability of the information needed to make choices. "Politics" is not included in the theory—it is indeterminate, contingent rather than lawful—except as introduced by the assumptions of the analyst ("If we increase protection here, what will the employment effects be?"), rather than in a theoretically determined way. Very little analysis is carried out on the basis of departures from these restrictive models. The work inspired by theories of industrial organization—Vernon on the product-cycle (1966), Hymer and Rowthorn on oligopolistic rivalry (1970)—constitute important achievements, but are only small incursions into, or exceptions outside, the boundaries of contemporary economic theory.

Realism of core assumptions aside, the biggest limitation of both classical and neo-classical economics is that it sees the division of labor as a result of static comparative advantage principles, despite some mention of "dynamic comparative advantage." The outlines of this theory are familiar to most people and go as follows. Countries specialize in (i.e., concentrate their labor on), and export products from, those areas in which they have a relative advantage (or relatively lesser disadvantage). On what does the distribution of comparative advantages depend? The answer generally is that comparative advantages depend upon the distribution of factor endowments (land, labor, capital) internationally, all countries having access to the same technologies. Thus, a country rich in natural resources will specialize in resource-intensive products, just as one rich in capital will specialize in capital-intensive products, and so on. Since resource endowments are naturally present in greater or lesser degrees, and since the market provides an effective mechanism for responding to relative scarcity and abundance, there is no need at all for governmental intervention.

The second body of knowledge we possess concerns the operation of the interstate system. The core of this knowledge revolves around the problems of anarchy, the security dilemma, and the attempts to reconcile the search for national (more accurately *state*) interest with the fluid, ruleless, coercive environment of the interstate system.

The kind of knowledge described above flows from the realist theory of international politics. The basic outlines of this theory include: a world divided into sovereign nation-states with jurisdiction over citizens within, but with little or no extraterritorial jurisdiction; a strong sense of domestic order, but anarchy among states; and, a monopoly on the legal use of violence by sovereign states. This is a "strong" interpretation of the realist theory of international politics, one not diluted by elements of world order. In addition, economic interdependence and dependence do not enter realist theory on a plane of importance equal with security concerns. Military-security concerns so dominate economic affairs on the world political agenda that the latter are treated as moving in a different orbit.

A third area of knowledge, more weakly developed than the other two, concerns the relations among family, culture, politics, and the economy. This area is composed of a number of disparate fields of inquiry, and no single discipline encompasses the activity that occurs within it; yet, we know that it includes family sociology, culture, elements of moral economy, and the articulation between all of the above and the formal and informal economy. With respect to these areas of inquiry, we know something about the family as a unit of reproduction and child-rearing, as a vehicle of primary and secondary socialization, and as a social unit that prepares individuals to assume positions in the work force. Marxist theory also tells us something about household labor, the role of such labor in the reproduction of the work force, and the production of use values that otherwise would have to be purchased on the market. Nevertheless, our ignorance in these areas is profound. We know nothing about some elementary questions. Why do some children become members of the working class, and others move up the class ladder? Why does such a high level of structured inequality exist along gender, ethnic, regional, and other lines? What are the basic forces—economic and political, as well as national and global—that might serve as agents of change of the current division of labor?

These are the areas in which we possess some knowledge: an economy without politics, an interstate political system that eliminates culture (by its assumption of universal actor rationality) and subordinates economics (by its assumptions of the centrality of security on the national agenda), and a microsociology in which family, culture, economy, and polity are only loosely connected. The areas in which knowledge are needed are, of course, provided by the mirror images of these gaps. Here I emphasize only the most obvious, and perhaps most challenging, of our needs, that of a theory (or theories) of political economy. Of course, to request that something so complex as a theory (or theories) of political economy come into existence is easy enough to do. The request itself comes with a very small price tag, and not necessarily with much appreciation of the difficulties to come.

By a theory of political economy I have in mind a general theory of the interaction of political and economic phenomena of which specific, ad hoc hypotheses relating political and economic variables are logically derivative. Such a theory could, of course, draw upon—indeed it would be premised upon—fundamental definitions of the economy and polity, and, in close touch with these definitions, it would build on a definite conception of state and nonstate political processes, as well as market and nonmarket economic processes. In addition, our prospective theory would, of necessity, include a specification of the relevant institutions (economic and political) in society and the ways by which the organized uses of political power condition and structure market behavior. The kind of political economy called for here is premised on the belief that the state must be seen as an active and creative agent in economy and society, and as much more than the silent guarantor of property relations, as in classical political economy (see Smith 1970), the provider of public goods in neo-classical economic theory (e.g., Baumol 1952), or the innocent, nonpartisan referee of the pluralist state.

Criticism of the theories mentioned should not be taken to mean that the state is not occasionally, or even frequently, all of these things. The argument is simply that it is much more. A conception of the state more in tune with some activities it historically performs is needed, and I say this with at least partial recognition of the complexity of state activities and the monumental problems associated with subjecting these complexities to the disciplines of a single theory.

What are some of these historically performed activities of which I speak? Included would be the selective use of state resources to aid particular industries or firms (Zysman 1977); attempts to foster concentration among firms within industries (Di Paliano 1970); efforts to provide protection to specific industries or, short of this, to provide relief, unemployment and restraining benefits, and perhaps most importantly, the purposeful creation of comparative advantages in the global political economy. Although the idea of "created comparative advantage" is certainly not new, it has yet to assume a central place in either neo-classical or Marxian economic theory, although selective recognition of its descriptive importance has been recognized. Zysman (1983) provides an excellent discussion of this concept, and grounds it in the historical experience of several countries, most notably Japan. As Zysman argues, "Policy-induced advantage can accumulate over time into real absolute advantage . . . as when abundant capital and protection allowed the investment in steel development which made Japanese producers preeminent" (1983, 39). The general point is this: the distribution of productive factors, relative endowments, and comparative advantages and disadvantages are not naturally supplied, at least not exclusively; they are also consciously created by state policies.

A second body of theory needed, and here only a brief comment can be provided, is one concerning the cultural economy. What I have in mind is theoretical knowledge about the ways in which ideas, beliefs, and ideologies, as well as patterns of affect and evaluative codes, structure the types of participation of various groups in the economy. Elements of this approach are present in the moral economy literature. The problem with some of this literature discussed earlier is that it tends to see the moral economy as concentrated too much in one sphere—the family—and the rational exchange economy as lying outside. Inside the family, affection, sentiment, and giving and receiving without strict accounts take place while the world outside holds to very different principles. Whatever the validity of this model for an earlier time, it seems decreasingly appropriate in parts of the advanced capitalist world where household work is increasingly commodified, where women increasingly move into various sectors of the formal workforce, and where "replacement costs" of household work are increasingly calculated by various economic actors, chief of which are insurance firms.

The call for a theory of political economy and one of cultural economy is a tall order; it is much easier to persuade others of their utility than to do the hard work required to bring them about. Although important progress has been made on several fronts (Keohane 1982, 1984; Olson 1965; Mandel 1962), there are good reasons for pessimism. The intellectual specialization of labor is well advanced. Economists are still rewarded for devising theorems and analytic proofs consistent with the orthodox paradigm; political scientists still advance within their discipline by replaying old themes without much theoretical advance (e.g., from governmental institutions to the political system to the state), or by producing (descriptively) new findings on interest groups, legislatures, or international organization. There is a great deal of overspecialization—itself a pathology of the division of labor—between economics, politics, and culture; this results in much "falling through the cracks," including, no doubt, political and cultural economy. Indeed, the intellectual division of labor is our own worst enemy when it comes to understanding the division of labor in the world.

The work of Marx, Durkheim, and Weber collectively spanned most of the nineteenth and parts of the twentieth century; in one way or another, all three dealt with the concept of division of labor. Adam Smith, before Marx, elaborated the importance of the detailed division of labor, which he saw primarily in the way it created efficiency and wealth. Marx stressed the importance of division of labor in a wider context. Indeed, he wrote about different types of division of labor: the social division, the class division, and that between town and country. His analysis made it possible to see the importance of the division of labor outside the technical realm, especially in the realm of class relations and exploitation.

Durkheim, the omission of whose work may seem odd for this chapter, wrote a book called *The Division of Labor in Society* ([1893] 1933). In many ways it was a deeply optimistic book, filled with hope about the possibilities for new forms of interdependence, as well as new possibilities for moral integration (professional ethics, importance of occupational groups) following collapse of the *conscience collective*. Durkheim certainly recognized the negative potential inherent in the division of labor; indeed, he devoted "Book Three" of *The Division of Labor in Society* to an assessment of "abnormal forms." Still, the division of labor, while it would involve growing pains and occasional pathological expressions, provided a fertile field in which to grow new organizational forms. Differentiation would lead to functional interdependence, replacing common sentiment as the social bond, and new forms of law and politics would emerge to accommodate the evolving social structures of society. The problem with Durkheim's analysis is that his interest in the division of labor is fixed only on the differentiation of occupational groups; it has no class content. For him, the danger of emerging modern society lay not in class antagonisms, but in the inequalities of status and economic rewards attached to different (occupationally defined) positions in the division of labor. In particular, the barriers (inheritance, social position) to eliminating the gap between natural and social inequalities were seen as the major problem (Sirianni 1984, 453). In a sense, Durkheim's societal ideal was a meritocracy allowing natural talents to express themselves. The contrast with Marx, who saw injustice and inequality themselves as natural, indeed intrinsic to capitalism, is obvious.

The importance of Max Weber, whose work on bureaucracy, parties, and the institutions of capitalism is of much relevance for contemporary discussion of political economy, has been greatly underestimated by (at least) social science in the United States. If Marx followed Hegel in accepting the separation of the state from civil society, Weber pursued this point to its theoretical conclusion. The state, differentiated from society, then develops its own differentiated structures; it cultivates its own tax-collecting institutions, war-fighting capabilities, and vehicles for delivery of services—in short, it develops its own means of administration. Weber takes great pains to show how the modern state grows in distinctive ways, first acquiring its own material base, its independent army funded by its own revenue sources, its own information base, and its distinctive code of loyalty. One might even argue here that, in part, the state creates its own social base, a possibility with important implications for the relationship between state and society.

While Marx "specialized" in elaborating the importance of the *means of production,* Weber's contribution lay in interpreting the importance of the *means of administration.* It is a fact of modern life that the operation of the political system, whether seen from a public goods or predatory perspective, requires specialized achievements in the means of administration; thus, the development of the political system is subject to much the same logic as that to which the economic system submits. Modern bureaucracy homogenizes; it levels social differences and unties the bonds between personal attributes and public outcomes. Modern bureaucracy produces "abstract power," just as modern capitalism produces "abstract labor" and "abstract production." As Marx talked about the levelling of idiosyncracies and stylistic variations in an ever more standardized production process, so Weber spoke of "the abstract regularity of the execution of authority, which is a result of the demand for 'equality before the law' in the personal and functional sense—hence, the horror of 'privilege'" (Weber, in Gerth and Mills 1946, 224).

Although Weber's work does not provide a full-blown theory of state-economy relations (i.e., a theory of political economy), it does suggest a corrective to simplistic ideas of how politics might join to economics. Reading Weber, it is difficult to imagine how the state could be simply "a material condensation of class relations" or "a referee impartially arbitrating conflicting group claims." The division between state and society, the emergence of independent staffs and resource bases, and the growing complexity of government itself all suggest a much greater degree of autonomy that does not rule out state bias in favor of particular group or class interests. In any case, a careful reading of Weber and Durkheim, in addition to the work of Marx and other classical political economists, is likely to prove useful in helping to meet the challenges ahead.

NOTES

I wish to thank a number people for a very careful reading of this manuscript: Robert Cox, Edward Greenberg, W. Ladd Hollist, Naeem Inayatullah, Haider Ali Khan, Alain Noel, and LaMond Tullis.

1. One of the most important sources is the book by Folker Fröbel, Jurgen Heinrichs, and Otto Kreye (1977), *The New International Division of Labour.* Also important are: Doeringer and Piore's (1971) *Internal Labor Markets and Manpower Analysis;* Edwards, Reich, and Gordon's (1973) *Labor Market Segmentation;* and Gordon, Edwards, and Reich's (1982) *Segmented Work, Divided Workers.* Writing from a World Bank (primarily neo-classical) perspective, there is Balassa (1979), *The Changing International Division of Labor in Manufactured Goods,* and Chenery and Keesing (1979), *The Changing Composition of Developing Country Exports.* Also important are the collections nicely edited by Bergquist (1984), *Labor in the Capitalist World Economy,* and Friedman (1982), *Ascent and Decline in the World System.* For a recent critical review of some of this literature, see Jenkins (1984).

2. I want to be clear that I am not criticizing eclecticism per se. Indeed, to do so is merely to commit a variant of the genetic fallacy, i.e., criticizing an argument by reference to its sources, rather than by reference to the strengths and merits of the argument itself. If a novel argument can be constructed out of previously separate theoretical sources in such a manner as to preserve—perhaps even to build—clear theoretical premises and coherent, reasoned arguments, there is not a thing wrong with this. Dogmatic critics of eclecticism presuppose pure theoretical archetypes, operating in airtight containers, from which all knowledge flows.

3. Although all three factors are important to the productive process, it is a central position of the labor theory of value that labor is the fundamental, indispensable element in this mixture. This argument, when it is not simply advanced as a definitional position, relies on a mode of reasoning that asks what happens if one pushes each of the productive factors to zero. With no raw materials or tools, labor can still

produce some things: entertainment, massages, therapy, etc. The other two productive factors are not in an equivalent position. All the raw materials and machinery in the world will produce nothing of value until acted upon by labor.

4. This point is often not given the important recognition that it deserves. External reliance is important not because it embodies a link to another country but because it contains a vulnerability—a capacity to be hurt should that link be broken. This capacity to be hurt reflects, in effect, the cost (or sacrifice) to dependent countries that would have to be sustained should that tie be broken. The implicit (but often only implicit) centrality of cost to the dependency theory's concept of vulnerability is pointed out most clearly by the fact that it is not the *magnitude* of external ties per se, but the *concentration* of these ties that counts. Concentration of external ties is important because it reflects a diminished capacity of the dependent country to adjust and to rearrange its external ties without absorbing substantial costs. To take the point even further, for precisely the same reason (i.e., that dependency contains the potential costs of reallocating external ties), there is a close link between dependency and power. Dependency implies power because, in at least an approximate way, the cost of breaking a relation implies a measure of potential powers that one actor can exert on the other. Alker (1973), Harsanyi (1965), Emerson (1962), and Keohane and Nye (1977) all write about power within an opportunity-cost tradition. Similarly, Buchanan's important essay, *Cost and Choice* (1969), clearly grounds the idea of cost in a rational theory of decision-making.

5. Some critics go much further, arguing that the segmented labor market paradigm has "grown" only at the expense of increasing incoherence. See Constance Lever-Tracy (1984).

6. For a useful survey and analysis of works dealing with these concepts, see E. K. Hunt's "The Categories of Productive and Unproductive Labor in Marxist Economic Theory" (1979).

7. The term "economic rigidity" is of course ideologically loaded. What is a "rigidity" from the standpoint of a perfectly fluid, frictionless economy is often a "security" for some group (e.g., workers trying to hold down a job). In this sense I agree completely with Piore (in Berger and Piore 1980) when he describes dualism as a "response to flux and uncertainty." But the basic point remains. To the extent that workers acquire security, the rest of the economy sustains a diminished capacity to reallocate productive factors.

2

Lynn Krieger Mytelka

Knowledge-Intensive Production and the Changing Internationalization Strategies of Multinational Firms

Capitalism is clearly in transition. Some have described its changing nature as postindustrial (Bell 1973), emphasizing thereby that the share in national output and employment contributed by manufacturing activity has declined relative to that of the service sector. Others have designated "late capitalism" as that period in which all branches of the economy have become automated (Mandel 1978, 191). Still others, notably the French *école de la régulation,* characterize contemporary capitalism in terms of its unique articulation between a mode of capital accumulation, in which the rate of technological change is accelerating, and a mode of consumption in which mass consumption norms, national and international, are adjusted to the dramatic rise in productivity generated by the process of intensive capital accumulation (Aglietta 1976, 1982; Lipietz 1982).

Despite their ideological differences, each of these approaches focuses upon the extent to which knowledge inputs have become increasingly more salient in the contemporary process of capital accumulation and its attendant mode of consumption. If we include in knowledge not only research and development (R & D) but also design, engineering, advertising, marketing and management, then present trends suggest that knowledge inputs may be displacing capital, land, and labor as the primary defining feature of the production process in advanced industrial capitalism. Much has been written, in this connection, about the growth of the service sector, particularly the expansion of engineering consultancy, data processing, banking and advertising (Pastre 1979; Spero 1983; Stanback 1981). The impact of automation on the labor process and on employment has also come under careful scrutiny in the literature (Garson 1975; Noble 1979; Forester 1980; *Scientific American* 1982). Less well examined, however, is the way in which knowledge inputs are affecting the growth strategies of firms, the nature of corporate competition and the internationalization of production.

In this chapter three new growth strategies of multinational firms are identified and their consequences for a changing international division of labor are examined. By way of introduction, section one analyzes the growing knowledge-intensity of competition, and its historical relationship to the process of concentration and internationalization. Sections two, three, and four then explore, through a number of specific illustrations, each of the three new growth strategies: (1) the decentralization and internalization of knowledge production via the creation of autonomous development units within the firm, the location of research and development laboratories in overseas subsidiaries and the introduction of world product mandates, (2) the delocalization of knowledge production to universities and institutes, and (3) the pursuit of joint ventures in design and production of high-technology products. The final section summarizes the arguments, and speculates briefly upon the consequences of these changes for the international division of labor.

THE SALIENCE OF KNOWLEDGE INPUTS IN PRODUCTION

In the eighteenth and ninteenth centuries, contact between scientists and industry was neither systematic nor institutionalized. This changed with the growth of the chemical and electrical engineering industries in the latter half of the nineteenth and early twentieth centuries (Landes 1979; Rosenberg 1972, 1982). Both product and process technologies, in these and newer industrial sectors, such as petrochemicals, electronics and biotechnology were based largely upon scientific discoveries and theories. The high cost of research and development in these industries made it increasingly difficult for the individual investigator to commercialize new products and processes without entering into collaborative arrangements with a manufacturing firm. As cost and complexity were prompting researchers to seek access to the resources of large industrial firms—their sources of funds, laboratory facilities and marketing networks—profitability considerations were inducing firms to create in-house professional research and development staffs (Freeman 1974). This was particularly true in the newer knowledge-based industries, in which innovation lay at the heart of the firm's profitability and in which control over the direction of research and ability to appropriate research results were thus crucial.

Within the multidivisional firms that began to emerge in the early part of this century, the integration of production also required increased knowledge inputs—this time in the form of centralized planning and administrative structures. The head office became the focus of these functions, as well as the center of research and development activities (Hymer 1975).

The growing importance of knowledge inputs in production is reflected in the large number of scientists and engineers engaged in research and development activities (table 2.1), and the magnitude of industrial research and development expenditures by firms in the advanced industrial capitalist countries (table 2.2). It is also evident in the accelerated increase in scientific and technical personnel and in R & D expenditures in Japan and Germany, two of the more technologically dynamic countries in the postwar years, as compared with the steady decline in these indicators experienced by the United Kingdom over the same period (Pavitt 1979, 1980; Walker 1980).

This change in the relationship of knowledge to production had immediate consequences for the nature of competition among knowledge-intensive firms and for the internationalization of production. First, in intermediate and capital goods industries, where economies of scale were important, the wedding of science and technology to industrial production either tended, as in the chemical and petrochemical industries (Freeman 1974) and more recently in semiconductors (Ernst 1981), to stimulate high levels of concentration or, as in the electrical industry, to encourage cartelization and patent-pooling (Lean, Ogur, and Rogers 1982; Newfarmer 1980). By limiting competition, each of these strategies served to reduce the risks in a knowledge-intensive industry where research results were not spread evenly over time yet sunken costs were high, and where firms were thus induced to guarantee

Table 2.1

Scientists and Engineers Engaged in R & D per 10,000 Labor Force Population--Selected OECD Countries and the USSR: 1965-80

Country	1965	1968	1972	1975	1978	1979	1980
Canada	n.a.	n.a.	n.a.	22.4	23.0	23.2	24.0
France	21.0	26.4	28.1	29.3	n.a.	n.a.	n.a.
Germany (FR)	22.7	26.2	36.0	41.0	n.a.	n.a.	n.a.
Japan	24.6	31.2	38.1	47.9	49.4	n.a.	n.a.
UK	19.6	20.8	30.4	31.3	n.a.	n.a.	n.a.
US	64.1	66.9	58.2	56.4	58.3	59.2	60.4
USSR[a]	44.8	53.5	66.5	78.2	82.9	84.2	85.9

[a]lowest estimate

Sources: National Science Foundation (1981), Science Indicators-1980: Washington: National Science Board, NSB-81-1, Appendix Table 1.1, 208; Statistics Canada, Annual Review of Science Statistics (1977, 1981 editions).

Table 2.2

Industrial R & D Expenditures by Firms in Selected OECD Countries for Selected Years: 1967-77

Country	National Currency in Millions	
	Business Enterprise R & D (BERD)[a]	BERD as a % of the Domestic Product of Industry
Canada		
1967	336	0.69
1971	468	0.70
1975	692	0.60
1977	841	0.60
France		
1967	6,292	1.42
1971	8,962	1.29
1975	15,617	1.37
1977	19,999	1.35
Germany (FR)		
1967	5,683	1.28
1971	10,521	1.54
1975	14,469	1.59
1977	15,717	1.64
Japan		
1967	378,969	0.84
1971	895,020	1.11
1975	1,684,846	1.19
1977	2,109,499	1.29
United Kingdom		
1967	605	2.00
1971	697	n.a.
1975	1,340	1.75
1977	n.a.	n.a.
United States[b]		
1967	16,385	2.49
1971	18,314	2.12
1975	24,164	1.98
1977	29,907	1.91

[a]Includes R & D performed in firms and funded by government.
[b]See also table 2.3, U.S. industry's expenditures for R & D in universities and nonprofit institutions.

Sources: National Science Foundation (1981), Appendix Table 1-9, 219; and Statistics Canada, Annual Review of Science, 1977 and 1981 editions.

their markets.

Second, in consumer-oriented knowledge-intensive industries, such as pharmaceuticals, risk reduction through concentration and cartelization was complemented by a systematic process of market segmentation through the establishment of brandname loyalty via high advertising expenditures (Lall 1975). To a large extent, R & D expenditures in these industries were reoriented to reflect this emphasis on product differentiation. Du Pont, where R & D expenditures in 1975 to 1977 averaged some $350 million annually, is a case in point. Their R & D expenditures were intended to

> generate product and process improvements and . . . [develop] new technology [but] new product introduction during the 1960s w[as] double [that] of the 1950s . . . during the first part of the 1970s, some two-thirds of R & D outlays supported modifications in existing product lines and processes. (Berhman and Fischer 1980, 144)

High research, development and advertising expenditures ultimately tended to create barriers to the entry of new firms in knowledge-intensive industries, although small firms might still survive in some of the newer industrial fields or in specialized niches, and some medium-sized firms might maintain themselves through state support in the form of procurement policies, R & D funding or export subsidization and (where this has proved inadequate) through nationalization (Boismenu and Ducantenzeiler 1983; Delion and Durupty 1982; Larue de Tournemine 1983; Steed 1982). Even then, the evolution of the computer and telecommunications industries, in the late 1970s and early 1980s, suggests that the process of concentration recorded above has continued to play itself out in successive new knowledge-intensive industries as firms in these industries moved beyond their initial innovative entry into second- and third-generation products (Duncan 1982; Roobeek 1984).

Third, the new relationship of knowledge to production also affected the foreign investment process. Whereas the search for new markets, market shares and secure sources of raw materials at acceptable prices had traditionally impelled large firms to invest abroad, knowledge-intensive firms were initially motivated to internationalize operations in order to fully utilize the market power that their monopoly of technological knowledge and organizational skills made possible. Through the *internationalization of production,* such firms could cover the high costs of innovation from the widest range of sales possible, while *internalization of the market* reduced the risks of price fluctuations and guaranteed final sales (Hymer 1976; Kindleberger 1979; Caves 1982; Helleiner 1981).

American firms, as technological leaders in the immediate postwar period, and operating within the context of a high-income home market, were first to take advantage of knowledge as a unique asset in their growth and internationalization strategies (Hymer 1976; Vernon 1966). But firms in other advanced industrial capitalist countries soon followed suit. Thus a study of French multinational firms found that, whereas in 1971 "exploitation of a technological advantage" did not figure among the principal reasons French firms located abroad, in 1981 this was cited by thirty-seven percent of the firms and ranked as the third most important reason for overseas investment (Michalet et al. 1983, 89).

During the postwar period, the process of capital accumulation within the large, multinational firm thus came to be characterized by a dialectical interplay between profit maximization strategies that focused on product differentiation and/or labor specialization and risk minimization strategies, which emphasized increased planning and control over knowledge and labor inputs and over markets. Underlying the whole, however, was an accelerated rate of technological innovation and diffusion, which periodically raised the specter of overproduction. In the 1960s, new pressures for change in corporate structures emerged. Dynamic sectors spawned a host of new competitors, and where these did not spring up of their own accord, states intervened to support national champions in key high-technology industries. Simultaneously, traditional industries faced a dramatic rise in competition from low-wage countries.

Augmenting these pressures were signs of an impending crisis, as the rate of productivity increase began to decline towards the end of the decade, making it more costly for governments to maintain high levels of mass consumption through Keynesian demand management techniques (Lipietz 1982). Responding to the new dynamics of competition and accelerated technological change to which their earlier actions had, in part, given rise, large corporations now devised two new strategic variants of their broader profit-maximization, risk-minimization strategy. Each of these variants, however, appears to have been short-lived, as we shall see.

The first of these, segmentation and delocalization of production, was a cost-reduction strategy made possible by technological innovations in unrelated industries and economic sectors. The microprocessor was the key, for it was with the development of microprocessors that a system for handling information became economically available and could be applied to production processes in hitherto traditional industries. The use of new control systems permitted the decomposition of complex processes into less skilled segments and this, in turn, implied that skilled and hence cheaper labor could be used without a reduction in efficiency. New transportation technologies, moreover, reduced the costs of moving goods across vast distances as innovation in telecommunications improved control and system efficiency, opening the way to an extension of control beyond a single factory floor (Fröbel, Heinrichs and Kreye 1980). A radical restructuring of industrial production on a world scale was now possible; the impetus to apply such innovations lay in the declining rates of domestic profit and the widening wage differentials between advanced, industrial capitalist countries and those of the Third World and Eastern Europe that emerged in this period.

During the late 1960s and 1970s, a delocalization strategy was adopted by many firms in what were then either labor-intensive industries (e.g., textiles and clothing) or labor-intensive segments of more capital- or knowledge-intensive industries, such as electronics and automobiles. By the mid-1970s, however, this strategy was approaching its limits. Within the context of continued economic crisis and high levels of unemployment, increased imports from delocalized production facilities contributed to mounting pressures for import protection. This was reflected, *inter alia,* in increasingly more restrictive multifiber arrangements and the imposition of voluntary export restraints (Aggarwal 1983; Balassa 1984; Dolan 1983). Those nondelocalized firms that opted for a modernization strategy, moreover, had become formidable new competitors in both traditional and knowledge-intensive industries. This was particularly evident in the automobile industry. It passed rapidly through a phase in which components for a standardized world car were relocated to low-wage countries in the 1980s and then to a production system in which robotized assembly lines slashed the labor time required to assemble a car and permitted reduced inventories that lowered the cost of storage but put a premium on locating component manufacturers within a ninety-minute radius of the assembly plant. Further, flexible manufacturing reversed earlier trends towards economies of scale by allowing a range of models to be produced competitively at lower volumes in a multi-model plant (Sekaly 1981; UNIDO 1984; A. Altschuler et al. 1984). Automation and the introduction of CAD/CAM systems began to produce similar results in the textile and electronics industries as well (Hoffman and Rush 1982; Mytelka and Mahon 1983; Kaplinsky 1984).

Whereas the delocalization of production aimed at profit-maximization, the second strategic variant, the formation of conglomerates, was oriented more toward risks reduction: for some firms in traditional industries, conglomerate mergers provided an alternative to the delocalization of production. Through conglomerate mergers, such firms could control forward linking markets, diversify into more dynamic sectors, reduce their tax burden and purchase existing plants and equipment for less than the cost (and risk) of new investment. But this was, at best, a short-term solution because such conglomerates, leaving production unrationalized, soon found themselves in serious financial difficulties—this was particularly evident in the French textile and chemical industries and the American steel industry (Mytelka 1982, Acs 1984). Conglomerates, moreover, do not have the flexibility to compete in a worldwide production and trading system in which the ability to respond rapidly to changing tastes, costs and patterns of competition has become the determinant in the survival of the firm. Ultimately even these firms found it necessary to adopt a modernization strategy.

The acceleration of technological change and the central role that flexible response plays in the growth strategy of knowledge-intensive firms have, in turn, raised both the costs and risks of knowledge production itself. This occurred for a number of reasons.

First, product life cycles in the most dynamic industries—microelectronics, telecommunications, ceramics, optical fibers—were shortening because the very nature of the products, their uses and the manufacturing techniques required for their production differed substantially from one product generation to the next. In the information processing industry, for example, more than half the products are less than five years old (Delapierre and Zimmerman 1984, 12). In the chemical and pharmaceutical industries, one out of every two products is less than ten years old (Bellon 1983, 158). With shortened product life cycles, firms need to spend *increasing* amounts on research and development to remain at the frontier of technological change in their industry. The need to expend increasing amounts on research and development in such industries is brought out in figure 2.1, which shows the relationship between product life cycle and R & D costs as a percentage of sales.

Second, with increased competitive pressure, the penalties for a failure to be first have also multiplied. Thus, Kaplinsky argues that the introduction of electronics-based automation technologies leads to a reduction in "product development lead time, a factor which not only cuts costs but also can be decisive in establishing market shares" (Kaplinsky 1984, 8).

Third, the risks in knowledge-intensive industries undergoing rapid technological change are also higher. This occurs because earlier strategies aimed at securing markets for products with high research and development costs do not work where the very conception of what might constitute the market for a new technology or product is unclear. Thus Delapierre and Zimmerman point out that:

> A l'heure actuelle . . . [l]es marchés nouveaux n'existent le plus souvent qu'à titre virtuel . . . les firmes ne peuvent donc plus se situer d'emblée sur un marché existant, facilement identifié par un ensemble de clientèle, une gamme de produits, un champs technologique et une population de concurrents. L'incertitude devient la règle et la souplesse et la rapidité de réaction des impératifs (Delapierre and Zimmerman 1984, 7).

The key to longevity in dynamic, knowledge-intensive industries, then, is to be in a position to control the transformation of the market, rather than merely respond to changes in it. From this perspective, it appears that competitive advantage in such industries is more a function of the rate of increase in knowledge than of an absolute increment to the stock of knowledge.

The escalation of research and development costs and risks that this new mode of competition presupposes has led firms in knowledge-intensive industries to develop a series of new growth and internationalization strategies. Each of these strategies, as we shall see in the following sections, represents an attempt to cope with the rising costs, risks and uncertainty of knowledge production.

Figure 2.1

Product Life Cycle (a) and Research and Development Costs (b)

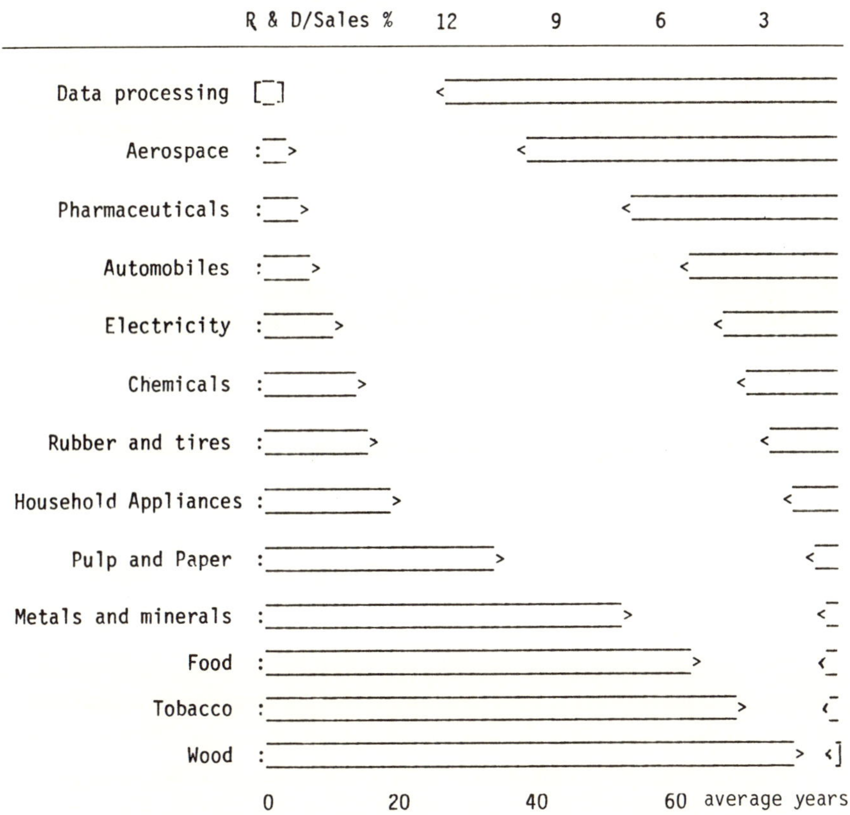

(a) product life cycle measured in average years
(b) R & D costs measured as a percentage of sales

Source: Canadian Council of Professional Engineers, Brief on Research and Development in Canada (Ottawa: CCPE, February 1983) 8.

THE DECENTRALIZATION AND INTERNATIONALIZATION OF KNOWLEDGE PRODUCTION

In the previous section, it has been argued that, during the nineteenth and twentieth centuries, control over the direction of research became central to the growth strategy of firms in knowledge-intensive industries. Initially, control and appropriation were ensured by bringing research and development activities within the confines of the firm and, wherever possible, patenting the results of such R & D activity. Where technical, financial and economic know-how replace embodied technology as the primary source of a firm's technological advantage, and where product life-cycles barely exceed the length of time required to secure patent protection, the ability to capture technological rents through patenting diminish and the importance of directly appropriating R & D results grows. These changes were reflected in the preference that firms in knowledge-intensive industries gave to direct foreign investment over licensing in their initial move abroad during the 1950s and 1960s. They were also a factor in the tendency of multinational firms to centralize R & D facilities in the parent firm (Britton and Gilmour 1978; Hymer 1976; Mytelka 1979; Vaitsos 1974). In the period 1967-1970, U.S. transnationals, for example, spent 97.4 percent of their total R & D expenditure in the United States, almost all of it in house (Michalet 1976, 164). As the costs and risks of knowledge production accelerated during the 1970s, however, large corporations began to decentralize, delocalize, and, in some instances, to internationalize research and development activities.

Decentralization of knowledge production has, thus far, taken three principal forms: the creation of autonomous development units within the firm, the decentralization of knowledge production to the firm's overseas research laboratories or the quasi-merger of dispersed research units through the establishment of data networks and the grant of a world product mandate to selected foreign subsidiaries.

The decentralization of knowledge production to autonomous development units within the firm responds to the growing need for flexibility and speed in bringing new products to market, as well as to the firm's need

> d'une part, chercher à multiplier les lieux de valorisation de sa technologie pour compenser la réduction du temps de valorisation par l'amelioration du progrès technique. L'avantage technologique est éphémère . . . [et] d'autre part, du fait de la présence du capital risqué, de s'éfforcer à retenir ses ingénieurs qui pourraient être tentés de valoriser par eux-mêmes les technologies disponibles dans l'entreprise et laissées inexploitées. C'est pourquoi . . . Control Data a décidé de faciliter la création d'entreprises par ses employés. Elle prend le plus souvent une participation dans ces nouvelles unités et s'éfforce de garder des liens d'affaires avec elles. (Delapierre and Zimmerman 1984, 14)

With this triple objective in mind, IBM has created thirty-five autonomous "special business units" within the firm. Xerox has set up a number of "strategic business units in which small engineering teams vie for the chance to take an idea from the concept stage to a feasibility model" (Dunk and Beinhorn 1984, 67). Hewlett-Packard has decentralized its R & D activities to sixty-six teams spread over fourteen of the United States (Dunk and Beinhorn 1984, 67).

Decentralization of knowledge production to the laboratories of foreign subsidiaries has also become more common in large multinational firms. Initially, overseas research laboratories were designed to modify products conceived in the firm's primary market, either to suit tastes in the new market of manufacture and sales or to match the design features or product quality of local competitors. Du Pont's paint laboratory in Belgium, for example, was established in 1962 once the local marketing group "realized that European customers would not readily accept the paint line used in the United States. Product adaptations were required, and some new products were needed . . . to match European types of paints and meet their qualities, which were fairly high. . . . The need for Du Pont to develop European paint qualities resulted from Du Pont's not being a market leader in Europe; competitors set the product pattern, forcing its R & D to be reactive" (Behrman and Fischer 1980, 166-7).

Similarly, the research facility established by Wang laboratories in Taiwan, in 1981, and staffed with over 50 engineers, is part of a "plan to begin serving the Far East market with products that can handle input and output in the region's ideographic . . . languages. This requires developing hardware and software to modify the design of the original system" (*Data Networks* 1984, 32).

Most recently, however, this traditional function has given way, in a number of instances, to a new role for overseas research laboratories as suppliers of technology to parent firms. Ciba-Geigy, a large Swiss chemical company, now spends more than twenty-five percent of its annual R & D budget in the United States, much of it on the development of new technology. Germany's Bayer AG "is using its two U.S. acquisitions—Miles Laboratories and Cutter Laboratories—to beef up its R & D effort in biotechnology." Foxboro, an American electronics firm, used the engineers' facilities in its British facility to develop a new semiconductor control chip (*Data Networks* 1984, 31-2). Similarly, Japanese, Korean, and Taiwanese firms have begun to take over American high-technology companies as a means of access to the knowledge resources such firms possess.

In the case of American multinational corporations, in a study of twenty-nine randomly selected overseas R & D laboratories representing several different industries and accounting for "about 10 percent of all overseas R & D spending by United States-based firms," Mansfield, Teece, and Romeo found that "about 47 percent of their 1979 R & D expenditures resulted in technologies that were transferred to the United States" (Romeo 1983, 5). This was particularly notable in the chemical industry, where 49 percent of the overseas R & D expenditures resulted in technologies transferred to the United States in 1979, up from 2 percent in 1965 and 22 percent in 1979 (Romeo 1983, 6). The "bulk of the transferred technologies" developed in these twenty-nine laboratories, moreover, "were new products, with product improvements a distant second" (Romeo 1983, 9), thus confirming the increasingly active role of selected overseas subsidiaries in new knowledge production.

The growth of data networks linking the geographically dispersed R & D facilities of a single corporation also reflects the need for flexibility and speed in the production of new knowledge, which the acceleration of technological change in knowledge-intensive industries has rendered essential to a firm's survival. Computer linkups of this sort, George Little of Foxboro pointed out, make "common resources available to widely distributed people" and they make "them available immediately" (*Data Networks* 1984, 31). Thus, Nixdorf Computers has linked its R & D centers in Europe and the United States; researchers at Bayer's pharmaceutical laboratories in Germany are electronically connected to their counterparts in Miles Laboratories, as are Digital Equipment Corporation (DEC) facilities in England and the United States.

THE INTRODUCTION OF WORLD PRODUCT MANDATES

A number of multinational firms have granted *world product mandates* (WPM) to selected overseas subsidiaries. Ideally, under the terms of a world product mandate, the local subsidiary is responsible for all aspects of research and development, including design and conceptualization, and for manufacturing and the international marketing of a particular product or set of operations (Atkinson 1985). As such, world product mandating is not simply "a new term for an old practice" and differs from earlier moves towards the decentralization of manufacturing divisions by such firms as General Electric, Westinghouse, or Philips (Rutenberg 1981, 592). Despite the fact that corporate headquarters continue to control key personnel and capital appropriation decisions there is an important contrast to be made between "the typically centrally organized multinational . . . [and] the far more autonomous organization required by the existence of a world product mandate" (Poynter and Rugman 1982, 54), or by present modes of competition as was argued above.

Much as the development of the multidivisional firm stimulated greater efficiency by inducing competition among divisions, and the introduction of multiproduct marketing increased market shares by covering a larger number of market segments, world product mandating increases the flexibility, reduces the costs and spreads the risks of R & D. It taps local R & D resources, including host government funding for research and development, use of public sector procurement budgets, investment tax credits and export subsidies. This is of particular importance in those countries in which the grant of public funds to a foreign owned firm can only be justified when that firm makes a significant contribution to the nation's R & D capabilities or its exports.

Given their unique combination of characteristics, world product mandates have come in for particular attention in Canada, where they are regarded as an innovative means to develop industrial R & D in a sector noted for its limited R & D activity and lagging manufactured exports (Britton and Gilmour 1978; Poynter and Rugman 1982; Science Council 1980). The Canadian government has thus actively funded firms that have received WPMs. For example, when it was granted a world product mandate to design and manufacture a new Cyber 170 computer, in the face of a dramatic rise in competition from low-wage countries, Control Data Canada received a significant portion of its funding for this project from the Canadian government's Enterprise Development Programme (*Financial Post,* 24 October 1981). Similarly, American Motors (AMC) (45 percent owned by Renault) is building an automobile plant in Canada that will have a WPM to produce a new series of intermediate-sized cars, the first of which is scheduled to roll off the assembly line in July 1987; the plant will be financed through a $121 million loan provided by the Ontario and Canadian Federal governments, to be paid back through a one percent royalty on sales over a 7.5 year period from the start of production. In addition, state participation was important in securing the support of a Canadian banking consortium (Nova Scotia, Canadian Imperial and Royal Bank), which is providing a $300 million loan. Of the total financing requirement only $343 million, in the form of equity, will come from AMC (*Globe and Mail,* 12 June 1984, B2).

The delocalization of knowledge production to university or inter-firm research centers fulfills three principal functions. First, it is a cost-reduction strategy; second, like the decentralization and internationalization of knowledge production to overseas subsidiaries, the delocalization of knowledge production to universities also enable firms to capture knowledge resources from a wider range of sources than the parent firm alone; third, participation in research pools provides access to future technologies that an individual firm cannot afford to develop on its own, yet may require in order to survive in the context of the technologically based oligopolies discussed later. Data on the magnitude of industrial funding of research in universities and nonprofit institutions in the United States are provided in table 2.3.

Although company-funded research and development in universities, colleges and nonprofit institutions amounted to a mere 1.3 percent of total company funded R & D in 1981, it was clearly on the rise; thus, whereas total corporation-funded research and development rose 113 percent in 1981 over 1967, United States industry's expenditures for R & D in universities and nonprofit institutions rose 281 percent during the same period. More recently in Britain, two major electronics groups have decided to finance chairs of molecular electronics and assist in the establishment of research laboratories at two universities, with the objective of ensuring a "more efficient technology transfer from university to industry" (*Financial Times,* 13 February 1983). In the United States over the next two years, supercomputer centers will be established at Cornell, Princeton, the University of California at San Diego, and the University of Illinois at a cost of $400 million, of which $200 million will come from firms such as IBM, Exxon, AT&T and Lockheed (*International Herald Tribune,* 27 February 1985). In France, a number of *conventions générales de collaboration scientifique sur programme* have been signed between public corporations and the CNRS (*Le Courrier du CNRS,* September-November 1983).

In the United States, most corporate funds are currently complementing seed money provided by the U.S. government's National Science Foundation (NSF) which, since 1973, has facilitated the establishment of university/industry cooperative research centers. A number of such centers have now been established in several of the most dynamically changing and hence riskier high-technology sectors—in polymers at Case Western Reserve and MIT, in robotics at Carnegie-Mellon's Robotics and Integrated Man-

Table 2.3

U.S. Industry's Expenditures for R & D in Universities and Nonprofit Institutions: 1960-81

	(Current U.S. $ Millions)	
Year	Universities and Colleges	Nonprofit Institutions
1960	40	48
1963	41	55
1967	48	74
1972	74	101
1973	84	105
1974	96	115
1975	113	125
1976	123	135
1977	139	150
1978	170	165
1979 (prelim.)	194	180
1980 (est.)	225	220
1981 (est.)	240	225

Source: National Science Foundation (1981): Appendix Table 4.9, 285.

ufacturing, in biotechnology at Washington University, in microelectronics at Stanford's Center for Integrated Systems, and at the Microelectronics Center of North Carolina (created by a consortium of universities):

> These centers investigate topics of interest to industry and promote technology transfer from lab to factory. In addition, corporate members receive access to center research and staff. . . . Martin Marietta brought researchers from MIT's Polymer Processing Center into its New Orleans Plant. Their mission: figure out how to process the special polymer used for thermal protection of the Space Shuttle's external tanks. Their . . . technique represents a potential cost savings of $25 million through the 1990s. (Ploch 1983)

Not only will the use of MIT staff save Martin Marietta money in the future, but it undoubtedly saved them considerable sums on the R & D that produced this cost-saving innovation. This is due to the fact that major overhead costs are born not by the firm but by the university, yet "the main criterion for research is its industrial potential," and the main beneficiaries are the corporate members of the research center (Ploch 1983). The latter point is brought out clearly in the recently concluded agreement between Hoechst A. G. and the Massachusetts General Hospital to create a Department of Molecular Biology at the hospital. Massachusetts General Hospital is affiliated with the Harvard Medical School, and most members of the scientific staff of the new department are expected to hold faculty positions at Harvard. Their work will focus

> on somatic cell genetics, microbial genetics, virology, immunology, plant molecular biology and eukaryotic cell gene regulation. MGM "agrees to do nothing" that might give any other entity a claim on work done by the department, staff members may consult only for nonprofit-making entities, and Hoechst gets exclusive world licenses—or the best possible licenses—for any commercially useful results. (Hancock 1983, I)

Although many U.S. university administrators see corporate financing as a boon, there is concern that academic research will be reoriented to serve short-term business interests. To the extent that such researchers "stop asking the tough questions, ones that will yield applications only twenty years from now, if ever, [and] skimp on their teaching duties [then] arrangements like this . . . constitute eating the seed corn?" (Hancock 1983, III-IV).

In addition to funding new university research facilities, U.S. corporate executives are actively seeking to rewrite antitrust legislation to facilitate greater interfirm collaboration in R & D. This is required, they argue, "in order to withstand the fierce competition from Japan, Germany and other countries whose governments encourage and, indeed, organize cooperation within industries" (Dunk and Beinhorn 1984, 69).

In Japan, for example, MITI and the Agency for Industrial Science and

Technology (AIST) have recently launched a series of long-term basic research programs in conjunction with private industry. One program, for which a budget of U.S. $75 million over the period 1979-1986 has been allocated, will focus on applied systems for measurement and control using a combination of fiber optics and electronics; the research will be undertaken by the association for the promotion of the "optoelectronic" industry, the collective laboratory for research in optoelectronics and fourteen private firms (CPE 1983b, 12-15). In the field of new materials and components, over the years 1981-1991, U.S. $104 million will be allocated for basic research to AIST's electrotechnical laboratory, in association with eleven private firms (CPE 1983b, 22-25).

Among U.S. firms, interfirm collaboration in basic research has begun through the establishment of such centers as the Semiconductor Research Corporation (SRC) and the Microelectronics and Computer Technology Corporation (MCTC). The former, with a projected budget of $30 million per year by 1986, was set up by the semiconductor equipment manufacturers' association to support basic semiconductor research in the United States. It brings together thirty-four firms, including IBM, Hewlett-Packard, Honeywell, Intel, Westinghouse, and Motorola (OECD 1984, 142); Erich Bloch, IBM's vice-president for research, is chairman of SRC's board. The board, with a budget of $50 million a year, is a joint venture among twelve high-technology companies. (Control Data, Honeywell, Motorola, Advanced Micro Devices, Harris, Digital Equipment Corporation, and National Semiconductor are members of both SRC and MCTC; major user companies, such as Martin Marietta Aerospace, RCA, and United Technologies, are also members of MCTC.) All patents and knowledge will belong to MCTC, and member companies will have first priority to license technology; member firms, moreover, will receive about 70 percent of all royalties, while MCTC itself will retain 30 percent (OECD 1984, 141). Intrafirm collaboration in nonstabilized, frontier technologies also occurs to the extent that no single firm can bear the costs of such research, and yet no firm can risk losing access to a new technology that membership in a R & D pool would provide. Thus Exxon, which is abandoning its efforts to enter the computer market, will nonetheless participate along with AT&T and Lockheed in a research center at Princeton University to develop supercomputers (*International Herald Tribune,* 27 Feburary 1985).

Although earlier efforts to develop in-house R & D had been designed to ensure privileged access to new knowledge, the current move to delocalize research activities to universities and interfirm institutes in no way diminishes the private appropriation of research results by individual firms. This is due in large part to the growing distinction between "base" and "key" technologies. A base technology

> is common to most industry participants and to most products of a business. Though essential, it is no longer critical to competitiveness because it is so widely available. . . . To a particular electronic terminals manufacturer, for example, the base technologies were integrated circuits and keyboards, whereas the key technologies were applications engineering techniques: 8-bit microprocessor applications technology; and manufacturing process technology for high-volume assembly of complex equipment (Lorenz 1981).

In the electronics industry, where product cycles are excessively short, the microprocessor, which only a few years ago was a "key" technology, has already "become a 'base' technology: it is [so] widely available [that] . . . it has ceased on its own to provide many equipment manufacturers with a substantial competitive advantage" (*Financial Times,* 2 March 1984, 6).

By delocalizing *research* on base technologies, firms liberate funds for investment in *development* activities that are more likely to enhance their competitive position. This shift in the composition of in-house R & D activities is further encouraged by the fact that research into base technologies in many of the most dynamic industries can generate a sufficiently large number of alternative development avenues, so as to make the private appropriation of development results for market advantage still possible.

By the end of the 1970s, both of these factors had led Japanese knowledge-intensive firms to significantly restructure their research and development activities. In the case of Nissan, for example,

> les différents laboratoires chargés des recherches de base (dans les domaines moteurs, véhicules, électronique, matériaux) occupent au total 1400 personnes. Le centre technique, chargé du developpement de produit, occupe quant à lui 3700 personnes, sans avoir pour autant d'activité de production. (SEST 1984, 8)

A similar reorganization was undertaken in the electronics industry by Toshiba, NEC and Casio (SEST 1984, 9). In each of these cases, using the "tree" metaphor common to Japanese descriptions of their current business strategy, the objective was to combine a number of diverse technological capabilities (the roots) into a solid technological trunk which, in turn, would open up the possibility for a wide diversity of product applications corresponding to the multiple branches of a tree, any one of which could be eliminated as changing circumstances require.

Under these changing conditions, the ability to determine when a technology is no longer a key technology becomes central to the competitive advantage of knowledge-intensive firms. This increases both the level of uncertainty in investment decision making and enhances the importance of flexibility and risk-spreading in knowledge-production activities. To cope with these new needs, a move toward the delocalization and, in some instances, the internationalization of knowledge-production activities through the establishment of joint ventures with other firms has also taken place. This new strategy, by recreating a form of oligopoly transposed to a technological base, enhances the ability of the participating firms to influence the shape of future markets.

THE GROWING IMPORTANCE OF JOINT VENTURES IN DESIGN AND DEVELOPMENT

Under contemporary conditions of transnationalized competition, firms in knowledge-intensive industries are required simultaneously to increase their flexibility of response to changing market and competitive conditions, and to position themselves in such a way as to influence the shape of future markets (Michalet et al. 1983; Madeuf and Ominami 1983). This dual concern has further accelerated the rate of technological change, obliging such firms to develop new growth and internationalization strategies that reduce the costs and enhance the flexibility of knowledge production. It has also put a premium on reducing the marketing risks and uncertainty involved in the generation of new products and processes. As in the past, a strategy that guarantees forward linking markets is ideally suited to this purpose. By incorporating rivals in a technologically based oligopolistic market structure, joint ventures in design and production of new products and processes do precisely this. Like the strategies for knowledge production discussed in sections two and three, joint ventures of this new type also permit a reduction in R & D costs and risks.

It is to the cost function that members of this business community appeal in their efforts to legitimate current moves to establish interfirm links across national boundaries. Thus Harry J. Gray, chief executive officer of United Technologies Corporation, argues that cooperation in research and development among high technology companies, no matter where they are located, has become essential:

> Growing technical complexity also means that research and development will have to be done cooperatively by groups of companies—within a particular country and even across national borders. The high cost of research and the rapid pace of product obsolescence make costs sharing necessary. A number of countries have recognized that companies can *cooperate* in research and development and still *compete* in the production, marketing and servicing of their products. (Gray 1983, 14)

What Mr. Gray does not point out, however, is the nature of that competition. "Strategic partnering," as McKinsey and Co. have termed this new form of interfirm cooperation, by implying a willingness of "competitors

. . . to join up with each other," represents a "quantum change" in a company's strategic position (Bickerstaff 1984, 42). In so doing, it goes beyond the joint ventures and arm's-length technology swaps characteristic of earlier phases of product-based oligopolization. Although interfirm collaboration thus reduces the costs, risks and uncertainty associated with rapid technological change, it also facilitates the centralization of capital, thereby raising profit levels for those firms able to appropriate rents generated by the production of new knowledge within an oligopolistic market structure. In essence then, joint ventures in design and development contribute to the formation of technological oligopolies by structuring the market, rather than by altering the cost structure of production.

Oligopolization has already begun in a number of knowledge-intensive industries, although its extensiveness is somewhat obscured by the fact that a large number of collaborative agreements involve no exchange of capital and nominally preserve the "independence" of both partners. Both the automobile and the telecommunications industries illustrate this phenomenon.

Following a period of concentration at the national level during the 1970s, as the automobile industry became more knowledge-intensive in the design of parts, final products and automation of production processes, international ventures in the design and development of components, engines and cars have multiplied. Table 2.4 provides a list of some of the most recent knowledge-related collaborative ventures in the design and development of automobile components. A major effort in collaborative research and development is also underway between American and Japanese car manufacturers: agreements have been signed between General Motors and Toyota for the production and development of small cars; between GM and Isuzu for the development of a new truck; between GM and Toyo Kogyo for the development of rotary engines, and between Ford and Kawasaki for the design of new production systems for motor assembly (CPE 1983, 26-28).

Insofar as the telecommunications industry is concerned, during the 1970s a link emerged between information-processing and transmission that required a mastery over both computer and telecommunications technology. Firms in neither industry, however, had such capabilities and the accelerated costs of R & D, given the short life cycles of these new telecommunications products, made it difficult for even the largest firms to create in-house R & D in both fields. Moreover, as product development costs soared, small and medium firms in the computer and telecommunications industries came under considerable financial pressure. At the national level these two developments induced a series of mergers, takeovers and joint ventures among computer and telecommunications firms that marked a growing oligopolization of both the domestic and international telecommunications industry.

In the United Kingdom, Standard Telephones and Cables (STC), in

Table 2.4

Knowledge-Related Collaborative Ventures in the Automobile Industry

British Leyland/ Perkins Engines	Joint contract	To develop high-speed direct-injection diesel engines
B.L. Technology/ Lucas Research Centre	Collaborative research	To apply CVTs in passenger cars
British Leyland/ Rolls Royce	Joint venture	To design and build transmissions for tracked military vehicles
British Leyland/ FIAT/Peugeot/ Renault/VW	Joint Research Committee	Set up to examine long-term research in combustion technology, corrosion, surface treatment, motor vehicle batteries, quality control, computerized engineering methods and new materials
Lucas/Chloride	Joint Venture	To develop and market high-performance electric vehicles
Lucas/Smiths Industries	Cooperation agreement	To develop a range of vehicle ignition electronics for fuel systems, sensors, transducers, monitoring vehicle conditions
Daimler-Benz/VW	Joint owners of DAG	To do R & D in the field of electric power
Lancia(FIAT)/ SAAB	Joint development	New four-door hatchback called the Type 4
FIAT/Peugot	Joint development	Ducato van
FIAT/Peugeot	Joint development	One-liter engines from components supplied by both
FIAT/Techumseh	Joint venture	To develop and pröduce a range of two- and four-stroke motors
Stanadyne/Motorola	Joint development	Production of electronic controls for fuel-injection equipment
Renault/VW	Joint development	Production of a new type of automatic gearbox from parts supplied by each firm
Renault/DEC/ COMAU	Joint research	Research into production activity control to close the loop between production planning and execution

Source: UNIDO (1984), 168-85; and Commission of the European Communities, ITTTF, Esprit Project Synopses, Computer Integrated Manufacture (Brussels: April 1986) 5-12.

which ITT, the world's second largest communications equipment market still maintains a 35 percent share, took over Britain's leading computer manufacturer, ICL, while Plessey and General Electric Co. (GEC) began to cooperate on the development of System X, a digital switching system for British Telecom. In Sweden, L. M. Ericsson, a world leader in public telephone exchanges, bought DATASAAB, the maker of small computers (*Financial Times,* 14 January 1985). In France, a series of state-guided mergers and takeovers in both the computer and telecommunications industries culminated in the nationalization of all major telecommunications and computer firms in 1982. Before nationalization, Thomson-CSF and CIT-Alcatel, France's two largest telecommunications firms, had accounted for over 55 percent of sector turnover (*Le Nouvel Economiste* 1983, 107). With the takeover by CGE, CIT-Alcatel's parent of Thomson's telecommunications activities, effective competition on the domestic market was all but eliminated, and CIT-Alcatel, which ranked tenth worldwide, moved to fifth place (*Business Week,* 24 October 1983, 146).

In the United States, deregulation initially appeared to increase competition by making it possible for AT&T and IBM to position themselves at the new interface between computers and telecommunications. After unsuccessfully negotiating with Canada's Mitel Corporation, IBM took over Rolm, a Silicon Valley digital PBX manufacturer, acquired 18 percent of ITEL (a manufacturer of semiconductor chips) and bought a controlling interest in Satellite Business Systems, owners of a long-distance transmission service. AT&T, moving more hesitantly into the computer industry, signed a cooperation agreement with Convergent Technologies for the development of 16-bit computers. At the global level, however, competition among the two U.S. giants has been a major factor in the formation of an international oligopoly in telecommunications; within two years, through a series of collaborative agreements with foreign partners, AT&T and IBM have secured bases in Italy, Holland, the United Kingdom and Spain, as tables 2.5 and 2.6 illustrate. In France, Thomson has agreed to collaborate with the French subsidiary of Hewlett-Packard (USA) (*Globe and Mail,* 13 August 1984). The recent discussions between CGE and ITT to merge their telecommunications operations will thrust the new CIT-Alcatel into the front ranks of the global telecommunications oligopoly (*International Herald Tribune,* 5-6 July 1986). Ericsson, Sweden's major telecommunications manufacturer, has linked up with Honeywell, a major U.S. computer manufacturer and British Telecan has taken over Mitel. In 1986 Germany's Siemans and the U.S. firm G.T.E. created a joint venture, leaving only AEG and Nixdorf Computer AG—insofar as their telecommunications operations are concerned—still on their own.

So extensive have these cross-national interfirm collaborative agreements become that they threaten to erode the fragile autonomy of Europe's

Table 2.5

List of IBM Recent Overseas Acquisitions and Joint Ventures (JVs)

Year	With Firm	Form	Purpose
1983	Matsushita (Japan)	Joint venture	To produce personal computers and office automatic products
1983	Toshiba (Japan)	Provides sub-assemblies	Production of a facsimile machine
1984	British Telecom	Cooperative agreement	To produce a cashless shopping system in the UK
1984	STET (Italy)	Triple agreement	A JV with Selenia-Elsag (STET subsidiary) 51%, IBM 49%, to develop CAD/CAM and computerized management systems (productique). Joint research planned in artificial intelligence, robotics and flexible manufacturing systems. In microprocessors: IBM will use SGT-ATES (STET subsidiary) inputs.
1984	Mitsubishi (Japan)	Two joint ventures	To study entry into Japanese telecom services
1984	Esprit - "AMICE" Project	Joint research	Through IBM-Europe [See table 2.6]

Sources: Roobeek (1984): 21-2; Le Monde (28 September 1984) 32; International Herald Tribune (20 November 1984) 13, 19; Financial Times (18 October 1984). Commission of the European Communities, ITTTF, Esprit Project Synopses, Computer Integrated Manufacture (Brussels: April 1986) 5-3.

telecommunications industry (*Herald Tribune,* 20 November 1984, 13; *Le Monde,* 24 October 1984, 17). One reaction to this is the recent agreement among four of Europe's largest telecommunications companies—Italtel, CIT-Alcatel, Plessey and Siemens—to reduce unnecessary duplication in research and development in digital telephone exchanges (*International Business News,* no. 194, 8 February 1985). A second is the European Community's ESPRIT program, designed to promote the development of common European telecommunications standards as part of a strategy to defend equipment manufacturers in Europe against the imposition of American and Japanese norms.

The emerging telecommunications oligopoly is not solely a function of

Table 2.6
List of AT&T's Recent Overseas Acquisitions and Joint Ventures(JVs)

Year	Firm	Form	Purpose
1983	Philips (Netherlands)	Joint venture	To produce public switching exchanges
1983	Olivetti (Italy)	Paid $260 million for a 25% share	Includes exchange of licenses, joint development of products, mutual sale of each other's products in home markets
1984	ICL/STC (UK)	Cooperative agreement	For provision of value-added network services
1984	British Telecom	Cooperative Agreement	To set up transatlantic telephone service between London-N.Y. and 13 other U.S. cities
1984	CTNE (Spain)	JV--$200 million	Being negotiated
1984	Nippon T & T (Japan)	Sale of equipment	60 Super-minicomputers for telephone traffic-monitoring
1984	KDD (Japan)	Joint venture	Set up by an AT&T sub sidiary, with KDD-Telecom monopoly to provide data communication services
1984	Mitsui (Japan)	Joint venture	To provide a value-added network (VAN) to link incompatible computers
1984	Esprit-"AMICE"*	Joint research	Through AT&T-Philips with 20 European firms to develop a European computer-integrated manufacturing architecture

*The partners include, inter alia, CAP Sogeti (F), GEC (UK), BULL (F), CIT-Alcatel (F), Siemens (Germany), ICL (UK), AEG (Germany), Volkswagen (Germany), and IBM Europe (Germany).

Source: Roobeek (1984) 24; Financial Times (18 October 1984); Commission of the European Communities, ITTTF, Esprit Project Synopses, Computer-Integrated Manufacture (Brussels: April 1986)3-5.

European-U.S. links—it is, in fact, global in scope; thus, a growing number of cooperation agreements between American and Japanese telecommunications firms are drawing the Japanese telecommunications industry into a structure of global oligopolistic competition. IBM, for example, has links through Satellite Business Systems with Fujitsu for the development of voice, data and video transmission with Nippon Telegraph and telephone (NTT) for the development of specialized circuits for voice and data transmission, with Matsushita for the manufacture of IBM computers adapted to the Japanese market under license, and the development of software (table 2.5). In expectation that NTT would lose its monopoly position in the domestic market in April of 1985, sixteen Japanese firms announced their intention to form a joint venture with AT&T to create a value-added network (VAN), which would enable otherwise incompatible computers to communicate with each other (*Financial Times,* 18 October 1984). Hughes Communications has also signed a memorandum of understanding with two Japanese firms, Itoh and Mitsui. The objective of their joint venture will be to study the Japanese telecommunications market and determine the possibility of creating a domestic satellite system (*Telecommunications,* November 1984, 8).

By the end of 1984, all of Japan's principal telecommunications firms had been drawn into cooperative relationships with the two U.S. giants and, through a series of connections between these and other firms, a dense network of interfirm research and development linkages has been established. Figure 2.2 traces these linkages but, by excluding "second-sourcing" agreements, it underestimates both Japanese participation in the emerging global telecommunications oligopoly and the extensiveness of such interfirm collaboration. "Second-sourcing" agreements, under which product technology is transferred from one firm to another, thereby enabling the latter to exactly duplicate the former's product, are used extensively in the semiconductor industy (OECD 1984, 52-3) and have become more common in the telecommunications industry (CPE 1983b). By reducing product variety, second-sourcing agreements ensure greater market stability than a more competitive environment would likely permit; they are thus important elements in the structure of a global telecommunications oligopoly. Their resemblance to licensing agreements, however, precludes their inclusion among the *new* knowledge-based strategies being examined here.

CONCLUSIONS

Underlying most views of the changing nature of capitalism is an implicit acknowledgement that knowledge inputs are becoming increasingly more important in the contemporary process of capital accumulation. While knowledge-intensity of production varies across industries, the conse-

Figure 2.2

Selected Linkages Among U.S. and Japanese Firms in Telecommunications and Informatics

```
                  Burroughs
                      :
       Harris[a] --- :: --- AMD[f]
                     :::
      Mostek[d] --- :::           Zilog[b] -- -- LSI Logic
                    ::::                      : :
   Signetics[c] -- ::::           AMS[a]     : : -- Standard ----- Toshiba
                   :::::                    : : : : Microsystems
                   :::::                    : : : :
* * * * * * * * *Intel----------------- NEC ---- Motorola --- Aizu-Toko
*                                           : :
*                  :                        : :
*                  :                        : :
*                  :           Hughes--        --Alcoa
* * * * SBS        :
*        :        :                            -- GE
*        :        :                           :
*        :        :                           :
IBM----- Fujitsu-------------------------Ungerman-Bass
:       :        :
:       :        :
:        -- TRW    -- Amdahl
:
:-------- NTT -------------Western Electric (AT&T)
:
:
:
: _ _ _ _  Matsushita
```

Notes:

*** Signifies ownership links   --- Signifies technological collaboration linkages

[a] American Microsystems (Gould)

[b] Exxon

[c] 100% Philips (Netherlands)

[d] United Technologies

[e] Linked through a joint venture with Matra (France)

[f] Advanced Micro Devices 20% Siemens (FRG)

Sources: CPE (1983)[a]; Roobeek (1984); OECD (1984): 134.

quences of the growing salience of knowledge inputs in production are being felt in all industrial sectors.

The changing relationship of knowledge to production has had numerous consequences for the nature of competition among firms and for their growth strategies. Initially, as production became more knowledge-intensive, control over the direction of research and ability to appropriate the results of that research stimulated the establishment of in-house research and development facilities. In knowledge-intensive industries, where research results are not spread evenly over time yet sunken costs are high, firms were also induced to guarantee their markets through concentration, cartelization, cross-investment and market segmentation.

During the 1960s, the rise of new cost-efficient competitors, the declining profitability at home and the widening wage differentials between advanced industrial and Third World countries led large firms to delocalize labor-intensive segments of the production process and/or to form conglomerates in an effort to diversify. Both of these strategies proved short-lived as neither dealt directly with the effect that the growing knowledge intensity of production was having on the global pattern of competition. Competition was increasingly knowledge-based; and, to the extent that it was, in the most dynamic industries product life cycles were shortening because the very nature of the products, their uses and the manufacturing techniques required for their production differed substantially from one product generation to the next. Firms were thus required to simultaneously increase their flexibility of response to changing tastes, costs and competitive conditions, and to position themselves so as to influence the shape of future, as yet indeterminant, markets. Not only did this raise the costs, but it substantially increased the risks and uncertainty of knowledge production.

Two broad strategies are being developed by firms to cope with the rising costs, risks and uncertainty of knowledge production. The first deals with the process of knowledge production itself. It includes the decentralization of knowledge production to autonomous development units within the firm—to the firm's overseas research laboratories or through the use of world product mandates to selected foreign subsidiaries and the delocalization of knowledge production to university or interfirm research centers. The decentralization, delocalization and internationalization of knowledge production increase a firm's flexibility of response. At the same time, they spread the costs and risks of response, along with the costs and risks of R & D, to universities and, through grants, subsidies, and state procurement policies, to host governments. The delocalization and internationalization of knowledge production, moreover, has the added advantage of enabling knowledge-intensive multinational firms to capture knowledge resources, frequently at lower cost, from as wide a range of sites as possible without inducing the migration of scientific and technical personnel, and without incurring the costs of reproducing such skilled manpower. Third World countries with a strong scientific and engineering base (e.g., Brazil, Argentina, India, Korea and Taiwan) are excellent candidates for the decentralization and internationalization of knowledge production by the large multinational firms, which are forming the core of a global oligopoly in these industries (Hobday 1984; Kaplinsky 1984; Rada 1985; UNCTAD 1978).

Advanced industrial countries such as Canada, the United Kingdom, Belgium and possibly France, whose firms are not at the technological frontier and/or whose domestic market cannot absorb the full range of product possibilities generated by the accelerated rate of technological change through political intervention can, nonetheless, negotiate to obtain world product mandates for products that complement the high-technology niches in which national firms can compete effectively.

The decentralization, delocalization and internationalization of knowledge production improve a firm's global flexibility and introduce a new element of autonomy into the structure of the multinational corporation, but they do not imply a loss of control over the knowledge-generation process. Rather, such strategies extend this control to incorporate knowledge resources not hitherto directly appropriable by private firms. In so doing, they reduce still further the domain of petty knowledge production, much as petty commodity production in agriculture and artisanal manufacture in industry have largely disappeared under the pressures of expanding capitalism. The current move to delocalize research activities to universities and interfirm institutes, moreover, in no way diminishes the private appropriation of research results by individual firms. This, it was argued, is largely due to the distinction that has emerged between "base" and "key" technologies, and to the fact that joint research into base technologies capable of generating a broad range of development possibilities liberates funds for investment in development activities that are more likely to enhance the competitve position of the firm.

The second strategy attempts to cope with the increasing market risks and uncertainties to which the accelerated rate of technological change in knowledge-intensive industries has given rise. As in the past, a strategy that guarantees forward linking markets is ideally suited to this purpose. Joint ventures in design and development of new products and processes, by incorporating rivals in a technologically based oligopolistic market structure, do precisely this.

Interfirm collaboration through joint ventures in design and development, like the decentralization, delocalization and internationalization of knowledge production discussed above, reduces the costs, risks and uncertainty associated with rapid technological change. They do this primarily by structuring the market rather than by altering the cost structure of production. By bringing together nominal competitors in the design and development of new products and processes, they go beyond the joint venture and arm's-length technology swaps characteristic of earlier phases of product-based oligopolization. By so doing, they determine the very shape of the future markets at the same time as they raise profit levels for those firms able to appropriate the rents generated by the production of new knowledge within an oligopolistic market structure. In this chapter, the development of a global telecommunications oligopoly, structured through a set of technologically based collaborative agreement among firms, was used to illustrate this hypothesis.

As knowledge-intensive industries are transformed into technologically based oligopolies, new barriers to entry are likely to be posed for latecomers, and the ability of small- and medium-sized enterprises to retain their independence diminishes. Indeed, the cherished notion of a "national" industry may be seriously out of date. The very logic of competition in knowledge-intensive industries suggests a gradual move from domestic concentration to international oligopolization and the survival of small and medium-sized firms seems predicated upon the establishment of technologically based collaboration agreement through which these "national" enterprises are progressively drawn into a global network of interfirm linkages, that, in the final analysis, structures their future development options.[2]

NOTES

Lynn Krieger Mytelka is affiliated with Carleton University (Ottawa) and CEREM, Université de Paris-X (Nanterre). Portions of this paper were published in French in "Le capitalisme fondé sur la connaissance et le changement dans les stratégies des entreprises industrielles," *Etudes Internationales,* XIV, no. 3 (1983): 433-52; and in "La gestion de la connaissance dans les entreprises multinaitonales," *Economie Prospective Internationale,* no. 20, 4ème trimestre (1984): 7-34. The author wishes to thank the Social Sciences and Humanities Research Council of Canada for their support in the preparation of this study.

1. The Centre d'études et de recherches sur l'entreprise multinationale (CEREM), Université de Paris-X, Nanterre, is examining the extent to which this process is currently structuring European knowledge-intensive industries.

3

Gerd Junne

Automation in the North: Consequences for Developing Countries' Exports

There has always been a time lag between real-world development of and academic reflection on what is going on outside the ivory tower of university departments and research institutes. When the book on *The New International Division of Labour* by Fröbel, Heinrichs and Kreye, which caused intensive international debate, first appeared in 1977, it quite adequately captured the most important new features of the changing international division of labor. When the book was published in English in 1980, the basic trend that the authors try to describe and explain was already changing again. Cheap, unskilled labor was no longer the main source of profit that multinational companies were looking for.

As a result of the worldwide stagnation in the second half of the 1970s, and especially as an answer to the recession in the early 1980s, new production processes have been introduced in the industrial countries. In order to capture unstable, quickly changing markets and to adapt supply to the demand of those groups in society whose purchasing power has not been affected by the crisis, more and more companies make use of *flexible automation*. Although many difficulties still have to be overcome on the way to total automation, the attention of large and small companies does very much focus on this trend, which will be described in the first part of this chapter. I do not argue that automation of production has already reached such a level that labor costs have become unimportant, or that such a level of production will be reached within a few years. I only want to stress that it is in this direction that companies are looking for a solution to their problems, and that the transfer of production to low-wage countries has become less attractive for many of them.

In the second part, the consequences of present trends toward automation of production for manufacturing exports from developing countries will be analyzed. The main question that this chapter addresses is *whether increasing automation of production in industrialized countries will lead to stagnation or even a decline of manufacturing exports from developing countries, especially the "newly industrializing countries" (NICs).*

Probably, the four "classical" NICs (Hong Kong, Singapore, South Korea and Taiwan) will be least affected by this development. There the warning signals were understood early enough to react—by automating, as well as by beating the West with its own means. But the second "layer" of NICs, those countries that tried to follow the example of the four "tigers" and sought a similar development in export-oriented industrialization, may be hit very hard. Most of them will have to fall back on their traditional role in the international division of labor as raw material producers.

The next wave of technological development, however, might undermine this position as well. New production processes will need less raw materials and fuel. Local resources in industrialized countries will be exploited more extensively, and recycling techniques will improve. As a consequence, not only exports of manufactured products will be threatened, but exports of primary products as well.

AUTOMATION OF PRODUCTION IN HIGHLY INDUSTRIALIZED COUNTRIES

A profit-squeeze as a result of increasing wages, a slowdown of productivity growth, and increasing competition from low-wage countries are identified as some of the reasons for the present worldwide recession by authors from different quarters. High wage levels have always stimulated the introduction of labor-saving technologies, and increased competition usually stimulates efforts to increase productivity. The high cost of traditional automation, however, could only be justified as long as sales prospects were bright. But the economic crisis of the 1970s and early 1980s did not encourage investment in expensive machinery, which could only work profitably if large series were to be produced.

Advances in Flexible Automation

A solution to this problem has come with the development of *flexible automation* instead of "hard automation."[1] Reprogrammable machinery can be used to produce a great variety of products and for profitable small batch production.[2] With the introduction of flexible automation, the link between automation and large-scale production is loosened. "Economies of scope" increasingly replace "economies of scale" (Bylinsky 1983). That means that, with the new equipment, a broad variety of (not too) different products can be produced with the same machinery at roughly the same cost per product as the output of large-scale production with hard automation equipment.

The centerpiece of flexible automation is industrial robots (reprogrammable mechanical manipulators); their use has increased greatly during the last years. The figures in table 3.1 show that in most developed countries the rate of increase has grown recently. The figures may be somewhat misleading, however. The impressive figures for Italy and France in 1982-1983 do not show that the introduction of robots is proceeding much faster in those two countries than in others, but that it has been especially slow in the years before with the effect that the actual increase is calculated on a very low basis. To some degree, this is true for all other countries as well: annual growth rates have been high because the number of robots installed has been small. Why this is the case (learning period) is explained later on. What is important for the argument made here is that the predicted rates of growth remain high. Although forecasts differ widely from each other (cf. OECD 1983, 52), it is only a difference between "bright" and "even brighter."

In the past, most robots have been used in the automobile industry, an industry that has not shown a strong trend toward transferring production for the world market to developing countries (Dankbaar 1983). Many observers expect a relocation of automobile production (or of parts production) to developing countries on a large scale to take place in the future (e.g., Kox 1981). However, a closer look at the investment plans of the large automobile companies reveals that they concentrate much more on the introduction of flexible automation in the production process in their home countries rather than on plans to transfer part of the production to developing countries. The most spectacular development will take place at General Motors, the world's largest producer of automobiles and the world's largest user of robots as well: in 1983, GM had 2,500 robots at its plants and ex-

TABLE 3.1

Average Annual Growth of the Robot Population in Various Countries (%)

	1974-1982	1981-1982	1982-1983
Japan	31	37	27
United States	23	39	28
Sweden	41	32	42
Germany	51	52	37
Italy	31	56	157
United Kingdom	48	62	52
France	54	20	126

Source: OECD (1983): 50; United Nations (1985): 42

pected to have 14,000 robots in place by 1990 (*Journal of Commerce,* 25 July 1983)—more than twice as many robots as installed in all the United States in the early 1980s (6,250 in 1982 [OECD 1983, 38]). A year later, GM had revised its plans and aimed at 20,000 robots by 1990, or 20 percent of the American robot population projected for that year (Gooding 1984). Other large automobile producers do not have any choice but to follow suit; the introduction of automation technologies has almost certainly been instrumental in preventing the migration of parts of the industry to low-wage economies (Kaplinsky 1984, 160-1).

The application of robots in the past has been limited because the first and second generation of robots could only be used for relatively simple tasks. The third generation of robots, however, is equipped with sensor capacity that allows them to recognize parts and to pick them up even if they are not positioned in exactly the way "expected." This allows the use of robots for assembly work, which accounts for about 40 percent of labor cost in manufacturing (Widl 1982, 12). These "intelligent" robots have become very attractive for the electronics industry, too. Here, robots do not replace the heavy, dirty or hazardous work in an environment such as the automobile industry, but rather the tedious assembly work, which, up to now, the nimble hands of female workers had done in developing, as well as developed, countries. In Japan, the electronics industry has already replaced the automobile industry as the most prominent user of robots: the share of the electrical machinery industry in the employment of industrial robots is 36 percent in Japan, compared to 29 percent in the automobile industry (Yonemoto 1982, 238). Robots are only the tip of the iceberg; they form just one step in a process toward the introduction of computer aided design/ computer aided manufacturing (CAD/CAM), which will allow almost complete automation of many production processes. There are experimental factories, where, during the day, only a few operators are present, and where production continues at night with a "ghost shift."

Although the process of automation does not advance in all sectors at the same pace, no sector of industry is excluded. A few activities remain rather recalcitrant to automation, such as sewing in the apparel industry (but design and cutting activities have become more and more automated). But here, progress is made as well, either by design of special robots, or by avoiding sewing altogether by the introduction of special adhesives to glue different parts of a garment together (Raasch 1985). In all sectors, storage and retrieval of components and spare parts, as well as packaging, lend themselves to automation. In some industries (fine chemicals and pharmaceuticals), these are yet the only activities not yet highly automated.

However, the introduction of robots and flexible automation has taken place at a much slower pace than many observers used to believe. A great number of obstacles still have to be overcome; but, as soon as (a) not only the general investment climate has improved, but also (b) better peripheral equipment is offered, (c) robots are equipped with better sensors, (d) the price of robots has declined, and (e) robots get used during more than one shift a day, there will be an even faster expansion of the number of robots in industrialized countries. Robots replace living labor; the amount replaced differs with the concrete use made of robots and with the number of shifts during which a robot is used. A recent study of robot applications in five different factories showed that one robot replaced between 1.6 and 6.2 workers (*Technische Hilfen* 1983, 218). If about 200,000 robots can be expected to operate in the United States alone by 1990 (*Technische Hilfen* 1983, 136), this would cause the destruction of about one million jobs. With General Motors alone, 80,000 of the 360,000 workers in the United States are expected to become redundant by 1986, because of the introduction of new technologies and new routine (*NRC Handelsblad,* 20 February 1984, 1).

The above sketchy remarks cannot replace a thorough analysis of the pace and progress of automation in industrial countries. The Economic Commission for Europe (ECE) of the United Nations is busy with the development of a methodology to allow the measurement of automation, and to help compare the advancement of different economies in this field. For the sake of argument in this chapter, it is enough to state that the evidence available corroborates the impression that the process of automating production has gained momentum, and that it will probably even speed up during the coming years.

The Acceleration of Automation from 1985

There are a number of reasons the process of automation will probably accelerate during the years to come: (1) "islands of automation" created hitherto will be linked more and more into integrated automation systems; (2) the learning period of the recent past will come to an end; and, (3) countervailing forces are in full retreat.

Integrated automation systems. In his recent book on automation, Raphael Kaplinsky offers a very enlightening classification of different types of automation that helps shed some light on probable future developments. He distinguishes between (a) *intraactivity automation,* which refers to automation occuring within a particular activity (for instance, replacing a specific human activity by a robot), (b) *intrasphere automation,* which refers to automation technologies having links with other activities within the same sphere, and (c) *intersphere automation* as the third and most complete form of automation, which involves coordination between activities in different spheres of production (Kaplinsky 1984, 21-7). The different spheres of production are *design* ("where the nature of the firm's output . . . is defined and new production processes are explored"), the actual *manufacturing* process ("in which the raw materials and intermediate inputs are stored, processed into final products and ultimately delivered"), and the sphere of *coordination and control* (e.g., inventories, marketing, financial control, wage payment, production scheduling).

Most earlier studies of automation refer to intraactivity automation, which is often called "island" automation. But present technological development allows for more and more intrasphere automation and even intersphere automation. The introduction of intersphere automation will especially make much labor redundant, because a large amount of work actually done consists of processing of information received from other spheres of production (e.g., adjusting machines to other types, designs or production schedules, collecting information on working hours, refilling inventories, etc.). The most prominent examples of intersphere automation are CAD/CAM systems, which in the future will also link design and production to the sphere of control.

End of the learning period. The integration of different islands of automation into wholesale automation systems will lead to far-reaching changes in all three spheres of production. These changes, however, cannot be realized from one day to the other; there is a long learning period necessary in order to let all echelons from top management to the shop floor adapt to these changes. Many companies foresaw the necessity of this adaptation and used the recession to experiment with automation equipment, even if they could not make immediate profitable use of it. They wanted to get their employees accustomed to the new equipment in several ways.[3] Managers had to learn how to plan integrated production processes, an activity that affords much closer cooperation between hitherto much more independent departments and divisions. Design engineers had to learn how to devise products that can easily be produced automatically, and production engineers became involved more intensively in the design phase of product innovation. Designers and production engineers, accordingly, have to learn to communicate much more intensively with each other. Technicians have to learn to repair and maintain the new equipment, and shop stewards have to adapt their demands to the new environment (e.g., to accept multiple shifts in exchange for general reduction of weekly working hours, see below).

In many companies, this learning period is nearing its end; companies have gathered experience with different kinds of automation equipment, and are better aware of the cost differentials of different types of production and problems connected to the equipment's introduction. Specialists have been trained for repair and maintenance of the new equipment. Workers have seen the introduction of robots and, in many instances, have been convinced that this is necessary to guarantee their company's competitiveness.

In that way, a basis has been laid to invest in the new equipment on a large scale. Now the recovery has somewhat gained momentum, better equipment is offered, and prices of this equipment have been slashed.

Countervailing forces in full retreat. The countervailing power of trade unions that might eventually be able to slow down the process of automation has declined radically in many countries (cf. Esser 1982). Trade unions have been weakened by the long recession and the large number of unemployed; but, they also suffer from the trends that will continue even during the upturn of the business cycle.

Increasing automation is linked to the erosion of traditional trade unions in several ways. The actual recovery will not lead to much new employment, just because much of the investment is in labor-saving devices. The kind of new jobs created as a result of technological development exposes the unions to an additional threat: the growth of high technology industries on the one hand and the introduction of electronical devices in almost all industries, on the other, leads to a small increase in the number of technology-oriented workers and "high-tech" occupations, and to a large increase of workers with little experience and education required, such as building custodians, cashiers, secretaries, and clerks.[4] Both categories of employees are rather difficult to organize. The structural shift in the economy forces workers to become more mobile, which will make them less inclined to participate in trade union activities. The potential of flexible automation leads to the creation of new factories that are much smaller than the traditional factories of the 1960s. Autoworkers in the South of the United States "contend that it is too difficult and too expensive to organize the small 200-men plants which are typical for the new sunbelt industries" (*Financial Times,* 10 April 1984).

It has turned out that it is less expensive to build completely new plants for the new automated production processes, instead of reequipping older installations. Many companies have taken this opportunity to rebase "themselves in agricultural regions tapping into nonunionized, and much cheaper, workforces" (*Financial Times,* 10 April 1984). Another reason for the decrease of union power is a change in mentality: people look at work in a different way than in the past. At least in Europe, work is no longer the central aspect of life for many people. With income having grown considerably in the past and a reduction of working time, other aspects of life have become more important for people who, accordingly, devote more time to these other spheres than to activities related to their work (such as trade union activity).

All these developments have contributed to the decreasing attractiveness of trade unions, which now face a dramatic decline in membership in many countries. In the United States, trade union membership as a percentage of the total labor force peaked in 1953 at 25.5 percent, fell steadily to 22.6 percent in 1970, and has since plummeted to 18.2 percent. In absolute numbers, private sector union membership reached its zenith of 17 million in 1973 and dropped to 14 million by the end of 1983; in the public sector, membership reached 6 million in 1976 and has since fallen to 5.5 million. The two key unions of the postwar era, the auto and steel workers, were hit the hardest: the autoworkers' membership in the United States topped out at 1.4 million in 1979, and had fallen to 998,000 by the end of 1982. The steelworkers, who reached a maximum of 1.1 million in 1975, have plunged to 617,000 (*Financial Times,* 10 April 1984). In the Netherlands, the decline of trade union membership has reached such proportions that representatives of *employers'* associations have started to worry about the eventual lack of a partner for discussion with sufficient numbers in the future. In Japan, robots had to become trade union members (for whom the company pays the membership fees), because the financial situation of the trade unions otherwise would have been in danger.

In many countries, trade unions have stopped fighting automation and are trying to make the best of it. Trade union struggle in Germany, for instance, centers on the reduction of weekly working hours. This is more an attempt to share the advantages of automation than to fight automation itself. Many companies (like BASF, or Siemens) have concluded special arrangements with the trade unions to reduce the weekly working time in experimental plants, in exchange for trade union consent to multishift work (*Fortune,* 14 May 1984, 136). The objectives of actual trade union struggle, therefore, are compatible with increased automation.

Another countervailing force, aside from the trade unions, might be found in the "green" parties and social movements that promote an alternative life style, fight for a less devastating impact by human activity on nature, and try to explore forms of social organization that lead to less alienation of the individual. This sometimes takes the form of protest against modern technology, and it shows a certain "Heimweh" with regard to predominantly agricultural activities of former times, with the accompanying organization of labor and integration of life into the rhythm of nature. One may ask whether this movement might have an impact on the pace of introduction of automation technologies in the highly industrialized countries.

There are two reasons this seems to be unlikely. The first is that the alternative movement itself is split over its attitude toward modern technology. Almost all groups are against the use of *nuclear* technology, but they take very different stands on other new technologies like microelectronics and biotechnology. The attractiveness of these new technologies to some in the social movement is that they have a much less negative impact on the environment (and even help to limit and repair damage done to the environment in the past), and that they provide new possibilities for the *decentrali-*

zation of economic activity. These new technologies, therefore, fit very well into the vision of a future society of many groups that often consist mainly of members with a "new middle class" background and a strong affinity for modern technology.

The second reason is that, although the alternative movement may perceive itself as a protest against modern capitalist society, it may more and more become a *necessary complement of the process toward increased automation.* Intellectuals who do not fit into this process in one way or the other can find a new identity in alternative life styles and in keeping themselves busy with a kind of labor-intensive subsistence economy. Instead of strengthening the protest against the new technologies, such a retreat may even absorb much of the critical potential and, in such a way, indirectly support the introduction of automation technology more than it will impede it.

Countervailing forces are also in full retreat because there is no alternative ideology or elaborated alternative utopia that could help to channel different forms of opposition. Obviously, the new technologies cannot be disinvented. They are there to stay (and to develop further), and social forces over the whole political spectrum in the industrialized countries have adapted to this idea.

CONSEQUENCES OF AUTOMATION FOR MANUFACTURING EXPORTS IN DEVELOPING COUNTRIES

Labor-saving technology will reduce the share of labor in total production costs and will change the structure of comparative advantages of many countries.[5] Availability of cheap labor will no longer be decisive in locating production facilities in the Third World. Export-oriented economies solely dependent on unskilled cheap labor may lose their comparative advantage in a relatively short time, with potentially severe balance of payments and employments effects. In some cases, there may even be some relocation of production facilities back to the industrialized countries. At a panel discussion of Swiss industrialists, for example, it was mentioned that Switzerland's disadvantages as an industrial location, due to high wages, were melting away because of increasing automation of production; it could be observed that certain production processes were retransferred to Switzerland.[6] The same has been reported for the Netherlands: a decrease in the cost differentials between products from low-wage countries and domestic products of about 20 to 30 percent during the last five to six years, increasing hesitation to place large orders (necessary in the Far East), insistence on fast delivery and increasing currency risks have led to a revival of the Dutch garment industry. This has hardly brought about more employment, but the financial position of the companies involved has improved considerably (*Volkskrant,* 20 May 1985). A real transfer of existing production back to industrial countries will hardly take place, just as little transfer of existing production from industrialized countries to developing countries has taken place in the past. What happens, however, is that *new* production sites will, more often than in the past, be located in industrialized countries, and that more plant closures will eventually take place in Third World countries.

Cheap labor was not the only reason to build up production capacity in the Third World; many authors have rightly pointed to the fact that, very often, highly capital-intensive production processes were installed in developing countries. The perceived comparative advantage of manufacturing activities in Third World countries is also based on *greater machine utilization,* made possible by the longer annual work hours characteristic of countries with high degrees of internal repression and severely constrained trade union movements (Ernst 1981, 211). This comparative advantage may even increase in a situation where the labor movements in the industrialized countries fight for less work hours per week. Workers in Singapore work forty-six hours a week, on the average, and workers in Hong Kong and South Korea work even forty-eight hours (Dresdner Bank 1983, 7). Therefore, a more intensive use can be made of the same machinery. However, this comparative advantage is also withering away.[7] As higher degrees of automation are reached, machinery in the industrial countries can be used around the clock with only a few supervisors present at night; maintenance tasks (e.g., reloading of magazines) can be done during the day shift.[8]

Difficulties in getting workers for night shifts will not necessarily lead to decisions to locate production in a developing country, but will only influence the specific way in which a flexible production system is operated: of the two flexible automation systems recently installed in the French car industry, for example, the one at Boutheon (Renault) is operated with three full shifts, whereas the one at Meudon near Paris (Citroën), where it is said to be more difficult to recruit workers for night work than in rural areas, two full shifts during the day and one ghost shift at night "operate" the plant (Bertrand 1982, 55). This demonstrates that operating time restrictions in industrial countries can be easily overcome.

Companies Prefer Automation to Emigration

There are not yet many automated factories in the industrialized countries. In Japan, the most advanced country in this field, there were seventy fully automated factories in 1980, and 200 in 1983, according to official sources (Ministerie van Economische Zaken 1984, 5). The figures are not yet impressive, but the fast growth of the number of automated factories is obvious.

Many more firms than those that have already invested in flexible automation equipment are deliberating such a step. I do not maintain that industries are already returning on a significant scale to the developed countries. However, there are more and more examples of companies that either return to the advanced industrialized countries, or faced with the problem to "automate, emigrate or evaporate," choose to automate. Facing "a horde of Far East manufacturers in the grueling competitive printer marketplace," Diablo Systems, Inc., a Xerox subsidiary, "has chosen to fight back by staying onshore and automating. Results to date include a 60% reduction in the direct-labor content of printers and a matching drop in average unit prices" (*Electronic Business,* February 1984, 178). But, still, Diablo is the only non-captive U.S. drive maker remaining "onshore." Twelve of the world's largest diskdrive manufacturers have set up factories in Singapore, "and more are coming in every month" (*Newsweek,* 12 March 1984, 36).

Other companies, however, move out of Singapore: this has been the case for Sord Computer Corp., a Japanese company that came to Singapore two years ago, but closed the factory there last year and shifted its business back to Japan. Companies like Hitachi, Fujitsu and General Motors are said to have moved assembly lines back home (*Newsweek,* 12 March 1984, 36), or will build up new capacity back in the advanced industrialized countries. In 1980, for example, "General Motors moved a major portion of its radio manufacturing out of Kokomo, Indiana to Singapore and Mexico. But by 1987, the company expects to expand again in Indiana, thanks to a combination of concessions from the United Auto Workers and a revolution in computer-driven technology" (*Newsweek,* 36). An example with more immediate impacts is given by Motorola: "Motorola, once wedded to Asian manufacturing, has built its latest computer chip plant in Arizona." According to a Motorola official, "Automation makes it possible for us to establish plants here, irrespective of labor costs" (*Newsweek,* 36).

There are also examples in Europe: Grundig of West Germany abandoned its television plant in Taiwan to concentrate production in Europe (*Fortune,* July 1983, 152). The large Swiss watchmaker Asuag/SSIH recently liquidated its subsidiary, Precision Watchcase Ltd., in Singapore that had employed 220 people; the same work is now done in Switzerland by fifty people. One year earlier, the Asuag subsidiary, Ebauches SA, had closed down Modutek, Ltd. in Hong Kong that produced electronic parts for watches; the parts are now made in Switzerland (*Tages-Anzeiger,* 21 February 1984).

What I want to put forward is that firms do concentrate their attention very much on further automation, and it seems that this perspective has become much more important for corporate planning than the expansion of offshore assembly plants in low-wage countries. This is supported by the interviews that Rada held with U.S. firms in the early 1980s; he found few who considered it likely that they would establish new plants in the Third World (Kaplinsky 1984a, 160).

Temporary Chances for Software Exports from Developing Countries

Whereas the chances that new manufacturing facilities for exports to the world market will be located in developing countries are diminishing, other chances may open up, at least for some developing countries. The development of new freely programmable automation devices of all sorts has increased the needs for programming and software development in the industrialized countries. The development of software has become one of the most serious bottlenecks on the way to further automation. Software actually accounts for seven of every ten dollars spent on computing (Fortune, March 1984, 64).[9] While prices for ever more intricate hardware are plunging, prices of software continue to rise (cf. Kaplinsky 1981, 84); this has led to an enormous demand for highly skilled programmers and software engineers. "The progressive automation of industrial production is running into an increasingly severe *shortage of skilled labor*" (Ernst 1984, 13). Computer manufacturers have tried to bridge the gap with an extension of in-house training and retraining programs (firms like Siemens spend at least three percent of turnover for this purpose), and by the recruitment of foreign personnel. Ernst mentions that "in the United States . . . at least 15 percent of the higher-level electronics engineers are from Third World countries" and 5 percent are Europeans (Ernst 1984, 14).

Caught in what Ernst calls an increasingly severe "human capital trap," Western firms have started to look for highly skilled labor in developing countries. In India, for instance, a great number of unemployed or underemployed engineers and programmers does exist that would work for about one-tenth the salary of their counterparts in the United States or Western Europe. With new telecommunications facilities, programming can easily be subcontracted to other parts of the world and immediately used anywhere else on the globe. The interest of multinational companies in cheap labor in developing countries therefore may shift: whereas they become less interested in unskilled labor in Third World countries, they seem to be more and more interested in the use of highly skilled but comparatively cheap labor from those countries. Software development therefore may be an area of interest for developing countries (cf. Hoffman and Rush 1980, 298-9). Software development remains a highly labor-intensive process, and software costs represent a large percentage of total production costs (Wad 1982, 684).

Will this development provide any compensation to those developing countries that lose their comparative advantage in the field of cheap and unskilled labor? Only in a few cases, and only temporarily. First of all, most of those countries that try to promote their exports by making use of their cheap labor reservoir do not yet have a large number of well-trained programmers and engineers. Therefore, this compensation will not go to all countries that have participated in the export run of labor-intensive manufactured products.

Even for those countries that will be able to export the result of their people's brains, this will only be a temporary chance. There are several reasons for this: one is computerized programming, i.e., the fact that programming and software development itself becomes more and more automated. Another reason will be a far-reaching change in the computer industry. This "transformation will be based on a fundamental idea: that the way to speed up computers is to divide the labor among many inexpensive data-processing devices rather than continue the present quest for ever faster single processors made with ever more exotic materials and techniques" (Alexander 1984, 62). Called "parallel processing," the technical changes inside computers turn out to be quite similar to changes that have taken place in the international division of labor in the past: "The new approach is analogous to mass-producing shoes with unskilled labor on assembly lines instead of handcrafting them with skilled workmen one by one" (Alexander 1984, 62). Traditional general purpose processors need a lot of software to let them perform all their different functions. "Parallelism will probably spawn many specialized types of computers with different species of processors connected in a variety of ways. Inherently general-purpose, the . . . traditional . . . computer relies on software programs to let it perform many different kinds of jobs. But almost any computational problem can be solved more rapidly with special-purpose hardware that uses a minimum of software. . . . Now that the cost trade-off has swung in favor of hardware, much of the complex software may be replaced by specialized parallel machines" (Alexander 1984, 64/65). The new generation of computers will be equipped with many specialized processors ("an architecture with a million processors arranged in a branching, treelike structure") to solve special problems, whereas the central processing unit will no longer be overburdened by countless tedious operations, but will "subcontract" them to specialized units better equipped to deal with the special kind of operations to be done.

Such a fundamental change in computer technology implies some change in the overall demand for software. Together with computerized software development, this may reduce the demand for software in such a way that little is left to be done by cheap programmers in developing countries, because the programming tasks that remain will consist mainly of the development of application software for specific customers. In turn, this will by and large have to take place where the customers are in the highly industrialized countries. Therefore, the opportunity to profit from the lack of highly skilled labor for software development and programming tends to be temporary. If developing countries want to keep up with the demand for specialized software, they have to invest heavily: "As software becomes more specialized and sophisticated to keep pace with new technological developments, there will be an increased demand for better programming skills, thus requiring any country following a 'software capability development strategy' to continuously upgrade such skills—which can be an expensive undertaking." And, "to keep up with the changing software demands associated with the technology requires a local capacity to monitor and analyze trends in the industry intelligently, which again requires a local technological and information capacity" (Wad 1982, 684).

Production Again Nearer to Major Markets

The preceding suggests that, while there is some chance to increase the export of software, the odds for export-oriented manufacturing are less favorable. With a declining share of labor in total production cost, manufacturing will concentrate more on locations near major markets. Not all analysts share this impression; Louis Emmerij, for example, acknowledges that the importance of the labor component in total production costs declines. He points out, however, that in spite of this tendency, differences in labor cost may still remain decisive for the location of production, because stiff international competition will force companies to take advantage of *any* significant cost differential in order to stay ahead of their competitors. Even if the share of labor in total production cost is reduced, it may still be important enough to guide the location decisions of multinational enterprises (Emmerij 1980, 303).

What Emmerij does not take sufficiently into account is that other factors may counterbalance the reduced wage advantage of developing countries. The four main counterbalancing factors probably are "currency risk," "political risk," "neo-protectionism" and "new management concepts." With the reduced impact of labor cost differentials, the final result of any location assessment will more probably end up under the threshold beyond (above) which location in developing countries would be preferred. Even for *purchases* from Asian countries, IBM, for example, follows an explicit policy of requiring savings of at least 25 percent to justify buying components in Asia and shipping them back to the United States (Ernst 1984, 9). If savings are less, the political risk of becoming dependent on outside suppliers from the developing countries is regarded as too high to compensate for the cost advantage.

How important "neo-protectionism" has become is underlined by the fact that companies from the so-called newly industrializing countries themselves have to open factories in the advanced industrialized countries. The largest Korean electronics company, Gold Star, built a plant in Huntsville, Alabama, with a capacity to turn out 500,000 color television sets and 400,000 microwave ovens a year. The company also bought a subsidiary in Silicon Valley. The second largest electronics company from South Korea, Samsung, is clearing a site in New Jersey to put up a plant similar to that in Huntsville (*Fortune,* February 1984, 68). Korean companies have also started to produce in Europe.[10]

This investment is, to a great extent, the consequence of Western protectionism; and, increasing protectionism is partly the result of automation in industrialized countries. Automation contributes to unemployment, and unemployment increases pressure on governments to protect the remaining industries. Imports of products from branches that hitherto have not experienced much automation, and where, consequently, low-wage countries still have an advantage, threaten the activity in industrialized countries that is still relatively labor-intensive. Given the fact that overall unemployment is already high, governments will, therefore, be especially sensitive to additional imports, because they might endanger a more than proportional share of employment (Kaplinsky 1984a, 157). Another link between automation and protectionism can be found in the demand for shorter working time. Wherever the working time is reduced in reaction to increasing automation, industry's international competitiveness threatens to decrease. In order to avoid any damage to industry (and employment), protectionist measures are suggested by the proponents of a reduction of working hours (cf. Kaplinsky 1981, 89).

Automation reduces the competitiveness of newly industrialized countries not only in reducing the comparative advantage of low wages but also by increasing pressures for protectionism. The diminished importance of wages—the share of direct labor cost in total production costs of American industry has declined from 25 to 30 percent to 10 to 15 percent during the last twenty years—has also given rise to new management concepts that strengthen the trend to concentrate manufacturing in industrialized countries. For instance, management aims at reducing those costs that now are responsible for the largest chunk of total costs. This often turns out to be *inventories;* therefore, new concepts work at reducing them as much as possible. High interest rates have sharpened attention toward working capital immobilized in inventories at all stages of the production process: inventories of raw materials, stocks of intermediate products, intermediate products on the way between one location and another, waste of raw materials and intermediate products for faulty products, and finished but unsold products.

As far as inventories of raw materials and stocks of intermediate products are concerned, companies try to solve the problem by "just-in-time delivery": they try to organize deliveries by their suppliers in such a way that inventories can be minimized. A good example is the Japanese car manufacturer that receives its seats twice a day from its supplier, or IBM that requires many of its suppliers to time deliveries to within hours of their being used in the assembly of display units and keyboards (*Financial Times,* 17 May 1985). Such a relationship demands close communication among the firms concerned, as well as short distances in order to provide the necessary flexibility. Many large companies, therefore, have started to demand that their main suppliers be located within a range of one day's trucking, or even within a radius of 80 to 100 miles in order to deliver at short notice (Kaplinsky 1984b). It is obvious that such a strategy is in contrast with a strategy of "global sourcing," involving suppliers from other continents. As far as intermediate products on the way between different plants of the same company are concerned, it is true that *transport costs* have decreased considerably. However, the important costs connected with a far-reaching internal division of labor between different subsidiaries of the same company are not the transport costs themselves; they are the costs of the additional time that unfinished products circulate inside the company and of additional inventories necessary as buffer stocks kept against irregular supply. These additional inventories make the production of parts in developing countries less attractive.

Another important management tool is the "zero defect" concept. In some companies, as much as 10 percent of total working capital is immobilized in raw material and intermediate products incorporated in faulty final products that either need much time and care to be repaired, dismantled, or that have to be thrown away. In order to introduce zero-defect standards, a relatively qualified and motivated work force is necessary. This puts some limits on the number of countries to which production processes can be transferred.

Finally, there are the inventories of finished but unsold products. In order to reduce these inventories and the connected risks, more and more companies try to follow the market and produce only what has been ordered already. This strategy demands a very flexible and streamlined production process to meet demand as quickly as possible, which will be difficult if production is scattered over a number of countries and production facilities distant from one another.

The conclusion of this analysis is that not only the decreasing wage component in total production costs reduces the incentive to locate world market production in low-wage developing countries. Given the smaller share of labor in total production costs, the attention of management has turned to reducing other important cost components, and these efforts, too, contribute to a shift of production activity back to the industrialized countries.

CONCLUSION

The main result of the foregoing argument is that the past increase of manufacturing exports of developing countries cannot be extrapolated into the future. Due to increasing automation of production in the highly industrialized countries, comparative advantages are changing again.

The introduction of *flexible* automation (instead of fixed automation of the 1950s and 1960s) has brought automation into the reach of smaller companies and of producers of capital goods, which sell small series only and not the mass products to which fixed automation is limited. The application of flexible automation is not limited to a few industrial sectors, but can be extended to all manufacturing of discrete products (and to the packaging and handling of the production that is the result of continuous processes as well).

With an improved performance of either the robots themselves (due to sensors and better software) or of the peripheral equipment, robots can be used not only for relatively simple jobs, such as painting and welding, but also for assembly and quality control. The range of applications has broadened and the integration of robots into integrated production systems has improved.

Robots are only the tip of the iceberg as far as flexible production equipment is concerned. The implications of the introduction of robots for employment will not so much depend on the robots themselves, but on their successful integration into manufacturing systems that integrate design, manufacturing, assembling, storage, transport, accounting and order administration. Many activities in present day factories consist of passing information from administration to the factory floor, from the shop floor to warehouses, from design engineers to production engineers and down to the machine operator. A large part of these activities can be made redundant by CAD/CAM systems, into which specific product parameters are fed only once and are then used throughout the system.

An increasing number of companies are approaching the end of the learning period in which they experimented with systems of partial automation in order to gather experience with the implications of new forms of production, to train management and work force, and to develop new design and production routines. As a consequence, it can be expected that the pace of automation will be maintained in the future or even accelerate.

Countervailing forces that could have slowed down the process of automation are in full retreat. Trade unions were weakened considerably as a result of the development of flexible automation. Not only had the labor market come under additional pressure, but changes in the composition of the labor force, the size of production units and their location brought additional difficulties for the unions. Their attractiveness has decreased in many countries as has their membership. In most industrial countries, they have stopped fighting automation and concentrated on demands that are fully compatible with the resulting increase of productivity.

As a result of flexible automation, the share of labor cost in total production cost is decreasing further. This reduces the incentive to transfer production to low-wage countries. Reduced cost differentials are only one reason for the more reluctant attitude of companies toward investment in world-market factories in developing countries. Increased protectionism in the industrial countries, large exchange rate fluctuations, increasing political uncertainty and the danger of unfavorable measures as a result of huge foreign debts are additional reasons.

Since direct labor cost often is no longer the dominant item in the calculation of companies, new management concepts concentrate on minimizing other cost factors. Inventories at all stages of the production process were identified as responsible for tying up a large share of working capital. Concepts that accordingly aim at a reduction of inventories such as "just-in-time" delivery, "zero-defect" production and "produce what is ordered only" also have implications for the localization of production. They make it less probable that production is spread around the globe and, instead, manufacturing in the future will probably be concentrated near the major markets.

What does all this mean for developing countries? Obviously, they will find it more difficult to attract foreign investment in export-oriented manufacturing, if the most important advantage they offer is only low wages. This development will not hit so much the so-called newly industrializing countries (especially the four Southeast Asian countries, Hong Kong, South Korea, Singapore and Taiwan). They offer much more than low wages (which are not so low any longer, compared to other countries in the region); they have highly qualified, experienced work forces, good infrastructure and increasingly important internal markets as well.

The victims will be those "second tier" newly industrializing countries that tried to follow the successful strategy of industrialization of the first generation of NICs—only to find out that multinational corporations have become much less willing to make use of their cheap labor force, and that the export markets in the industrialized world are already occupied by the countries whose strategy they wanted to follow—and do not expand any longer. Many developing countries, therefore, will be caught, more or less exclusively, in the position of exporters of raw materials. However, automation in industrialized countries and other technological developments threaten to undermine this position as well.

Computer-aided design will lead to less waste of raw materials, and zero-defect strategies will lead to fewer faulty products that have to be thrown away. The next wave of technological development, the application of biotechnology, probably will contribute even more to economizing on raw materials; biotechnological production processes that can substitute for many chemical processes will need less raw material and fuel. Local resources in industrialized countries eventually will be exploited more extensively, and recycling techniques probably will improve. As a consequence, not only exports of manufactured products ultimately may be threatened by automation and the application of other new technologies, but exports of primary products as well.

NOTES

1. "Hard automation" (in contrast to "flexible automation") consists of the installation of machinery that (without extensive mechanical changes) can only per form the one task it has been built for. "Flexible automation" means the installation of machinery than can be reprogrammed. The tasks performed do not depend only on the "hardware" (the machine) but also on the "software" (the program) used.

2. At Hewlett-Packard's South Queensferry plant, where professional electronic systems are made making use of computer-integrated manufacturing, some 840 different printed circuit board types are involved and *batch sizes can be as low as ten. Financial Times,* 20 May 1985.

3. Many of these points were mentioned during an interview with managers of Volvo Car in the Netherlands.

4. The U.S. Bureau of Labor Statistics expects employment in high-tech jobs in the United States to increase by 46 percent between 1982 and 1995, but since employment in high-tech occupations was only 3 percent of all employment in 1982, the additional employment will only account for 6 percent of the new jobs in the economy. The occupations with the fastest absolute growth differ substantially from those with the fastest rate of growth. None are related to high technology. The occupations that will provide the greatest number of new jobs are building custodians, cashiers, secretaries and clerks, cf. Rumberger/Levin 1984.

5. The stream of innovations in the textile industry, for example, means that an individual garment is made in 50 percent less time than ten years ago. "Fashioned by computer," *Financial Times,* 14 February 1984.

6. Asked on which evidence this statement was based, one of the participants of the panel discussion mentioned the example of transistor production by Philips in Hong Kong, which has been relocated because of changes in production techniques. Schweizerischer Bankverein, 1983, 21.

7. In order to create additional employment, electronic component manufacturers at Hamburg got special permission to work at night and during the weekends. Raasch 1985, 11.

8. An example is the plant of Yamazaki Machinery Works, Ltd., that produces turning lathes. It is almost fully automated, with six persons operating the plant in daytime (whereas a conventional plant would need 215 workers instead), and nobody—with the exception of the watchman—working there during the night. Production continues for twenty-four hours a day and seven days a week. Ministerie van Economische Zaken, 1984, 2.

9. According to estimates by Input, a California based market research firm, sales of software packages in the United States were expected to top $10 billion in 1984 (against sales of computer hardware of more than $30 billion). The market for software will continue to grow much faster than the market for hardware: by 32 percent a year until 1988, according to the same sources. It may reach $30 billion in 1988 (compared to $60 billion in sales of hardware). These figures are compatible with the seven-to-ten ratio mentioned in the text, because they only include the sales of software-packages and not the expenditures on in-house programming. cf. *Business Week,* Special Report on "Software: The New Driving Force," 27 February 1984, 54-5.

10. "Like the Japanese, the Koreans are finding that to sell in Europe means having to produce there, too. . . . Samsung Electronics has a factory in Lisbon and is negotiating to build a television and microwave oven plant in Britain, with plans to double its exports to the European Community to $100 million, as a way of lessening dependence on the U.S. market. But Samsung's major rival, Gold Star, finds Europe too difficult to target." *Business Week,* 20 February 1984, 32.

4

John Kurt Jacobsen

Peripheral "Postindustrialization": Ideology, High Technology, and Dependent Development

Although their luster has dimmed lately, the newly industrializing countries (NICs) have achieved impressive aggregate growth rates, hefty hikes in exported manufactures, diversification of industrial structures, and a multiplication of trade outlets.[1] The developing countries'share of global value-added edged upward only 3 percent between 1965 and 1980, but ten NICs recorded almost 75 percent of the gain. As of 1975, seven NICs—Hong Kong, Taiwan, Singapore, South Korea, Argentina, Mexico, and Brazil—were sources of more than 60 percent of the South's manufactured exports (*IDS Bulletin,* 1982, 2). The product-cycle virtuosity and the industrial "deepening" of the NICs is evident not only in steel, textile, shipbuilding, and some other "mature" industries but also in "high-tech" sectors such as electronics, in which the Asian "Gang of Four" (Hong Kong, South Korea, Taiwan, and Singapore) boosted their share of the South's exports from 60 percent in 1967 to 80 percent by 1980 (*IDS Bulletin,* 1982, 24).

Although beset today by Northern protectionism, foreign debt, authoritarian regimes or precarious transitions from them, the NICs demonstrated that "late-comers" are not condemned by any immutable iron law to perform as hewers of wood, drawers of water, and assemblers of final-stage products in peripheral enclaves linked regressively to the world economy. Contrary to bleak "dependentista" prognoses, a few Third World nations strode briskly from import-substitution and consumer goods phases to the production of intermediate/producer goods and of consumer durables. Brazil, Mexico, and India—endowed with requisite natural, human, and organizational resources—developed capital goods industries, and are shifting (as are smaller NICs) into "more skill- and technology-intensive areas of production" (Ruggie 1983, 9).

In his volume surveying outward-oriented development policies, Ruggie contends that liberal economists and dependentistas alike "overstate the determining impact of the international division of labor on national welfare." Liberals "tend to ignore the critical importance of, and dependentistas to discount the generative potential in, domestic political structures (Ruggie 1983, 39). Worse are neo-Marxists who allegedly ignore "the opportunities in developing countries created by new institutional arrangements for indigenous entrepreneurs, the state, and the process of local accumulation" (Ruggie 1983, 481; also see Smith 1979, 69, 77; and Poznanski 1984).

Such charges appear peculiar in light of the neo-Marxists' obsession with the role of the state; it is also true if one troubles to scan the vituperative critiques exchanged among dependentistas and between them and neo-Marxists (see especially Warren 1982 and Brewer 1982). Fernando Cardoso long ago spurned "overly static, mechanistic views of the relationship between the polity and the economy," urging scholars to focus upon the political forces and policy possibilities unfolding within dependent developers in terms of "double determination"—a task requiring the "formulation of concepts linked to the effort to explain how internal and external processes of domination relate to one another" (Cardoso 1973, 143). Cardoso and Faletto (1979) cite the dynamic developmental role, class composition, institutional structure, and the consequent internal and external sensitivity of states that have indeed achieved wider "margins of maneuver" afforded by the changing international division of labor.

Dismissive appraisals of dependency literature too often confine themselves to ritualistic statements of scorn for the stagnationist theses of Paul Baran and of André Gunder Frank.[2] Nonetheless, critics of dependency (and world-systems) analyses have made welcome efforts "to contextualize the economism of the debate in larger institutional terms and frameworks" (Ruggie 1983, vii). Analysis is trained on local factors and social forces, which promote or hinder supple adjustment to changing patterns of global production and trade. The prescriptive implication is that peripheral polities—instead of prattling on about imperialism, repressed alternatives, and quixotic aspirations for national autarky—more prudently ought to put their own houses in order so as to maximize the substantial benefits that the capitalist world-economy offers to the adept. Thus, fertile research agendas have evolved that strive to explain the differential impact of exogenous events upon local producer groups, disaggregated sectors and branches, institutional structures and networks, state strategies, and their implications for coalition formation.

But political and social elites, when undertaking the tasks of adjustment, will try to guide the manner and to limit the extent to which socio-organizational changes required to upgrade the economy occur, so that policy measures designed to increase the rate of accumulation will not upset the internal distribution of power. (Specifying conditions under which these vital if inexact trade-offs occur between economic adjustment and power-retention, and their consequences, has been the special concern of the literature on bureaucratic authoritarianism [O'Donnel 1973, 1978; Collier 1979]). *An implicit or insufficiently explicit premise in recent studies of the political dynamics of adjustment is that global economic shifts rarely are presented to the state in the form of an unambiguous "stimulus," demanding an invariant policy "response;" rather, such impinging events, in effect, are appropriated through the interpretive (ideological) capacities of domestic coalitions and actors to reinforce their dominance, or else to weaken or displace that of rivals.* Global shifts *signal* the need for internal adjustment, but these signals, and the very real pressures accompanying them, are converted by ideological mediation into programmatic *messages* to the citizenry as to the exact form the policy response should take. Cardoso and Faletto adumbrate this thesis in their depiction of the state not only as a vigorous agent (in the Gerschenkronian sense), but also as a crucial field of contest for groups and classes with competing "projects" whose success will be determined "by how international conditions are used in the internal power game, rather than by the particular economic conditions themselves" (Cardoso and Faletto 1979, 175).

In a study of the determinants of policy response to global market forces, particularly by a democratic, dependent developer (the Irish Republic), I elaborate conceptual means by which the role of ideological activity can be incorporated into explanations of choice in the politics of adjustment. A related concern is in the consequences of these ideological struggles (in which developmental "projects" are cast in the most persuasive terms, so as to gain consent of groups who are crucial to the outcome of policy debate) for the limits of state autonomy, as well as consideration of the meaning of state "autonomy." Finally, I argue that the Irish case exemplifies a syndrome of wider significance, "peripheral postindustrialization."

Peripheral postindustrialization denotes: (1) the policy-induced diffusion of "postindustrial" industries within peripheral nations; (2) a truncated form of development (minus linkages and a local technology-generating capacity), wherein developing states latch onto the more labor-intensive phases of industries with a "postindustrial" vocation (electronics, pharmaceuticals, etc.); and (3) an *ideological* strategy for extending hegemonic developmental schemes against challenges presented by global economic trends and from local counter-elites.[3] The Irish Republic is an especially intriguing case because it is an ex-colonial nation, with uncharacteristically durable democratic institutions. It embarked on export-led industrialization in the late 1950s and, since 1975, has chosen electronics as a basis for pioneering a new local structure of "complex-factor cost industries" (which I call "postindustrial") that, ideally, will maximize its competitive advantage of skilled labor against lower-wage export platforms vying for markets and for foreign investment.[4] The Irish experience, like that of other European "intermediaries," may shed light "on the predicaments facing both the large, advanced industrial states" and the "less-developed countries" (Katzenstein in Ruggie 1984, 93).

STATE-SOCIETY RELATIONS AND POLICY CHOICE

Dependentistas (excluding crude determinists) and nondependentistas (excluding "mainstream liberals") agree that the state is a pivotal actor with interests and resources of its own, but they differ in analytical depictions of state-society relations (see, e.g., Moran 1978; Foster-Carter 1976; Biersteker 1979; and Ruggie 1983). Nondependentistas favor a "statist approach," which posits that strong states like South Korea, Taiwan, Mexico, and Brazil can shape the policy preferences and behavior of societal groups so as to serve state-defined ends.[5] The stronger a state is, the more autonomously it acts, and so the more likely are the preferences of potent societal groups to be overruled when conflicting with the most pragmatic course plotted by formal policy makers. Such states may appear to act as autonomously as Frankenstein's creature, but studies usually yield more ambiguous findings. In their "statist" analysis of the South Korean experience, Haggard and Moon note how the state "relied heavily on domestic entrepreneurs to perform the miracles" and, more tellingly, that "the business-State alliance has proscribed thoroughgoing liberalization" politically as well as economically (Ruggie 1983, 161). Duvall and Freeman (1984, 375) find that "state entrepreneurship" occurs where the private sector is unable or unwilling to undertake developmental tasks or may "generate some substantially undesirable patterns of development." New public assets are deployed so as to complement private activity, and profitable public assets may be sold off. In the view of some dependentistas, the state here appears intent on creating or "reinventing" a bourgeoisie that gradually will acquire control over the state itself.[6]

Dependentistas tend to explain this evident "bias of statism" in terms of structural marxist models (Jessop 1982; Carnoy 1983). The reproduction of capitalist relations requires a relatively autonomous state apparatus, whose managers must attend to the often times divergent tasks of promoting conditions that enhance *accumulation, legitimation,* and *security.* The weight policy makers attach to each "function" depends on the balance of class forces and the intensity of class struggle (penetrating all branches of the state), as well as on state strength. An important implication is that state managers can act not only against the short-term interests of "particular capitals," but also, under certain sets of conditions or "conjunctures," adopt programs endangering the capitalist dominance.[7] The state, then, is a curious entity (a "material condensation" of class conflicts but not *reducible* to them) that is capable of playing or buying off class-based organizations, class fractions, or societal groups in order to realize goals designated according to the policy makers' calculus. Even when situational factors appear to augment state autonomy, state managers do not do just as they please because at least tacit alliances are needed to assure civil compliance with policy changes. (Analysts also must attend to the class origins, positional interests, and ideological stances of formal policy makers and of "technobureaucrats.") Obviously, the state's resource base constricts the range of viable responses to global market changes, but the level of resources policy makers actually can summon is contingent on the kind of cooperation they are able to elicit. The *quality* of cooperation—from consent to coercion—is itself a resource. In other words, politics really matter.

For advanced industrial and newly industrializing countries, one can posit that *accumulation* goals are realizable by several strategies that pose different consequences for the distribution of the benefits of development and the burdens of adjustment. The form of the emergent policy response will be guided according to the implicit *legitimation* scheme of state managers (who may be impelled by social resistance to reappraise whose oxen they can least afford to gore). Pragmatism is at its zenith when state managers, motivated by economic exigencies, come to support policy packages, based on new coalitional formations, which challenge the interests of hitherto dominant groups. ("Pragmatism" is a term more evocative of the crucial blending of political entrepreneurship with brokerage that usually portends policy change; capitalist states, with certain vile historical exceptions, are never purely "autonomous.")[8] What remains is to identify conditions that enable or precipitate "pragmatic" state action, and to examine *how* one is linked to the other.

Among these conditions are foreign debt crises, the exhaustion of industrialization phases (e.g., horizontal import-substitution), mismatches between internal production structure and international marketing patterns, and other forms of severe pressure to adjust in costly ways. International influences will be investigated here, as Cardoso and Faletto urge, as "endogenous variables," whose local expression enables us to understand, anticipate, and perhaps predict the content of policy responses by nations on the weak side of asymmetries. Perhaps one useful means for invigorating the flagging "dialog" between dependentista and nondependentista is for the latter to apply the "sensitivity-vulnerability" distinction to *intrastate* relations (between and among components of the state "apparatus," which interact with societal groups) as well as to interstate affairs, and proceed to inquire how changes in "sensitivities" affect national policy formulation, economic performance, and the distribution of power and wealth. But even this enterprise is likely to neglect crucial determinants that do not lend themselves to easy transcription into statistical tables and graphs. The most resistant is ideology.

INTERESTS, IDEOLOGY, AND POLICY STRUGGLES

John Odell's study of U.S. international monetary policy (1982) argues that a cognitive perspective (which claims that reigning ideas exert an "independent effect on policy content") ought to be considered in a multiple explanatory framework, including four other perspectives: security, market, domestic structure and bureaucratic politics; he traces ways in which the explanatory foci interpenetrate, and cites conditions under which their relative importance changes. A cognitive perspective is least significant for explaining policy response by states under extreme market or other "situational" pressure; it is most useful when studying states twice-blessed with structural power and domestic tranquility that, together, allow a "breathing space" wherein ideas play an accentuated role in shaping decisions. The scope of choice is conditioned not only by global impacts and domestic forces, but by the pool of policy "ideas" that are intellectually available, economically viable, and politically permissible. I say *conditioned* rather than *constrained* because critical conjunctures can draw authoritative attention to "ideas," which will enlarge the conventional pool of choices.

Given the esoteric nature of international monetary issues, Odell restricts his analysis of cognitive factors to the "circulation of policy ideas in Washington." His approach is less useful when dealing with issues where a wider public audience readily recognizes the stakes they have in policy outcomes. More helpful clues for investigating how these explanatory foci interrelate are contained in the work of Antonio Gramsci, whose writings on hegemony are gaining currency among non-Marxian students of political economy (Keohane 1984, 84; Burnham 1982, 14, 266). Hegemony occurs in a socio-organizational "phase in which ideologies, which were germinated earlier, become 'party'" and enter into struggle until one (or a combination) of them

> tends to predominate, to impose itself, to propagate itself throughout the whole social sphere, causing, in addition to singleness of economic and political purpose, an intellectual and moral unity as well, placing all questions around which the struggle rages not on a corporative, but a 'universal' plane and creating in this way the hegemony of a fundamental social group . . . the ruling group is coordinated concretely with the general interests of the subordinate groups and State life is conceived as a continual formation of unstable equilibriums (unstable within the ambit of the law) . . . equilibriums in which the interests of the ruling group predomi-

> nate but only up to a certain point, i.e., not as far as their mean economic-corporative interest would like. (Gramcsi 1971, 181-2)

The state is ideologically an "educator" and, in the economic field, an "instrument of rationalization" (Gramsci 1971, 247). He argued that counterhegemonic parties should engage in a wide-ranging "war of position" to garner support and, in effect, surround, as well as penetrate, the state because economic crises do not, and the formal assumption of state power cannot, guarantee "transformative" or socially progressive results.[9] Gramsci (1971, 182) notes that "the fact that international relations are interlaced with these internal relations of a nation-state, creating new, original and historically concrete combinations," which, for some, present opportunities. He emphasizes both the systemic sources and conflictual undercurrents because "it is at the level of ideologies that men become conscious of conflicts in the world of the economy."

For analysis of short-term, nontransformative situations ("second-stage" struggles occurring inside the "fundamental existing framework"), more suitable but related concepts are needed and, in this capacity, Albert Hirschman has contributed the notion of "propensity to defer" to "economic exigencies," which he judged abysmally low among Latin American elites (Hirschman 1979, 65). Taken a step further, societal actors will have differing "propensities to defer" both to global market conditions and to state policy responses. *I will refer to the propensity of a given group, class or organization to defer to the adjustment prescriptions of prevailing policy wherever the term "propensity" henceforth appears.*

Why do actors defer? The reasons are usually interrelated: rewards, coercion, organizational impotence, lack of persuasive alternatives, costs and risks of opposition, apathy, "poor" information, and outright approval. The lattermost depends on ideological predispositions that enter into the calculus of self-interest; hence, one witnesses the resonance of the phrase, "Stay the course," even among those most mauled by the "magic of the marketplace." While state managers and dominant coalition members obviously may differ in their attachment to the mixed product of their negotiations, I will focus here on subordinate groups, and *the "propensity to defer" should be understood as being imbued with Gramsci's acute sense of the powerful material underpinnings of prevailing ideology.* This depiction is not, of course, exclusively Marxist. Schumpeter's remarks on the manipulation of ideas and of public opinion are most familiar. Lindblom (1977) examines the institutional sources of "constrained volition" in polyarchal systems that result in a "lopsided competition of ideas," and Burnham (1982) discusses the "politics of excluded alternatives" in the United States. We would be astonished, as Barrington Moore Jr. (1972, 144) observed, if social systems did not propagate core beliefs favorable to elites, insofar as these beliefs preserve the "absence of a demand for change." A *high* propensity to defer is defined operationally by this "absence" because all a dominant coalition needs is acquiescence, not love. A low propensity is indicated by standard measures of protest and dissent: strikes, demonstrations, rapid rises in support for chief opposition and fringe parties, and knitting together of the various elements of resistance. Dispersed and inchoate protest is no challenge; organization is the key concern.

Policy makers are spared any test of their skills if there is high public confidence in the state's ability to cope efficiently and (more or less) equitably with economic setbacks or transitions. If this public confidence (or propensity to defer) is low at the outset or diminishes rapidly after the onset of economic adversities, the state undergoes a "policy crisis" whose outcome will be determined by the severity and duration of adjustment, the strength of the given state, the capacity of dominant groups to repress or appease opposition, and the capability of counterelites to mobilize support for their alternative programs (Jacobsen and Hofhansel, 1984). If policy crises are acute and protracted (and conflict sharpens within the dominant coalition), state managers have the opportunity to exercise political entrepreneurship to the extent that new alliances are formed with formerly subordinate groups promoting alternative adjustment schemes. This ultrapragmatic scenario is less likely to unfold where a "triple alliance" reigns; it is more likely to occur in societal corporatist frameworks where the alliance is, if warily, a "quadrupled" one (i.e., includes an independent and assertive labor representation).[10]

The Irish case fits Peter Evans' (1979, ii) definition of dependent development as a "special case of dependency," characterized by "capital accumulation at the local level accompanied by increasing differentiation" of industrial structure. But Evans and the bureaucratic-authoritarian literature focus on repressive renditions wherein "ambivalent alliances" of (a fraction of) the local bourgeoisie, multinationals, and the state rule. The Irish Republic resembles the small European corporatist polities where consent must be managed through democratic institutions. When the "hard choices" appear on the policy horizon, elites will resort to material concessions and ideological appeals long before bayonets are considered. If the elite's favored policy choice is portrayed successfully as a Hobson's choice, or else the wisest one, then "the openness of an economy provides the means to combat the demands of the working class for higher wages and for economic and political reforms" (Block 1977, 3). But even where "the logic of economic vulnerability prevails over the logic of worker militancy," democratic structures provide incentives for bargaining on other bases (e.g., investment controls over "wages foregone" [Lange 1981]). Of course, policy crises untended can flare into systemic crises that no prudent elite desires.

To reiterate: international market forces signal the need to adjust, but the precise *form* of adjustment will depend on how such signals are converted by social contestants and institutions into programmatic messages to the citizenry. One should not suppose *a priori* that these (diagnostic and prescriptive) messages reflect only the narrow interests and redound to the benefit of elites. Nor should one suppose that the state always obeys elite preferences (even when unambiguously offered), especially if they are hotly contested and, in system-maintenance terms, differ only marginally from other programs. Further, we must not assume that counterprograms are inherently less congruent with international economic shifts or are inferior to the adjustment schemes championed by dominant groups. The reverse may well be the case. If so, and the opposition is strongly organized (and crafty), a policy crisis ensues that will pose an interesting trial for the pragmatic capabilities of state managers.

DEPENDENT STATES AND HIGH TECH STRATEGIES

The OECD Inter-Futures Report (1979, 336) portrays microelectronic technology as a "decisive qualitative leap forward," such that "the electronics complex during the next quarter of a century will be the main pole around which the productive structures of the advanced industrial countries will be reorganized." Among so-called postindustrial industries are computers and software, semiconductors, lasers and fiber optics, electronic consumer goods, biotechnology, and ancillary activities. Although research and development (R & D) and other sophisticated functions are metropole-centered, the strategic fragmenting of standardizable aspects of production has brought the heady taste of the "micro millennium" to poorer climes.[11] Envisaging many silicon valleys, glens, and enterprise zones, several NICs and peripheral European states (the Irish Republic, Scotland [or its Development Offices], Spain, Portugal, and Greece) either have selected the electronics sector as the cornerstone of their development schemes or else have it figured prominently among their aims. The stirring success of the "East Asia edge," during the 1970s, with more standardized forms of electronics goods production, was widely noted, and with annual expansion of the market proceeding at a rapid rate, the rush was on to share the bounty.[12]

The South Korean and Taiwanese states actively direct their economies so as to attain an (elusive) R & D-based competitive structure. Ireland and Scotland are "catalytic" in approach, attracting foreign industries whose cumulative implantation on native soil will form not only an integrated network, but also prod local entrepreneurs to supplement, complement, and perhaps surpass them. A "catalytic" mode of state intervention is ineffective if local entrepreneurial elements are weak (because of high risk, uncertainty, higher rates of return elsewhere, etc.), but states tend to strike different balances among intermingling modes over time.[13] These societies are not content to await the expiration of product-cycles (nor, for that matter, are foreign manufacturers). Job creation and higher investment may be the immediate but secondary goals; the ultimate aim is to create a base of gleaming "postindustrial" industries and to endow themselves with R & D resources that can give their products a "cutting edge" in the global market. This ambition is consonant with the assumption that as a state's "capacity for action" (administrative skills improve, industry diversifies, entrepreneurship improves, saving and investment rates rise, etc.), so too is the state all the more motivated to pursue the goal of "alleviating dependence on foreign capital and technology" (Freeman and Duvall 1984, 375).

Liberal economists score points in questioning the welfare-enhancing wisdom of too zealous a pursuit of this aim, and states do trade off a degree of autonomy in order to reap the benefits of economic interdependence. But there are distinctly domestic reasons why autonomy cannot be consistently pursued, and these reasons can be characterized in the form of two satisficing bargains, *elite* and *consensual. What is "satisficed" in these bargains is the goal of autonomy. A consensual* bargain is endorsed across cleavages because *autonomy goals are really a means to other ends* (full employment, rising living standards, economic opportunities) that may be achieved by embracing interdependence. In an *elite* bargain ("triple alliance," comprador coalitions, state corporatism, and some forms of societal corporatism), dominant groups resist any policy shifts that portend erosion of their shares of power and wealth. Thus, ideologically linked societal interests (or the "pact of domination") will seek to impose policies that not only consign autonomy goals to oblivion but also harm nonelites by sacrificing their most salient concerns (jobs, living standards, social services) which, if improving, otherwise induce consent. Nonelites may be better served by policies promoting autonomy (e.g., enhancing indigenous R & D, more active state coordination in the commercial and financial arenas, shading the developmental emphasis toward local resource bases). Here Freeman and Duvall (1984, 391) argue that "there is no reason to believe that the state's activities are an effective means of achieving control over industrialization and of alleviating dependence on foreign capital and technology." *Empirically* sound, this verdict founders analytically on the premise of invariantly high "propensities to defer" by subordinate strata whatever their organizational capabilities, whatever the feasibility of alternatives, whatever the level and form of socioeconomic conflict, whatever the strength and "pragmatic" capacity of the state. Of course, *situational factors can press so powerfully that no alternative to orthodox adjustment prescriptions is possible;* even so, the analytical tack urged here requires consideration of counterfactual alternatives, which serve to sharpen any interpretation. These theoretical concerns will be fleshed out in the ensuing analysis of Ireland's peripheral postindustrializing strategy.

IRISH DEVELOPMENT AND THE COLONIAL HERITAGE

As England's first colony, Ireland was integrated into the core economy in the seventeenth century, as in function and effect, a "vast cattle ranch." Rebellious natives were dispossessed of land until only 14 percent remained in their (Catholic) hands by 1703. English legislation stifled industrial competitors (and, more briefly, cattle exports) through the eighteenth century. Ireland was forcibly united to the core after the 1798 rebellion, and the result was "a colony—not of the classical English form, but rather of the style of Algeria, nominally part of the United Kingdom, but in practice governed on different principles" (Greaves 1974, 36). While industrialization did occur in the northeast corner, exposure to free trade harmed incipient industries elsewhere, so that Ireland became, as Marx remarked, "only an agricultural district of England, marked off by a wide channel from the country to which it yielded corn, wool, cattle, industrial and military recruits" (Marx 1958, 8-9). Capital as well was yielded in the form of rents and of investments to the more lucrative and developed money markets across the channel. A singularly adverse effect on Irish development was the fourfold rise in cattle prices relative to grain since George III's reign.

> The expanding Irish cattle-exporting industry, by supplanting other agricultural enterprises with a high ouput/acre, caused a decline in demand from the land-intensive export sector. Simultaneously, competing exports were depressing nonexport industries. The combined effect was greatly to reduce total demand, scale of operations, and hence overall efficiency in labour and capital-intensive industry in Ireland. (Crotty 1979, 227)

As unit production costs rose due to declining scale, the "remedy" of wage reduction aggravated the fall in local demand. Meanwhile, the expanding cattle trade ("on the hoof" for mainland value-adding) was displacing small farmers and tenants, who were crowded onto ever smaller parcels of land. The stage was set for a gruesome display of "propensity to defer"—the great famine of 1845-49. A Malthusian tragedy prompted by Manchester liberals, the famine made emigration the fatalistic substitute for social radicalism, an invaluable "prop" for the stationary social order. (Population fell from 8.5 million in 1845 to less than 5 million at the turn of the century.) Still, struggles for land reform intertwined with the Home Rule movement several decades later. Incremental concessions culminated with the 1903 Wyndham Act, which created a new class of peasant proprietors who, like the large "ranchers," undertook an undercapitalized but socially conservative existence. Home Rule was frustrated by a league of English and Ulster Tories (supported vigorously, indeed virulently by Protestant underclasses) and a minor insurrection in 1916 eventuated the Anglo-Irish War of 1919-1921.

In the 1922-23 civil war, the new Free State defeated rebels who opposed partition, and had also beaten wage levels below those during the infamous 1913 Dublin lockout. Bereft of the industrial northeast (containing 40 percent of taxable capacity, 30 percent of population, and a third of port trading), the new regime presided over a primary commodity-exporting economy.

Technically a dominion, the new state was a re-creation of British institutions and economic ideology. Party cleavages occurred over civil war (i.e., nationalist) affiliations, enduringly so. The Catholic church, source of solace and identity in plainer colonial days, guarded the gates against Bolshevik demons and bawdy authors, while emigrants poured out.

Designating agriculture as the motor for the growth of secondary industries, the first government "aimed at the reduction of all costs of production in order to enable exporters to compete successfully abroad; this entailed low taxation and low expenditures" (Orridge 1983, 353; Mennan 1972). "Abroad" meant Britain, and "exporters" meant the cattle ranchers. "Law taxation" meant low direct taxes only, and "low expenditures" meant misery, migration, and self-prescribed "low stateness."

> In 1926, 57.1% of the male working population were employed in agriculture and in 1929 33.7% of the national income was earned by this sector. In the same year, 88.99% of exports by value were agricultural and 42.08 % came from the main export to Britain, mainly cattle; 92.3% of exports went to the United Kingdom . . . 58% of imports by value were manufactured goods and 78% of imports came from the United Kingdom. (Orridge 1983, 364-5)

Despite emigration, unemployment never dipped below 6 percent. By 1930 Irish investment in British industry was twice that of the reverse flow. An ardently *antidirigiste* government was impelled to create "state-sponsored bodies" to fill the entrepreneurial gaps in the economy—utilities, credit, transport, and, later, commercial public enterprises.[14] But the "great spurt" of industrial development under organized direction, noted elsewhere by Gerschenkron (1962), occurred in sporadic dribbles in Ireland. Why?

The "advantages of backwardness" were superceded, in part, by the "advantages of dependence" for particular strata. Dominant rural and petit bourgeois interests shunned Sinn Fein party's reveries of national self-sufficiency, and were better served by free trade. Liberal economic orthodoxies were embedded in the institutions inherited from Britain. The "island behind an island" felt no pressing military threat that might motivate state-directed development and, as a marginally privileged member of the "Celtic periphery," Ireland was *insufficiently* backward because of earlier British infrastructural investments (albeit to facilitate particular patterns of trade and traffic) and political reforms (Hechter 1975, 123). How the inclusion of industrial Ulster might have changed the character of an all-Ireland state is a much pondered matter.

As in Latin America, the depression made a necessity of the Sinn Fein virtue of import-substituting industrialization (ISI), which a newly elected populist government (Fianna Fail) intended to pursue in 1932. Irish exponents of Friedrich List's gospel never imagined that infant industries were nurturable during contractions of agricultural trade—aggravated by an "economic war" with the United Kingdom over retention of payments for previous tenant-purchases, funded by British government stock. The value and volume of cattle exports fell more than a third by 1935, while dependence on the United Kingdom changed not one whit. The dispute was resolved in 1938, but, in the midst of it, the Fianna Fail government (comprising most of the defeated rebels in the civil war) tapped an aggressive populist nationalism to increase state autonomy vis-à-vis "prometropolitan" interests which were motivated by economic losses to flirt with a clumsy and ultimately impotent fascist movement (Orridge 1983; Manning 1972). While the global economy foundered and emigration outlets were clogged, a populist government upset the preferences of elites for free trade to pursue autarkic policies.

Under ISI, industrial employment rose from 100,589 in 1931 to 166,513 by 1938, while industrial output increased by 40 percent (then skidded quickly with the exhaustion of "easy" opportunities). In the absence of exchange controls and specific policies to induce use of indigenous raw materials or to direct linkage patterns, prices rose in a complacent industrial climate. Tariffs and low taxation won assent from both small-scale industries and from agricultural exporters for the new policy. (British investors were undaunted by a singularly porous Control of Manufactures Act, which decreed that firms must be Irish-owned).[15] By the mid-1940s, Fianna Fail, the radical populist phase spent, had become a classical "catch-all" party presiding over development strategy (Garvin 1981; Rumpf and Hepburn 1977). While creating public enterprises in peat production, sugar, chemicals, steel, airlines, and food processing, the party's deputy leader asserted that "private enterprise should be supported by the state until it matured and that private enterprise, if strong and willing, should then be permitted to take over public enterprise." The state did not entertain "scale-down" tariff designs to improve efficiency; nor was there an effort to rationalize firms or coordinate relations between private and public sectors in order to enhance economies of scale and factor utilization. Capital-deepening was not on the agenda, although producer goods, imports and the overall ratio of imports to national income *rose* in the Sinn Fein haven of the 1930s through the 1950s.

From 1946 to 1951, industry created one job for every thirty job seekers; total employment had risen 1 percent since 1926 despite the emigration of one out of every three citizens. In a saturated home market, industrial production (and the volume of agricultural exports) was static from 1953 to 1958 and, while the population had declined, unemployment was rising. Balance-of-payments problems were met with non-Keynesian responses, which only exacerbated the crisis of 1956-58. (Kennedy and Dowling [1975] argue that, given signs of an export upturn, an expansionary policy could have fostered an export drive off the protectionist base.)

But by 1958, with the Common Market forming, dollars converting, and transnational firms roaming, Irish policy makers abandoned (in no small measure, self-thwarted) autarkic ambitions for industrialization by invitation. As the legitimacy of economic nationalism bled arterially away in emigrants and capital, state managers utilized the crisis and international market forces to subdue any resistance from a weak bourgeosie—although they sugared the pill with requipment subsidies and formal discouragement of internal sales by grant-aided foreign firms. Agricultural exporters were eager for EEC markets and prices. Since the anemic "propensity to defer" by subordinate strata was expressed quite literally by "exit," the "voice" in the policy switch belonged primarily to pragmatic state elite during this instructively labelled "Whitaker-Lemass revolution." (Whitaker was Secretary of the Department of Finance; Lemass, formerly Minister of Industry and Commerce, was premier from 1959 to 1966, and the "revolution" was a mild updating of economic orthodoxy to fit the Rostovian-ECLA age.) Coinciding with a world trading boom, the policy shift paid off handsomely from 1958 to 1964 with a 4 percent GNP annual growth rate and a 7 percent industrial growth rate. In this period, foreign firms accounted for 70 percent of start-ups, 85 percent of new investment, and 77 percent of new industrial jobs—provoking apprehensive, if ugly, rural sneers in high places. Quoth one discussant:

> The cry that industry is "away" and all because a few Japs, a few Jews, and a few Negroes come in here for the taxpayers to build factories for them, contribute to the cost of machinery, give them slave labour—if it can be got—protect them on every side so that they can export their goods to other countries under the label "Irish," I warn the minister that they will pack their bags tommorrow or the day after and clear off, and they can tell this government or any other government where to get off. (Parliamentary Debates, 1961)

But jeremiads, racist or otherwise, were rare; that such comparatively modest growth was declared an "economic miracle" speaks volumes about the gravity of the 1950s crisis. Over the 1932-1957 era, quasi-autarkic policies proved ultimately incongruent with international market forces and so were socially insupportable in terms of providing the "material bases of consent" (Przeworski 1980). State autonomy increased as state managers were forced to devise an immediately effective response to the long-exhausted, "easy"

ISI phase. In the absence of popular mobilization behind alternative programs (the Labour party was and is notoriously weak), the policy shift occurred in timid accordance with modern capitalist precepts about indicative planning, active macroeconomic policy and unhampered trade. State authorities saw themselves, in effect, as "Leninists of the bourgeoisie" whose mission was to enlighten and aid myopic private entrepreneurs in realizing their long-term interests. As economic nationalism was shed, the dominant coalition was reinvigorated by a more consensual policy course, exportled industrialization, from which a legitimating stream of benefits flowed. In this respect, the consequence of the Irish policy shift accorded with the verdict that "while the apparent determinants of state action may involve the political defeat of the bourgeoisie," the effect is "to reproduce and to reinforce that class" (Esping-Anderson, Friedland, and Wright 1976, 183).

Was there an alternative course? Yes, but only in the outermost reaches of counterfactual speculation. Emigration, which in the 1950s was equivalent to one-seventh of the population, was both indicator and dampener of crisis. No substantial support could be drawn from any quarter for more dramatic state intervention, expansion of public commercial activities, and more forceful measures to upgrade native firms so as to mount a home-market-based export drive.

INDUSTRIAL RENAISSANCE AND SYSTEMATIC TECHNOLOGY GAPS

Like Chile and Uruguay in the 1960s, the Irish aimed to improve a small-scale industrial base, expand and diversify exports, and thereby diffuse dependence. Foreign firms were envisaged as "pump-primers" for an *Irish* dynamism. Some efforts were made to encourage primary export-substitution (exporting goods that previously had been substituted), but these shrank to an ineffectual defensive posture against strong competitors swarming across the lowered tariff walls (because of mutual tariff reductions with the United Kingdom in the mid-1960s, and culminating five years after the 1973 EEC entry).

But the response of indigenous firms to free trade was sluggish, almost resistant. In 1961 only 31 firms employed 500-plus workers and produced 28 percent of gross output while over half of total firms employed fifteen or fewer workers and accounted for 6 percent of output (NESC, 1980, 61). Glittering real growth rates in GNP (4.2 percent over 1960-1970) and industrial exports (17 percent over 1964-1974) were attributable to foreign firms that garnered three-fourths of state subsidies, but likewise contributed 75 percent of new industrial jobs. The proportion of exports in national industrial output rose from 13.8 percent in 1961 to more than 30 percent by 1972. Rising internal demand brought reprieves, not pardons, to local firms using standardized technologies, minimal export orientation (10-20 percent), a relatively nonexistent research base, and archaic managerial practices, which were, in most cases, more import-intensive and less value-adding to local primary resources than the incoming firms (NESC, 1980). The level and range of state inducements—"adaption grants," a Management Institute, an Industrial Research Institute, etc.—failed to counter the private prerogative of searching for the highest or least exerting rate of return (in real estate, services, foreign investment, and some defensive investment, rather than aggressive adjustment to stern challenges). The state mollified, and more than modified, local capital via equipment aid, export-encouraging subsides, eventually a fifty-fifty split of grants, and in 1981 a flat 10 percent tax on *all* manufacturing activity.

But, basking in the early glow, state managers (1) dabbled with "economic programmes," (2) depoliticized the development process by investing responsibility in a technobureaucratic entity, the Industrial Development Authority, and (3) attempted to contrive corporatist arrangements, expressly including trade unions in order to influence wage restraint. As Kaufman observed elsewhere:

> Manufacturing exports of any sort arguably require policies which threaten a variety of domestic populist interests: devaluation and subsidy burdens on urban consumers; requirements of low labor costs and union discipline; liberalization of import policies; and stable expectations about price and exchange level—in short, many of the requisites of predictability and stability that O'Donnell suggested were necessary for deepening. (Kaufman 1979, 212-3)

Corporatist experiments fizzled. The small scale of industry inhibited both managerial adjustments and the organization and ideology of the labor force. Neither labor nor capital was organized sufficiently to "deliver" on commitments. Although the Irish Congress of Trade Unions (ICTU) eagerly participated in the National Industrial Economic Council, this tripartite body collapsed at the decade's end when the ICTU, seeking *quid pro quo* investment guarantees, balked at other income policy proposals. Under statutory threat, the ICTU agreed in 1970 to engage in annual "national pay agreement" bargaining. Governed by Fianna Fail, or else by an even more conservative Fine Gael party (in coalition with a hapless Labour party), the state gave short shrift to Labour's pet idea of a national development corporation intended to coordinate private activity with the public commercial sector (which, in 1970, accounted for 8 percent of GDP, 6 percent of employment, 37 percent of public employment, 15 percent of gross investment, and 46 percent of public gross investment). Ignoring the latter's roles in underwriting local demand, generation and use of local resources, infrastructural and welfare value, and of "socializing" some private sector risks, the highly ideological and economically illiterate cry that "four private jobs support each public job" was quite resonant.

Foreign firms became the driving force. In 1966 grant-aided firms (78 percent of foreign) accounted for 9 percent of industrial jobs, 42.5 percent of manufactured exports, and 11 percent of gross output. By 1973, the respective figures were 29 percent of jobs (10 percent in the United Kingdom, 22 percent in West Germany), 62 percent of exports (24 percent in the United Kingdom and 30 percent in Belgium), and 30 percent of output—though two-thirds of increased export revenue stemmed from other sources, invisibles and agriculture (Jacobsen, 1978; McAleese, 1977; and NESC 1980). The bulk of FDI was British, American, and German, with American investment prodominating by the mid-1970s. The decisive role of FDI in Ireland was expressed bluntly in a government-sponsored report, which warned critics that if these sources were discouraged, "Irish people will still have to work with capital that is not owned by Irishmen—but they will be working with it outside Ireland rather than at home" (NESC 1976, 20). This celebration of the disciplinary virtues of emigration—together with exhortations to restrain wages so that capital could "renumerate, renew, and expand"—became the battle cry of the new developmental ideology.

The 1972 referendum over EEC entry presented the next pivotal moment in which the Labour Party's struggle to present viable alternatives was overwhelmed by a combination of official and private pro-Common Market forces. Labour spokemen argued that associated status served Irish needs equally well, while preserving state discretion over the timing of tariff scale-downs and industrial upgrading schemes; but, the Finance Minister demurred, balked "for the simple reason that foreign investors would not regard the two situations as equivalent" (Parliamentary Debates, 1968). A massive pro-Market propaganda campaign carried the vote exactly in line with party shares: a Fianna Fail and Fine Gael total of 83 percent for entry versus Labour's 17 percent against. Contrary to stereotyped dependentista claims, the international market and foreign firms dictated nothing; rather it was indigenous interests, persuasively converting "market signals" into programmatic messages, that determined the precise form of policy response. The active state direction implied in Labour's program was shunned. Hence, this analysis is consistent with the "recurring dependency syndrome" by which Duvall and Freeman (1983) describe an inverse relation between growth and state entrepreneurial activity. Rather than focus on technobureaucrats, I argue that this syndrome is explained by outcomes of broader social struggles for the political power to define the development project.

The argument that state-aided, untaxed industries provided the otherwise unemployed with the privilege of paying taxes seemed pragmatically sound, if not strikingly equitable. But this tactic became a substitute for the vaunted upsurge of private initiative that the policy was intended to trigger;

official reports recognized that "repeated injections" were needed to sustain the developmental project. So the Industrial Developmental Authority (IDA) ingested funds and issued "job projections" which, while they were credible, conferred political capital on incumbent governments. But the IDA was running too many races: against demography ("youngest and fastest-growing population in the EEC"), job loss from import competition, rising expense of capital-intensive technology, and other rivals for footloose capital.

Concerned over the final-assembly bias and abysmally weak local linkages of foreign firms, the IDA responded in the mid-1970s by targeting high-tech electronic firms abroad for attraction to Ireland to create a secure web that might transform the Emerald Isle into a silicon island. However, obscured by energy crises and global recession, the benign consensus-generating basis of the "peripheral postindustrial" project was eroding as a result of systemic technology gaps—systemic in terms both of internal socioeconomic organization and of international exchange relations. The sources and effects are identified briefly:

1. *Foreign control over the terms of technology transfer* is the most familiar problem. Duty-free technologies give rise to balance-of-payments strain. Imported with the technologies is their "interest-composition," i.e., their design embodies the criteria of potent social interests elsewhere. Among potentially inappropriate criteria are:
2. *Capital-intensity bias and "segmentation"*. Though never realizing full employment in its history, the Irish state is not so directly situated relative to labor-surplus Third World economies. Trends toward industrial and service automation should not necessarily be disadvantageous for a relatively developed society that produces a surplus of science and engineering graduates in addition to a skilled labor force, but nonetheless they have taken a toll. Segmentation is the allocation by parent firms of partial, specialized production processes among a variety of sites. If "final-assembly," they are low-skilled, as early critiques had noted. Segmentation retards host state capacity to make Vernon's "obsolescing bargain" obsolesce, and also militates against linkage. A related concern is:
3. *The "volatility" of new technologies* also hampers any turn of bargaining advantage to the host. That parent firms of foreign affiliates retain control over R & D for rapidly changing sophisticated products is too well documented to dwell on here. If local firms and the state are unable or unwilling to match (presumably in product lines of specific competitive advantage) these R & D outlays and organization, product cycles virtuosity suffers. If so, reliance on high-tech foreign affiliates will only exacerbate these cited effects. Finally,
4. *1, 2, and 3 are interrelated,* and their negative impact is intensified by global economic downturns *and* by "standard" global competition, especially so when the state is restricted to a catalytic role and

> the local bourgeoisie lacks what Evans nicely terms a "vocation for hegemony." In downturns, R & D is devoted to tasks of rationalization (producing a similar level of output with less labor) rather than product innovations which provide a basis for capacity-extension (and more jobs). But in the latest upturn, high-tech firms are more likely to locate affiliates in Asian rather than European low-wage areas. The competition for the mobile capital to feed the "peripheral postindustrial" path is keener than ever.

The effects of automation were evident before the oil embargo and energy price rises: between 1966 and 1974 new grant-aided firms "accounted for 59 to 68% of the increase in gross output and 24 to 33% of the increase in exports, all of which was *achieved with a lower labour force than in 1966*" (McAleese 1977, 25). Another Irish economist observed that a curious feature of the economy during the 1960-1973 "miracle" years

> was the very high level of investment (averaging 19 + % of GNP over the period and the poor performance on total employment which rose from 1,052 thousand in April 1960 to 1,066 in April 1974. . . . In the more recent period 1974-77, investment has averaged almost 25% of GNP. (Durkan 1978, 47)

Despite a rise of investment to 30 percent of GNP (compared with 14 percent in the United States, 17 percent in the United Kingdom, and 31 percent in Japan), *total employment fell to the lowest level in the history of the Irish state.* By 1984, the unemployment rate exceeded 16 percent (and, even in the 1960-73 heyday, averaged a discomfiting 6.5 percent). State spending rose from 35.8 percent of GNP in 1962 to 53.0 percent in 1974 through regressive taxation policies that triggered massive street demonstrations in 1979 (and recurrently afterward) for reforms. (Capital taxes amounted to less than 1 percent of total revenue while the share contributed by tax-at-source wage earners rose from 62 percent in 1970 to 90 percent by 1980.)[16] The consensus-generating aspects of the strategy were eroding, a fiscal crisis was looming, and an elite satisfice (of foreign and local exporters, some small Irish "supplier" firms, elements of the bureaucracy and the two main parties, and some skilled branches of the trade unions) was forming before the onset of more drastic global adversities.

THE "PUSHBUTTON" REPUBLIC AND THE POLITICAL EXHAUSTION OF INDUSTRIAL PHASES

Diagnosis

When some problems of pursuing a "peripheral postindustrial" path were cited, an IDA official replied that the Republic was so compact, population so skilled and educated, economic and political climate so obliging that surely there would be enough push buttons to go around for Irish fingertips (in an interview, January 1977). Similar optimism informed the "new strategy" of the PNP and Fomento in Puerto Rico, which hoped to lure enough high-tech firms to emerge as the "technological axis" of the Carribean (Carr 1984, 227; Vilamil 1978). South Korea and Taiwan undertook "statist" direction of their economies toward production of high-tech equipment, and other Third World states followed even though this route "is just about the most difficult and least effective way of entering industrial production." The dice are loaded against the newcomer that has a small home market, is short of capital and skilled manpower, and is rich in unskilled labor (*IDS Bulletin* 1983, 25). Even the experience of relatively privileged Scotland, an early "peripheral postindustrial" path taker, has duplicated, in often a more aggravated way, the Irish adversities. Viewing a Scottish scene of poor linkages, automated unemployment, and foreign firm departures, a scholar asks if

> indigenous firms have not *yet* escaped commercial dependence upon the local multinational sector. However, the fact that external investment in electronics manufacturing in Scotland has been taking place for nearly 30 years casts doubt upon this explanation, especially in light of the small size of this group (native firms provide 9% of total electronics employment). (McDermott 1979, 304; also see Hood and Young 1982)

The most damaging appraisal of the Irish strategies was composed in 1982 by an independent consulting agency. Pertinent to the waning consensual nature of the Irish project, Telesis observed:

> Irish industrial policy aims to create jobs. As it is now designed, it expends too much energy creating job "approvals". . . .Only 30% of the jobs approved in foreign-owned firms between 1972 and 1978 were actually on the ground in 1981. . . . An even greater discrepancy exists for indigenous industry. Sustainable jobs as a percentage of job approvals is only 14%. (NESC 1982, 33)

Telesis reported the good news for indigenous firms that the "shake out" attending EEC entry was nearly over; the bad news was that few Irish firms had adjusted to competitive conditions (Puerto Rican job figures, incidentally, were worse). The Telesis report criticized the state for encouraging a "businessman's dole mentality" among small firms, and noted "most of the largest and strongest Irish companies are investing abroad in businesses only minimally related to Irish employment and export." As to ambitions to create an integrated electronics industry (60 percent of job "approvals" in 1978-80 were in electrical and mechanical engineering firms), Telesis found "manufacturing satellites performing partial steps in the manufacturing process" whose skill demands and linkages were "limited," as in Scotland, Puerto Rico, Singapore, and other cases. Telesis laid the blame upon "timid"—futilely "catalytic"—government, which failed to press vigorously for creation of a "corporate base with sufficient resources and time horizon to undertake removal of obstacles" to more indigenously based export growth. The report cited the "ultimate limiting factor" on the Irish strategy as the rival strategies of parent multinationals, but another comment truly hits the mark of structural constraints.

Telesis noted, "private capital, both Irish and foreign, would find better opportunities in other countries if market forces alone were dictating their choices" (NESC 1982, 185). This constraint is a potent stimulant of a high "propensity to defer" during turbulent adjustments when elites call upon subordinate strata for sacrifices. But this high "propensity" is submission or agreement to an *interest-based depiction of economic exigencies,* where alternative schemes of dividing the burdens of adjustment are possible. The patent need to adjust is distinct, in the cases at hand, from the struggle to formulate an acceptable allocation of "austerities" among the population. A class, organization, or group does not exhibit a high "propensity to defer" when simply accepting the least worst of all possible policy choices, but rather when it accepts a narrowly defined set of options that serve the interests of either another class or the ruling bloc. In this case, the subordinate population accedes to a "surplus" burden in an adjustment process which is nationally necessary.

The ironies of chasing progress in this "information age" are painfully evident. Elites inform job holders that, in order to catch up with EEC living standards, they must deliberately lag behind the rates of wage (and, by extension, social wage) growth among the trading partners because the external environment demands it. The living standard gap between Ireland and the EEC average increased since entry, and only the admission of Greece buoyed Irish standards, wages and social services up from the bottom of the Common Market charts: a further one-fourth to one-third of the citizenry lives in poverty while one-tenth holds two-thirds of all wealth. In the absence of proof of "wageled" losses of jobs or competitiveness, elites incessantly admonish workers to restrain wages even while the productivity gains are robust. These admonishments testify to the *exculpatory* and *extenuating* functions of a hegemonic ideology, which portrays international economic conditions as omnipotent forces requiring invariant reactions from a blameless private sector. If this characterization is found credible, no decline in "propensity to defer" will occur, but neither this characterization nor the "peripheral postindustrial" strategy are garnering credit.

Workers are instructed to invest—via wages foregone and rising taxation—in job-destroying productivity measures. The bulk of Irish-owned firms, reliant on internal demand, suffers more from ebbing demand than they gain from wage "relief." As Elsenhans (1983) nicely illustrates in historical perspective, investment will decline because demand is more vital to capitalist calculations than are wage scales per se. Still the message is driven home that Irish workers are implicitly competing with *Asian* wage level: when the IDA is luring new high-tech affiliates. (The Central Statistics Office reveals that the average wage for "high-tech" employees in Ireland is slightly *less* than the overall average manufacturing wage. [*Sunday Tribune,* 17 February 1985]). In turn, the state responds by raising aid and incentive levels through further revenue extraction from fewer wage earners—until fiscal crisis, as it has, erupts. External "shocks" quicken but do not, by themselves, cause the crisis.

One may object that rising demand elsewhere will stimulate export-oriented investment; but, the trends analyzed here are arrested and the material basis for support of the state strategy is restored only if sustained trade growth occurs, and if the local economy is equipped to take full advantage—both dubious assumptions. Belgium recorded productivity increases of 90 percent from 1970 to 1980 but, with fewer workers producing a roughly constant output due to demand conditions, it passed even Ireland to top the EEC unemployment statistics (Merrill 1982, 22). Multiplier effects are weak in Ireland, and the microchip's impact on tertiary employment should not encourage those interested in attaining even politically tolerable levels of unemployment—and it is the *political* exhaustion of industrial strategies which is the analytic concern.

A second objection is that a "lump of labor" fallacy is promulgated; that is, the analysis ignores the demand creation attending the progressive cheapening of products. This is an open question. The least skeptical investigators foresee mismatches between the labor-shedding effect of process innovation and the timing of product innovations—which have not appeared in gratifying profusion (Stout 1980; Nora and Minc 1981). An OECD study in 1980 found that consumption "of information goods and services is still playing a fairly minor role in the budget of the average household."[17] Another disturbing factor is the current "shake-out" in the electronics industry: Atari and Storage Technology recently closed shops, while Mostek "deferred" plans to locate a new plant in Ireland.

Export-oriented investment, in the absence of vigorous external demand, converts "peripheral postindustrialism" into a subset of dependent development, defined by Evans as excluding local consumers due to the export-based strategy. The process is regressive in a way akin to Frank's notion of underdevelopment. Unlike Frank, this analysis stresses the *indigenous* sources of support for this *choice* among responses to international forces; the consequent fragility of the ideological basis of the dominant coalition (which Cardoso regards as the "state"); and, the effects on the limits of the state automony in democratic politics where adversely affected subordinate groups are less reliably—because more ideologically—contained than in the authoritarian NICs.

Borrowing rose precipitously in the 1973-76 period to offset energy prices and otherwise depressed consumer spending (which, however, is import-oriented when high). The Irish never considered an "indebted industrializing" tack with a view to expanding public commercial firms. As the former premier of the 1973-77 coalition government explained, although he had "no prejudice one way or another," any "completely different deployment" of state-sponsored bodies risked "alienating the investment on which our future depends." The 1977-81 Fianna Fail government increased borrowing for short-term electoral reasons (as analyzed by Tufte), but also in the belief that private investment would be stimulated, and borrowing was the only option for a democratic state whose development strategy yielded diminishing returns and a shrinking pool of revenue sources.[18]

But by 1982 borrowing was 18 percent of GNP, borrowing (mostly foreign) equalled GNP, and debt service consumed over a quarter of revenues.[19] The "propensity to defer" remained high over three elections fought during 1981 and 1982 as parties competed for the right to impose deflationary programs that differed only marginally. Austerity packages were portrayed in the media as a secular pilgrimage, a repentence for "sins" that barefoot treaders of (as a Fine Gael minister evocatively phrased it) the "rough, stony path" may not recall having committed. They are induced anyway to feel guilty because the international marketplace, like God, moves in mysterious ways that demand perfect obedience.

Deflationary policies feed the vicious cycles, and erode the sources of regime stability. The "peripheral postindustrial" strategy will aggravate, not arrest, the erosion. By 1983 the "average earner" paid 43 percent of income to taxes, while hikes in indirect taxes further depressed purchasing power—and the fortunes of local businesses. The real level of personal consumption was 15 percent lower in 1984 than in 1979 (and overall investment fell by nearly a third in the same period, while the foreign debt was rising fivefold). Irish economists find it "something of a paradox" that, despite a stricken domestic market, manufacturing output rose 5 percent in 1983 and by 17 percent in 1984 so that economic recovery, such as it was, had been "all output, no jobs" (*Sunday Tribune,* 8 January 1985). Unemployment rates passed the 16 percent mark. By 1984 "leakages" into debt service and profit repatriation amounted to 10 percent of gross domestic spending, reducing a 4 percent GNP growth year to a 2 percent rise in GNP. The beneficiaries of a 10 percent growth in world trade were certainly the "high-tech" firms, primarily U.S. ones. United States direct investment in Ireland grew from 986 million Irish pounds to 3.8 billion between 1977 and 1983—an annual reinvestment rate of 24 percent. In their most recent profitable EEC outlet, U.S. manufacturers recorded a 24 percent real rate of return compared to an average of 5.6 percent elsewhere in 1984 (but this differential is substantially due to transfer price mechanisms directed toward the favorable Irish tax climate). Benefits do not trickle down to consumers and job seekers.

The espoused solution is to do the same things, only somehow better. Thus a minister decries "unreal wage *demands,*" and argues that future productivity gains will be rewarded not by vulgar wages (as opposed to refined profits) but, incredibly, in "the satisfaction and security of a long-term job." This minister admitted that management efficiency, marketing expertise and new product development were more crucial to Irish competitiveness than wage curbs, but paused for no thought on the implications of infringing upon private prerogatives in order to correct these deficiencies. The emphasis on wages diverts attention from more serious questions regarding industrial strategy and state intervention. But this cannot be construed simply as an expression of base self-interest by "capital" if only because so many Irish businesses are harmed (and voters annoyed or alienated). Ideological "lag" better characterizes the problem; however, the "lag" is conditioned by an institutional environment that keeps "nondecisions" at bay. The dissident voice of the small Labour Party is, of course, well muffled during periodic coalitions with Fine Gael in government. So by itself, "lag" is an insufficient explanation; those who prosper through the current strategy tend to know very well where at least their immediate interests lie.

The Role of Ideology

An investigator of the Peruvian case has argued that a "new bourgeoisie" may arise as a "hegemonic candidate" in dependent developers. Particularly (though not solely) where "bonanza" resources appear, domestic industrialists' liberal fear of the state

> as a restrictor of entrepreneurial initiative diminishes in direct proportion to their self-transformation from an individualist to an organization-based class; to the restructuring of the state apparatus along technical-managerial lines and the infusion within it of the managerial ideology, and to the growth of the 'bonanza,' which enables them to enjoy the advantages of a strong local state without paying for it. (Becker 1983, 329)

If unblessed by a "bonanza," a "mature" and developmentalist" bourgeoisie can engineer the integration of the working class into the capitalist order by reliance on the spread of high-productivity enterprises which enable a rising wage basis for accommodation of trade unions (Becker 1983, 278). But our analysis of "peripheral postindustrialism" identifies disturbing features that vitiate this progressive scenario. Wage "givebacks," work rule erosion and union-busting efforts so recently evident in advanced industrial states testify to the very contingent nature of "mature" private enterprises when opportunities to "roll back" labor power arise. Whether "rollback" or sophisticated bargaining will occur in a specific case depends not on the enlightened ideology or new scruples of management but, foremost, upon the relative strength of the contestants and their capacity to enlist the support of the state.

High sensitivity to international market conditions will induce corporatist-style "consensual" bargaining (e.g., wage controls in exchange for job guarantees, public employment and project expansion, tax reforms, and monitoring of investment) only if (1) the requisite conditions of centralization and concentration among and within the bargaining groups obtain, (2) propensity to defer (to an interest-based depiction of economic "exigencies") is diminishing rapidly, and (3) the level of organization enables a counterelite (seeking, where possible, allies) to promote credible alternatives that influence state policy. The political exhaustion of an economic policy course can then impel formal policy makers (or new incumbents) to search out new coalitional arrangements.

Gourevitch, too, argues that crises "render politics more plastic," emphasizing how the "international situation" shapes internal group behavior according to varying sectoral locations in the global division of labor. The conditions for the cohesion of a dominant coalition give way, opening up possibilities for new coalitional configurations (a process which "political entrepreneurs" may or may not guide, depending on the resources they can summon, or to which they are *forced* to resort). My argument is that just how "plastic" politics becomes during crises will be retarded or accelerated by ideological interpretations of the response "demanded" by economic exigencies. This is a vital supplement to the more sociological approach of Gourevitch (1984, 99), who writes,

> A given policy preference is not necessarily in the "interest" of the actor. On the contrary, it is possible to posit a calculus or frame of reference that could make a range of conflicting policies reasonable from the standpoint of different strategies. . . . The way out of this interpretive trap is to be sociological, to ask what sorts of strategy various groups actually did prefer.

The "interpretive trap" had sprung on the *actors* before the crisis; the "way out" is confined by the prevailing frame of reference; and the latter may be swamped by international market forces so that the "calculi" of various groups become indeterminate; although the opportunity may be missed, a critical moment occurs during which the governing coalition loses adhesion, becomes porous vis-á-vis subordinate group demands, incorporates new and/or sheds old components, and in which the preferences of coalition members (and their weighting) changes with obvious implications for the design of adjustment strategy (Jacobsen and Hofhansel 1984).

A high "propensity to defer" is in effect an *ideologically induced vulnerability* that serves the interests of an export coalition, but also is based on the diffusion of real material benefits to other groups (hence the relevance of Gramsci's work). Waning deferentiality is by no means irreversible, nor are counterelites always poised to exploit it. The British miners' strike of 1984-85, an essentially defensive struggle, failed because they had no positive program by which to galvanize wider public support (indeed losing union and Labour Party support), and because they faced a well-prepared Tory government (deploying superior resources) that proved adept at promoting its own "definition of the situation," and were easily outflanked and overwhelmed in the media. In the Irish case, adversities sparked massive demonstrations for tax reform, worker sit-ins in shut-down factories, and repudiation of coalition Labour Party policies by trade unions for its "anti-working class measures" (*Sunday Tribune,* 15 December 1985). But, so far, these indications of a declining "propensity to defer" amount only to sporadic grumbling.

Prescriptions and Counterhegemonic Content

Finding "catalytic" state activity ineffectual, the Telesis report urged adoption of an alternative strategy of industrialization and adjustment that might provide a basis for restoring a consensual developmental bargain. Telesis advised the state to maximize skill barriers (versus low-wage rivals) by reallocating a third of public expenditure from foreign firms to indigenous exporters and subsuppliers. A "national enterprise agency" should service as a "corporate shell" for Irish firms because "the industrial infrastructure does not exist in Ireland and *the network of subsuppliers has to be created in a more planned and organized way*" (emphasis added) (NESC 1982, 232-3). The state should encourage mergers, rationalization, joint ventures, and private-public coordination, while phasing out low-wage sectors, à la the Swedish policy pattern. The state must emphasize competitive advantages in exploiting native raw materials—food processing, fisheries development, processing of mineral deposit finds (small oil strikes have been made offshore), and research capacities expanded for "selected" industries, including small-batch production of capital goods. This requires a "carrots-*and*-sticks" approach to private industry, and the creation of coordinating mechanisms and forums (by implication, a revival of societal corporatist efforts).

Telesis did not dwell on the role of public commercial enterprises; given the caustic diagnosis of local capital's shortcomings, one may chalk it up to ideological tact. But the Telesis recommendations provide a programmatic basis for new coalitional possibilities, and can prove profoundly subversive because there is scant reason to believe that the *degree* and *kinds* of intervention suffice to meet social goals. A supplemental program, such as the Cambridge School recommendations of selective import controls, devaluation, and incomes policy, tied to investment monitoring, is a probable addition. As the "peripheral postindustrializing" path takes its toll, one can anticipate splits inside the dominant coalition over policy strategy, enabling a new coalitional configuration to arise (the trade unions, left groups, hard-pressed small businesses, "technobureaucrats" who can swing either way, and authentic pragmatists in the major parties). Relevant here is the Stephens observation on Jamaican politics (1983, 405): that where popular loyalties are primarily "clientelistic" rather than ideological, "the party leadership is allowed a greater flexibility to change its ideological stance without alienating (or educating) its supporters"; and, envisioned is a "democratic-entrepreneurial state," which also goes by other, more emotive labels. The ideological basis of the current strategy can be broken or bent to support an alternative policy design during the course of a long-term political struggle, so it really is important to inquire why it is "people in that situation [are] likely to think that way" (Gourevitch 1984, 128).

However, the potential resistance is quite powerful; the dominant export coalition is justifiably apprehensive of the pragmatic path urged by Telesis—seeing it as the "camel's nose beneath the capitalist tent." A weak Irish bourgeoisie knows it needs the state, but will fear the state "acting for itself" or, less metaphysically phrased, "acting for others." Small business shares this view (although the 1981 French election is an interesting exception) and is primed to join the antistatist chorus when key industrial, financial, and agricultural groups begin it. A "recurring dependent development syndrome" can come into play, of course, if aggregate growth resumes (primed by world trade expansion), but only if a satisficing level of employment—anything under 10 percent unemployment these days—and rising living standards occur. In the short term, social pressures on elites tend to be "populist," centered around no specific programs and so are manipulable. If elites are unwilling or unable to defuse popular protest through concessionary measures, the threat of a concerted movement can grow as economic adversities continue—and, so does the option of an authoritarian response.

CONCLUSION

I have argued that international economic forces alone do not determine either the precise response engendered in a given state or the varying definitions of interest made by internal actors as to the policies they prefer the state to initiate. *This obviously presupposes some degree of choice, and the presence of resources that make choice possible.* Global economic shifts and shocks are "interpreted" through mediation by dominant coalitions in ways designed to uphold their social power versus challengers who stand to benefit from altered patterns of policy and state activity. Powerful groups may even exacerbate sensitivity when the means for diminishing it are present. External forces become (not totally tameable) pieces to deploy on the social gameboard. When acute and protracted, economic adversities, however, can erode the propensity of subordinate strata (and of separate components of the dominant coalition) to defer to the prevailing development policy and adjustment schemes, triggering a "situation of indeterminacy" (regarding policy content and outcome) within policy networks, within the dominant coalition, and between the latter and nonelites, if they are mobilizing, and between these shifting influences and the receptiveness of formal policy makers.

The "politics of debt" in Latin America offers further material for the study of state responses to declining "propensities to defer." The IMF can provide welcome internal leverage for some groups over the demands and resistance of others. The IMF is not the only agent that can be invoked for such purposes, of course, and this function is not invariably a malign one. In the case of an exceptional debtor, Washington applied pressure on Israeli leaders to put their finances in some semblance of order. "The message Peres and Modái tacitly convey is that they welcome Washington's discipline," a commentator observed. "It helps them make a case for austerity in their bids for consensus at home" (Viorst 1985, 304). But when mysterious market forces become institutionally embodied in such agents, the market becomes, in popular eyes, coteries of affluent aliens who determine, over their tax-deductible lunches, whether and how long the citizenry must be starved. Market forces no longer appear intangible and inexorable. Restive publics in Argentina, Brazil, Venezuela, and the Dominican Republic have forced governments to tread warily toward fiscal propriety; Mexico has counted on ruling-party ties to trade unions in enforcing severe austerity measures.

In the Bolivian case, an ultimatum by the Bank of America, on behalf of creditors to the nation, to resume interest payments was not acted upon by either party. "It's not a case that we ignored the deadline," a bank negotiator explained afterward. "There was no one to talk to" because the country was undergoing its ninth cabinet change in little over two years, not to mention five general strikes (*New York Times,* 5 February 1985). Social distress does not disturb bankers, but institutional instability does. Banks are forced to consider conciliatory actions when the perceived capacity of states to enforce rules is diminishing. A declining "propensity to defer" among subordinate strata permits a breathing space for governments (whether they want it or not), when dealing with international leaders; it *may* also stimulate a search for alternative adjustment packages that broaden the scope of "orthodoxy" in the international regime (but this remains an extremely speculative point). The political implications of a widespread decline in "propensity to defer" is not lost on local elites; even where their own misfiring strategies are most blameworthy, dominant groups can co-opt populist pressure into a "nationalist" course that restores their authority. The international implications are cited by the Latin American Debt Commission:

> In virtually every Latin American and Carribean country, there are major pressures to turn inward, to reject cooperation with the IMF, to turn their backs on existing obligations and to look to solutions which stress a higher degree of protectionism and state control. (*New York Times,* 11 March 1984)

Popular attention may be diverted successfully from internal shortcomings by pointing fingers at external agents, but any act tantamount to repudiating international market forces is a rather hazardous precedent for local capital to set. Although local capital and foreign bankers alike may wish the Pinochets to proliferate, both Chicago-style economics and the military option are at least temporarily discredited in the larger debtors (Kaufman 1985). This enhances the question of how "situations of indeterminacy" regarding state strategy, coalition formation, and debt negotiation are contained or exploited by domestic contestants for politcal power.

This chapter, however, has focused on democratic states pursuing, and coping with the consequences of, "peripheral postindustrializing" development. This term denotes: (1) a policy-induced diffusion of high-tech affiliates on the periphery, with the objective of installing them as the leading local sector; (2) a truncated form of such development (low linkages, meager R & D, less sophisticated elements); and, (3) an ideological extenuation of prevailing policy, designed to counteract the political exhaustion of the development pattern. The lattermost was indeed a strong motive of Irish elites, given that alternatives of a state-capitalist kind were ruled out by the hegemonic ideology. The negative effects of a "peripheral postindustrial" development course are most aggravated in states employing "catalytic" policy instruments, but the problems cited earlier are manifested across the spectrum of regime type, levels of development, mode of intervention, and state-society configuration (Jacobsen 1987).

South Korea and Taiwan take a strenuously statist approach to promotion of electronics industries, but remain reliant primarily on Japan for technology generation (the "cutting edge" technologies being withheld) (Cumings 1984; *IDS Bulletin,* 1982). By incorporating microelectronic advances into older industrial processes, the advanced industrial states threaten to "roll back" the Third World's comparative advantage in cheap labor; "the scope for offshore activities is decreasing," even for standardized segments of production (Rada 1981, 50; Junne, this volume). The increasing concentration of control by transnational firms over such products is associated with decreases in offshore production; and, the skill mix and the complex "systems nature" of innovation—which must underlie a successful pursuit of this strategy—pose formidable barriers to even the most capable of imitators.

The prospect of rolling back Third World advantages in cheaper labor should not be a source of good cheer to First World work forces. In the United States, the Federal Bureau for Labor Statistics expects between now and 1995 that high-tech industries will create from 3 to 17 percent of new jobs. The EEC Brussels Office estimated that, in 1978, 7.5 percent of the EEC workforce was employed in the electronics industry, broadly defined, but that since 1969 these firms have shed an average of 20 percent of labor.[20] The impact of the automation on tertiary activities is far from encouraging, at least in the present global text. Ultimately, demand growth must outpace productivity gains to sustain or raise employment levels, and the fabled forces of the market are not very evidently poised to accomplish this. "Trade," as Nathan Rosenberg writes,

> means a willingness to accept new patterns of specialization as the industrializing countries establish new competencies and displace more advanced industrial economies from traditional niches based upon earlier, but now eroding, comparative advantages. These adjustments, however, are coming into increasing conflict with other domestic goals, such as high employment, strong expectations about the continued growth in real wages, and increasing sensitivity to the distributional aspects of adjustment processes when left to the marketplace.[21]

The present interaction of "high-tech" development with international market patterns will exert pressures on states to adopt protectionist measures or to engage in creative policy adjustments domestically, and perhaps explore new cooperative arrangements internationally over the allocation of niches in the changing international division of labor. Certainly, market mechanisms and the remarkable advances in high technology both offer indispensible benefits. But as the current scramble for advantageous niches continues (despite a cyclical downturn in high-tech industries), political pressures will mount for leads to devise means to avert the negative aspects of this chase. "Perhaps the profoundest problem that faces modern society," Paul Goodman noted two decades ago, "is to decide in what functions the automatic and computer style is not relevant—and therefore to curtail and forget it" (1968, 76). The same may be said for the role of the market, and when "propensity to defer" to what Gailbraith terms the "conventional wisdom" is declining, these social tasks effectively begin.

NOTES

1. "Countries commonly given 'newly industrialized' status [the NICs] include Argentina, Brazil, Greece, Hong Kong, Republic of Korea, Mexico, Portugal, Singapore, Spain, Taiwan, and Yugoslavia" (Lewis and Kalleb 1983). Lists vary, depending on the criteria applied. Some rankings exclude OECD nations by virtue of the exalted affiliations. In others, Israel is occasionally cited, and I include the Irish Republic. In any case, the list above is not exhaustive or indisputable.

2. E.g., Paul Baran (1957) and Andre Gunder Frank (1969). The thrashing con-

tinues. See Frank's plaintive reply (1983).

3. I emphasize that the term "postindustrial," as employed here, refers only to science-based, research intensive industries. A "postindustrialization" strategy uses such industries as the cornerstone of economic development. This analysis and usage in no way subscribes to the particulars associated with Daniel Bell's forecasting venture (1973).

4. On strategies for creating "complex-factor cost industries" and maximizing competitive advantages, see Magaziner and Reich (1982). Magaziner heads Telesis Consultants, an organization that figures prominently in later discussion.

5. The most comprehensive argument for the "statist approach" is Stephen Krasner (1978); a critique is presented in Jacobsen and Hofhansel (1984).

6. Here, I refer to states as "catalytic" if they rely upon market mechanisms and nondirective incentives to guide the economy; as "complementary" when engaged in substantial public commercial activity and planning, more or less, in tandem with private capital (indeed abetting the latter); and as "entrepreneurial" only if the state undertakes directive planning, public-private coordination, and commercial activity in a manner superordinate to the private sector. A genuinely "entrepreneurial" state would be a risk taker in a dual sense: with respect to international marketplace challenges, and with regard to challenges from internal economic elites. On the ambiguous relation between state and capital in "state entrepreneurship," see Evans (1982).

7. For another analysis of what we dub the "pragmatic hypothesis," see Hamilton (1979).

8. On political entrepreneurship, see Mollenkopf (1983, 4-11).

9. In Jurgen Habermas's (1975) schema, a "rationality crisis" occurs when the state appears unable to manage the economy effectively. If prolonged and unalleviated, this can grow into a "legitimation crisis" wherein the state's capacity to reproduce the capitalist system is threatened—although the outcome is unpredictable; also see Jennifer Todd (1979). A "policy crisis," stemming from what Habermas terms a "rationality crisis," refers to sudden or gradual departures from previous harmonious accord over specific policy areas among members of a dominant coalition and/or between these private interests and state policy makers, thereby creating opportunities for new or weaker groups to influence policy content and outcomes. See Jacobsen and Hofhansel (1984).

10. The "triple alliance" is a complex coupling "between elite local capital, international capital and state capital" in peripheral societies thereby incorporated into the international economy (Evans 1979, 11). For a most interesting exercise in tracing the causes and consequences of changing "equilibrium mixes," see Freeman (1983).

11. On metropole control of technology, see Mytelka (1978); Vaitsos (1976); Stewart and James (1982). On the Indian effort to counter this problem, see Parasothi (1979) and Grieco (1982), wherein an antidependentista conclusion is drawn from remarkably ambiguous evidence. For some peculiar reason, Poznanski, in his critical review article (1984), regards even Grieco as something of a dependentista.

12. Incorporating China, North Korea, and Japan in their analysis, Hofheinz and Calder (1982) provide Kiplingesque exemplification of nondemocratic "propensity to defer"—indeed a tribute to it. Noting how sparse democratic activity is in regions "where East Asian officials form a caste of oligarchs vying with one another to exer-

cise authority over a deferential and productive society," they continue undismayed and objectively to observe, "citizens of East Asia, especially the businessmen, are comfortable knowing their governments do not change" (1982, 71-2). See the rather more critical essay by Cumings (1984).

13. Hypothetically, these modes might co-vary with the changing "equilibrium mixes" among state, elite local, and foreign components of capital in a given dependent context; see, e.g., Freeman (1983).

14. "By 1951, state-sponsored bodies controlled 25% of investments, and employed 5% of all employed workers at a wage 40% higher than average" according to Ellis (1972). If so, much room existed for friction with small capitalists unhappy with the comparatively profligate example set by the state. Even so, "10% owned 66.7% of land and capital in 1953 by E. T. Nevin's estimates," and that percentage has not since been redistributed downward, according to subsequent studies (1972, 291).

15. Sweeney (1973) estimated that more than one-half of "Irish" manufacturing assets were foreign-controlled (mostly British) by the mid-1950s.

16. *Hibernia Weekly Review,* 23 March 1979; also Ken O'Brien, "Will Marching Change The Tax Bands?" *Irish Times* (14 April 1983).

17. Cited in Friedrichs and Schaff (1983, 197). A more scholar-oriented version of several papers in the above cited volume appear in Berting (1979).

18. During this period, farming income dropped precipitously, so that the raising of farm taxes was off the agenda (of the government, if not of the trade unions). The government had introduced the 10 percent nominal manufacturing tax in 1981. Tax protests, which brought as many as half a million people into one-day street demonstrations, also discouraged raising "average earner" tax rates. The easiest and most tempting "way out" for a government with a thin electoral edge was to continue to borrow.

19. See Frieden (1985) for a breakdown of Irish debt, and a more pessimistic projection of political consequences than that presented here.

20. Merritt (1982, 65). In the U.S. electronics industry, the figure is 4 percent, and for high-tech, broadly defined, about 10 percent as of 1979.

21. Rosenberg (1982, 277). On business views on this issue, see the glum survey by *Business International* (1979, 68); an American executive observes: "Every businessman I know is trying to run his business with the least number of people. It's understandable. And yet I don't know of a place in the world where finding meaningful employment isn't perhaps the number-one problem. Now these two things are absolutely inconsistent."

5

Mette Skak

The New International Division of Labor and East-South Relations

The 1970s saw a process of stark economic differentiation among Third World countries and regions, marked by the advent of powerful cartels such as the Organization of Petroleum Exporting Countries (OPEC) and new, dynamic industrial producers, the newly industrializing countries (NICs).[1] The emergence of NICs capable of penetrating the markets of "Northern," i.e., Organization for Economic Cooperation and Development (OECD) countries with manufactured goods, chemicals and steel was a qualitatively new trend in world economic exchange later referred to as the "new international division of labor" (NIDL).[2]

This contribution deals with the issue of NIDL from a controversial, regional point of view. What follows will be an attempt to analyze the significance and character of NIDL in the relationship between the NICs and the European members of the Council for Mutual Economic Assistance (CMEA).[3] The emergence of NICs has played a distinct, but indirect role in East-South relations. Due to the intricate problems for the European centrally planned economies in generating "intensive growth," and hence CMEA's continuous position in the world economic exchange as a representative of an intermediate level of development, NIC-manufactured exports tend to undermine previous complimentaries in East-South economic relations. NICs appear as the most direct competitors to CMEA countries on the Western markets; therefore, the Eastern views of NICs vary between perceptions of challenge and of new political options. Consensus prevails, however, on the recognition of the primary importance of Third World economic differentiation processes which, by implication, means recognizing that political differentiation is only of secondary importance.

Before we enter into the discussion of actual CMEA relations to the Third World and CMEA theoretical perceptions of NIDL and NICs, we should consider East-South relations against a background of more general economic issues. A focal point is the problem of rationality in East-South relations and, in connection with this, the question of whether the concept of NIDL applies to relations between CMEA and NICs. A relevant point of departure is the general trend of CMEA foreign economic policy from the 1970s, namely the attempt at combining intensified intra-CMEA interaction (integration) with intensified world economic exchange after twenty years of relative autarky.

CMEA IN THE WORLD ECONOMY AND CMEA INTERRELATIONSHIPS

Concerning the role of the CMEA in the world economy we could cite CMEA's combined share of world industrial production, which (according to official UN statistics) is presently, in 1982, around one-fourth, or 40 percent of the industrial production of developed market economies. Throughout the 1960s and 1970s, CMEA growth rates in gross domestic product (GDP) and industry were higher than those of the developed market economies. But when it comes to more qualitative measures, such as the level of development in terms of technology, the *intermediate* position of the CMEA in the global division of labor becomes clear.[4] U.N. trade statistics show that, whereas the share of manufactured CMEA exports to LDCs was some 45 percent in 1980, CMEA-manufactured exports to the developed market economies was only 35 percent of total CMEA exports to this region, and, conversely, the percentage of CMEA-manufactured imports from the West was nearly 60 percent of total imports. This pattern would become even more outstanding in an investigation of the actual technology content in the respective trade flows.

The less dynamic role of the CMEA region in the world economy can also be seen in the scope of foreign economic exchange. CMEA countries account for a decreasing share of world trade (below 9 percent), where the major part is intra-CMEA trade, and East-South trade accounts for 1.5 percent. Some 60 percent of East-South economic interaction is accounted for by the Soviet Union. Interestingly enough, East-South trade plays a greater role for the CMEA than for the LDCs themselves. In 1982 13 to 14 percent of CMEA's foreign trade was with LDCs whereas, for LDCs, imports from and exports to CMEA, on an average, accounted for 5.3 percent and 2.5 percent respectively. CMEA-LDC exchange has, however, expanded considerably since the 1960s and, according to Soviet sources, CMEA countries now have regular commercial links (via bilateral trade agreements) to over ninety LDCs. By 1983, East-South trade amounted to $53 billion (according to GATT; UNCTAD sources have a higher figure: $64.6 billion).

On the other hand, both trade and aid patterns of the CMEA display concentration on certain key LDCs such as India, Iraq, Iran, Libya, Egypt, Argentina, and Brazil. On average, OPEC (and especially Arab oil-producing countries) has been the most dynamic regional group in East-South relations throughout the 1970s, whereas the role of NICs, especially Asian NICs, has certainly been much less significant. The Hungarian economist Istvan Dobozi sees CMEA's relations to NICs as a case of blundering on the part of CMEA (Dobozi 1983).

In order to give a fair evaluation of CMEA's NIC policy, we should examine the demand structure and export/import capacities of the CMEA in more detail. As is commonly known, the actual economic strategy of the CMEA has been to rely heavily on Western transfers of technology, for lack of effective innovative structures in the planned economies. Originally, CMEA countries planned to repay these imports with CMEA industrial exports; in fact, a switch to a more export-oriented growth was anticipated.[5] However, as economic rivalries among OECD countries, as well as competition between OECD and LDCs flourished, the CMEA found itself unable to catch up with its competitors on the Western market. As a result, the CMEA was caught in a squeeze between Western protectionism, NIC competition on Western markets, and rising CMEA technology and energy demands. External and internal pressures have thus destabilized the CMEA countries' foreign trade, so that they are now caught up in the global economic crisis without having the LDCs' option of getting preferential treatment. The result of the CMEA trade deficit in its dealings with OECD countries has been aggravating indebtedness,[6] which has produced austerity measures, including cuts in LDC imports (see table 5.1). Seemingly, deficits in East-West trade are offset by surpluses in the East-South trade. Now, it should be borne in mind that East-South relations are still, to a large degree, characterized by clearing, barter, and other noncurrency exchange arrangements since technical-scientific assistance (development aid) is an integral part of trade flows. In other words, CMEA surpluses from East-South trade cannot automatically be used in CMEA debt servicing vis-à-vis the West. But, clearly, CMEA has sought to lessen imports and heighten exports.

For various reasons, the small Eastern European countries' demand for Western technology has been higher than has that of the Soviet Union. One reason is Eastern Europe's acute need for increased export earnings in order to pay the rising energy import bill vis-à-vis the Soviet Union; except for Romania, the Eastern Europeans depend on the Soviet Union for about 80 percent of their energy imports and about 90 percent of their oil. Following the OPEC price shock of the mid-1970s, the Soviets began to press for a better deal in their oil and energy exports. In 1975, a new pricing mechanism was introduced in the CMEA, which meant a further approximation to world market prices, the result of which has been sharply deteriorat-

Table 5.1

CMEA Balances of Trade with the West and with LDCs Respectively, 1977-1982 (Figures in Billions of Rubles)

	Trade with the West			Trade with LDCs		
Year	Export	Import	Balance	Export	Import	Balance
1977	17.291	22.833	- 5.542	8.230	5.535	+ 2.695
1978	17.884	24.623	- 6.739	8.966	5.332	+ 3.634
1979	23.798	28.354	- 4.556	10.065	6.172	+ 3.893
1980	29.539	32.192	- 4.556	11.785	8.978	+ 2.807
1981	30.570	34.218	- 3.648	14.521	10.882	+ 3.639
1982	34.854	34.985	- 0.131	17.492	10.440	+ 7.052

Source: Compiled from Statisticheskii Yezhegodnik stran-chlenov SEV, various editions, CMEA Secretariat, Moscow.

Note: Figures for Romania are not available.

ing terms of trade of the small Eastern European countries with the Soviet Union, as well as in relation to other trade partners. (See table 5.2.) To put it another way, the Eastern European countries are experiencing much greater difficulty in their debt servicing, as they are caught in both a Soviet and a Western *trade deficit trap.* Thus, the cumulative trade deficit of the small Eastern European countries in relation to the Soviet Union, from 1976 to 1983, amounted to around 12.2 billion transfer rubles which, according to the official ruble/dollar exchange rate, is equivalent to around $16.5 billion (Hohmann 1985, 23).

One possible alternative has been to diversify energy and fuel supply sources, now that marginal costs of Siberian resource extraction are rising. Even more disturbing for the Eastern Europeans than the mere rising of prices (where there still is a decisive margin of competitiveness for Soviet oil, compared to world market oil prices) have been the signs of a stagnation in Soviet oil exports to Eastern Europe. From the point of view of CMEA demands, the most dynamic area of East-South relations is the fuel and mineral imports, which will probably accent the OPEC focus. Thus, table 5.3 shows the actual trends of CMEA fuel and mineral imports from LDCs throughout the 1970s.

The table documents a sharp increase in CMEA fuel and mineral imports from the Third World so that, by the early 1980s, around 25 percent of

Table 5.2
CMEA Terms of Trade, 1960 to 1979[a], and Trends in Eastern Europe's Terms of Trade with the Soviet Union, 1975 to 1985[b]

	1975=100						1970=100				
	1960	1965	1970	1974	1979		1975	1980	1981	1982	1985*
Bulgaria	107	108	104	102	83		90	76	71	66	49
Czechoslovakia	(108)	(108)	110	110	84		86	77	71	65	48
German Democratic Republic	115	113	115	104	99		85	74	69	63	47
Hungary	113	117	120	108	86		81	68	64	60	44
Poland	96	97	98	100	97		95	83	78	74	55
Soviet Union	114	103	94	109	123						
						Romania	103	86	85	83	61
						Eastern Europe	89	77	72	67	49

Source: a) 1981 Yearbook of International Trade Statistics (New York: United Nations, 1982) vol. 1, special table B. Figures in parentheses from the 1979 Yearbook of International Trade Statistics, special table G.
b) J. Vanous, "East European Economic Slowdown," Problems of Communism, July-August 1982, Table 3, page 5.

*Estimated

Table 5.3

Fuel and Mineral Imports of the European CMEA Countries from the Developing Countries

	1971		1980	
Commodity Group	U.S. $ Million	Share of LDC Imports in CMEA Imports of Respective Commodity Category (%)	U.S. $ Million	Share of LDC Imports in CMEA Imports of Respective Commodity Category (%)
Crude fertilizers and minerals (SITC 27)	47	14.5	256	12.6
Metalliferous ores and metal scrap	163	22.5	577	27.7
Mineral fuels and related materials (SITC 3)	140	7.4	4507	22.6
Nonferrous metals (SITC 68)	13	1.8	281	10.6
Total fuel and mineral imports from LDCs	363	9.9	5621	21.1

Source: After I. Dobozi, "Arrangements for Mineral Development Cooperation between Socialist Countries and Developing Countries," *Natural Resources Forum* (New York, 1983: 340).

CMEA fuel and mineral imports were provided by non-CMEA sources. Although certain demand-limiting measures, such as energy savings, have been introduced so that Eastern European economists now tend to have a less alarmist view on future import needs (Dobozi 1984), it goes without saying that the central import items for the CMEA will continue to be raw materials. In other words, a conventional division of labor can be expected.

Although the table is incomplete for showing actual CMEA-LDC trade flows (e.g., CMEA exports do not always total 100 percent), the trend throughout the 1970s has been a preservation of previous patterns of raw material versus manufactured goods flows. Concerning CMEA exports of manufactures, the table suggests a decreasing CMEA role in the Third World, which may be explained by a combination of lessened CMEA competitiveness and the economic crisis in many LDCs. Lessened CMEA competitiveness, in turn, may be partly explained by the rapidly increasing foreign economic presence in other LDCs of certain NICs, notably Brazil and South Korea, together with India.

There is a remarkable parallelism in the manufactured export potentials of industrializing developing states and CMEA, which does not only mean that the demands of the two groups for each other's industrial products in general is rather vague, but even that East and South (NICs) are in-

Table 5.4

Structure of Foreign Trade of CMEA Countries with Developing Countries, 1970, 1980 and 1982(%)

CMEA Imports by Commodity Group:[a]	1970	1980	1982[b]
All food items (SITC 0+1+22+4)	39.4	41.9	36.6
Agricultural raw materials (SITC less 2-22-27-28)	19.2	7.3	6.8
Ores and metals (SITC 27+28+67+68)	12.6	9.3	7.6
Fuels (SITC 3)	2.2	16.4	7.0
Manufactured goods (SITC 5 to 8 less 67+68)	26.1	24.6	40.9
CMEA exports:[a]			
All food items (SITC 0+1+22+4)	9.0	7.7	4.7
Agricultural raw materials (SITC less 2-22-27-28)	3.7	3.9	5.7
Ores and metals (SITC 27+28+28+67+68)	8.5	6.2	10.6
Fuels (SITC 3)	6.2	15.5	26.6
Manufactured goods (SITC 5 to 8 (less 67+68))	53.9	45.4	51.2

Source: UNCTAD Handbook of International Trade and Development Statistics, 1983, International Trade Data Base of the United Nations Statistical Office, quoted after TD/B1003/Add., 31 July 1984.

[a] Including China. The shares exclude exports or imports for which the country of destination or origin, as well as the commodity class could not be identified.

[b] Calculated on the basis of incomplete data.

[c] Figures based on national statistics for Czechoslovakia, Hungary and Poland and on partner country statistics for the other CMEA countries.

creasingly *competing* in third markets, as shown in table 5.5.

The table illustrates the point that, although CMEA exports of more sophisticated goods to the West have been rising, they *fail to match the export expansion of LDCs,* i.e., notably NICs, as LDC export growth is much more dynamic. However, it must be stressed that there are fundamental differences between the small Eastern European CMEA states and the USSR concerning the impact of the NIC process. The foreign trade demand structure of the USSR is similar to that of an OPEC (OAPEC) country, with a high percentage of energy exports (around 50 percent of total exports, and over 75 percent in exports to the West in 1981), combined with a large share of food and fodder imports (24 percent by 1982). It is exactly this commodity group that can be assumed to be the most dynamic for Soviet LDC imports, following the rather permanent agricultural crisis in the Soviet Union.[7] In the field of manufactures, the main Soviet potential is within heavy industry,

Table 5.5

CMEA and LDC Exports of Manufactured Goods, Machinery and Transport Equipment, Chemical Products, Steel, and Iron to the Industrialized West, 1970 and 1979, in US$ Millions, Expressed in Market Shares

		1970	SHARE %	1979	Share %
Manufactured goods (SITC 6+8-(67+68))	CMEA	977	2.2	5578	2.5
	LDCs	4267	9.5	34737	15.6
	Latin America	410	0.9	3497	1.5
	South/Southeast Asia	3415	7.6	28590	12.8
Machinery and transport equipment (SITC 7)	CMEA	630	1.1	3638	1.3
	LDCs	756	1.3	11826	4.4
	Latin America	191	0.3	1754	0.6
	South/Southeast Asia	518	0.9	9551	3.5
Chemical products (SITC 5)	CMEA	373	2.6	2166	2.6
	LDCs	522	3.7	2857	3.4
	Latin America	325	2.2	1602	1.9
	South/Southeast Asia	82	0.6	736	0.8
Iron and steel (SITC 67)	CMEA	593	5.3	1793	4.5
	LDCs	263	2.3	1824	4.6
	Latin America	78	0.7	715	1.8
	South/Southeast Asia	85	0.8	831	2.1

Source: UNCTAD Handbook of International Trade and Development Statistics, 1981 (New York: United Nations, 1982).

power plants, etc., leaving significant import demand to the sphere of light industry and sophisticated equipment, which has been Eastern Europe's, as well as certain industrializing countries' (notably India's), main access to the Soviet market. In other words, Soviet trade with LDCs follows a less "colonial" pattern than that of Eastern Europe.[8]

Conversely, in terms of foreign trade potentials and demands, the Eastern European countries might be termed "socialist NICs," as Eastern Europe's exports to the EEC apart from agricultural goods, metals, etc. consist of chemicals, cars, textiles, footwear, furniture, household appliances, and other consumer goods. Here, the low level of technical sophistication and fashion/style-designing becomes critical for CMEA exports, and Eastern Europeans have had to resort to dumping. As the demand for these products is diminishing, NICs themselves increasingly switch to high technology productions, such as pocket calculators, digital watches, radio, television, and other electronic equipment, so at least the Asian NICs have already bypassed the CMEA.

To sum up, this section has stressed general trends and problems in the foreign economic situation of the CMEA with respect to consequences and prospects for East-South cooperation. The emphasis was on a discussion of the role of NIDL in relation to East-South cooperation. CMEA's intermediate position in the global division of labor, as well as the marginal role of East-South flows, was emphasized, although East-South cooperation has been expanding since the 1960s—but, the prospects for enhanced East-South exchange are meager, following the serious intra-CMEA economic problems. On balance, the USSR appears to have greater potential for cooperation with industrializing LDCs than have the Eastern European countries, both in terms of economic surplus and demand structure. But generally, the division of labor pattern of East-South flows can be expected to be a continuation of previous trends which, in terms of CMEA exports, implies focus on technology transfers to LDCs.

What can be concluded is that NIDL has had an indirect, but nevertheless remarkable impact on the CMEA. CMEA's position as "socialist NICs" aiming at expanding industrial exports creates problems similar to those of the NICs (e.g., the problem of finding export outlets). This parallelism has meant trade competition with the West, and may reduce East-South complementarities so that a certain competition arises on this level too. After this broad outline of the problem, we will now turn to a discussion of actual CMEA-NIC interaction.

CMEA INTERACTION WITH NICs: THE RECORD

In this section we will examine CMEA-NIC interaction in more detail, in order to identify trends and prospects of CMEA future links with NICs. As the

NIC group is in no way homogeneous, a distinction between at least Latin American and Asian NICs seems proper. For reasons of comparison, we will also refer to CMEA trade with OPEC countries and with India. The pattern of CMEA-NIC trade is displayed in table 5.6.

At the outset, it should be said the NICs are certainly among the newcomers as partners in East-South relations, partly due to distance and partly due to the outspoken Western economic and political orientation of NICs. From that perspective, the low level of CMEA interaction with NICs is really no surprise; however, table 5.6 points to interesting trends and new developments in CMEA countries' economic relations to NICs.

First, the table reveals a remarkable and stable CMEA deficit in trade with all NICs, in stark contrast to trade with other LDC regions. In other words, it is certainly not the NICs that are used as levers in balancing East-West trade, as referred to above; rather it is OPEC countries, in spite of the rising CMEA oil and mineral imports from Arab countries. Thus, the table underlines the point that CMEA technology exports to NICs are confronted with domestic competition, and have failed to penetrate the NIC market. From the CMEA perspective, this is a sore point in East-South relations, which can also be seen in frustrated Soviet commentaries on the low technology import inclination in Latin American NICs (Zhuravleva 1983, 44-8). Although Soviet Latin Americanists prefer to be optimistic concerning future balancing of trade patterns by citing *inter alia,* Soviet hydroelectric power stations erected in Brazil, it remains doubtful whether CMEA will have the required export flexibility and efficiency to really match NIC technology import demands in the future.

Second, the table shows that cooperation with Latin American NICs is far ahead of cooperation with Asian NICs. In recent years, Latin America has actually surpassed OPEC as the primary CMEA import market, due particularly to rising Soviet food and fodder imports from the region. Trade with Asian NICs is marginal except for trade with Malaysia, from which CMEA traditionally imports rubber. Also, CMEA trade with other Asian NICs is characterized by CMEA imports of tropical raw materials. Asian NICs would appear to be an even tougher export market for the CMEA to enter into than Latin America, since these countries often do not have the same political ambitions as have some Latin American countries (e.g., in relations to the United States) and they are quite protectionistic in their industrial policy. Moreover, a fear of communism does seem to play a role in their interstate relations—in contrast to patterns in Latin America. Although one could cite South Korea's steel industry as a theoretically promising field for cooperation with the Soviet steel industry, the practical and political obstacles are enormous. Because of political circumstances, CMEA is cut off from developing significant ties with the most advanced NICs of them all: the "gang of four"—South Korea, Taiwan, Hong Kong, and Singapore. Admittedly, CMEA

Table 5.6

CMEA Trade with Latin American and Asian NICs, OPEC Countries, and India, 1965 and 1983 ($ Millions)

CMEA Exports To	1965	1983	CMEA Imports From	1965	1983	1983 CMEA Balance of Trade
Latin American NICs	87.8	526.6	Latin American NICs	263.5	3517.0	-2990.4
Argentina	29.6	71.9	Argentina	108.4	1933.9	-1862.0
Brazil	54.3	413.7	Brazil	84.2	1490.0	-1076.3
Mexico	3.9	41.0	Mexico	70.9	93.1	-52.1
Asian NICs	7.3	170.2	Asian NICs	129.7	687.6	-517.4
Malaysia	0.1	30.0	Malaysia	124.6	401.9	-371.9
Philippines	...	23.7	Philippines	...	79.3	-55.6
Singapore	2.9	67.2	Singapore	...	106.0	-38.8
Thailand	4.3	49.3	Thailand	5.1	100.4	-51.1
OPEC countries[a]	277.4	7101.1	OPEC countries	131.3	5797.2	1305.0
Iraq	47.7	2239.3	Iraq	4.3	869.2	1370.0
India	354.4	2064.0	India	309.9	1855.8	208.2

Source: UNCTAD document no. TD/1003/Add., 1(31 July 1984) tables 13 and 14 (based on national statistics of CMEA countries). Please note that data are only indicative or provisional for 1983, as CMEA statistics are often incomplete.

[a] I.e., Abu Dhabi, Algeria, Ecuador, Gabon, Indonesia, Iran, Iraq, Kuwait, Libya, Nigeria, Qatar, Saudi Arabia and Venezuela combined.

exports of digital watches, pocket calculators and computer parts from Hong Kong, Taiwan, and South Korea may take place (via third countries); but, there is reason to believe that many CMEA technocrats would like to see a genuine industrial cooperation evolve in relation to exactly these countries. For the time being, this is certainly future music.

Third, the table shows that CMEA experiments with formal LDC association have played a marginal role, if any at all, in developing CMEA-LDC interaction. What is referred to here is the "Agreement Concerning CMEA Cooperation with the Republic of Iraq" of July 4, 1975 and the "Agreement Concerning CMEA Cooperation with the United States of Mexico" of August 13, 1976. These two documents marked the first attempt at establishing CMEA *en bloc* (multilateral) relations with LDCs, which was one of a series of new CMEA initiatives to intensify East-South cooperation in the 1970s. The agreement with Iraq may be termed a logical development, following years of growing economic links between this Arab country and all CMEA countries, and a parallel to the signing of the Soviet-Iraq Treaty of Friendship and Cooperation, in 1972. But the agreement with Mexico marked a new trend in East-South relations, namely the expansion of trade with the Latin American region. Interestingly enough, trade with Mexico shows a stagnating trend when compared to trade with Argentina and Brazil, which has really boomed. It is tempting to term the agreement with Mexico an alibi for expanding trade with Brazil and Argentina, as no multilateral cooperation between Mexico and CMEA countries worth mentioning is going on. Mexico herself may well have been the partner to show no interest in diversifying foreign economic links but, in any case, this attempt at a CMEA breakthrough in relation to a NIC could not be called a success. Relations with Mexico, as well as experience with Iraq, show that CMEA as an institution has extremely limited power to attract LDCs to orient their trade eastwards. In contrast to EEC association with LDCs, CMEA multilateral agreements with LDCs mean only formal tariff preferences (i.e., with little or no effect on trade, due to foreign trade systems of planned economies with differing foreign trade and domestic prices), and no multilateral credits but centralized channels of contact.

Although CMEA has no such formal multilateral agreements with India, India is a primary LDC partner of nearly all CMEA countries and is probably

Table 5.7

CMEA Development Assistance to Latin American and Asian NICs, 1954 to 1983 (in Millions of U.S. $)

	1954-1983	1980
Latin American NICS	1,530	250
Argentina	552	27
Brazil	933	223
Mexico	45	-
Asian NICs	65	-
Philippines	65	-
Total LDC assistance	35,252	5,522
Total NIC assistance	1,595	250
Total NIC in % of total LDC	4.5	4.5

Source: 1954 to 1981: "Soviet and East European Aid to the Third World, 1981," Department of State (Washington, D.C., Feburary 1983), table 10; 1982 to 1983: "Soviet, East European and Western Development Aid 1976-1983," Foreign Policy Document No. 108 (London: Foreign and Commonwealth Office, December 1984).

Table 5.8

CMEA Foreign Investment in Latin American and Asian NICs, End of 1983 (Number of Instances)

	Bul-garia	Czechos-lovakia	GDR	Hung-ary	Poland	Romania	Soviet Union	Total
Brazil	0	2	0	2	3	0	0	7
Mexico	0	5	1	1	0	1	0	8
Singapore	2	1	0	0	2	0	6	11

Source: Based on a table furnished by Carl E. MacMillan, COMECON Foreign Investment Project, Carleton University, Ottawa, "Geographical Distribution of CMEA Overseas Investment in the South," end of 1983 (Ottawa, 1984). Some of the investment cases may no longer be operational.

the developing country with the most sophisticated level of cooperation. Not only had India industrialized to a large extent on the basis of CMEA technology imports, but it is also hosting significant East-South and East-West-South industrial cooperation ventures, and even acts as a subcontractor to Soviet industrial projects in third countries. Also, in monetary terms, India's links to CMEA appear to be relatively balanced in comparison to other LDCs. In other words, India is probably *the* case of a mutually beneficial relationship, with both sides actively interested. Therefore, traditional partners like India are much more likely to develop their CMEA relationship in a more and more advanced direction than the NICs, their technological capacities notwithstanding.

From the above discussion it can be seen that CMEA trade and other fields of cooperation are closely intertwined. Strictly commercial links coexist with more advanced types of cooperation, based on treaties of scientific and technical cooperation. Let us briefly address the latter, which is the CMEA parallel to aid. The CMEA type of aid consists of long-term intergovernmental development credits for the purchase of CMEA equipment and services; certain grants appear, too (e.g., drought aid, educational scholarships, etc). Data on CMEA aid projects in NICs are displayed in table 5.7.

The table documents the marginal role of CMEA as a development assistance partner for NICs, especially as far as Asian NICs are concerned. Disbursements to Brazil, however, do deserve mention, as Brazil hosts certain large Soviet-built power stations. Certain NICs have also been the focus of CMEA foreign investments (see table 5.8).

The table illustrates one of the new developments in East-South relations, namely the emergence of joint East-South production projects or CMEA-owned assets within the service or trade sector in LDCs. The former type of joint venture prevails in Latin American NICs, whereas the latter is prominent in Singapore. Thus, the Moscow Narodny Bank has a subsidiary in Singapore, where trading or shipping offices of CMEA countries may also be found.

A natural question to ask now is whether this type of CMEA-NIC interaction is a promising access for CMEA to NIC markets, as the record for this type of cooperation, so far, is much more impressive than for ordinary types of development cooperation. CMEA foreign investment in these two types of joint ventures tends to be a more flexible and efficient type of cooperation than traditional interstate links—on the basis of the above mentioned treaties of technical and scientific assistance. They are more decentralized, although mostly at the level of foreign trade corporations and not on an actual firm-to-firm basis, and they may include commercial or export credits, furnished more flexibly than is the case of state loans, but also on less concessionary conditions. So, the answer to the question would be "yes" insofar as NICs themselves show interest in the given CMEA project, and certainly this may not always be the case.

The general conclusion from this section would therefore be that CMEA-NIC interactions have expanded and may grow further in the future, but are also marked by stark imbalances, financially as well as structurally. On balance, NICs seem to have the upper hand in their relation to CMEA countries, as they have more to offer to CMEA than the reverse. Directly and indirectly, the unfolding of NIDL has, therefore, not left the CMEA unaffected. An interesting topic in connection with this is the Eastern theoretical perception of NIDL and related developments in the Third World, as they shed light on CMEA perceptions of future options in the world economy. This is the object of the following section.

EASTERN EUROPEAN PERCEPTIONS OF NIDL AND OF NICs

The reader may be in a state of confusion after this exposition of the East-South interaction. What has become of the well-known Soviet radicalization of her Third World links, the growing militarization of Soviet political and aid relations, of Soviet interventions in the Horn of Africa and in Afghanistan? Of course, I do not mean to deny the well-documented radicalization of Soviet Third World policy throughout the 1970s. On balance, however, it seems that CMEA ties to and competition with economically prosperous, but politically "moderate" LDCs have had far greater impact. The interesting thing is that a closer examination of Eastern European theoretical and politico-programmatical literature reveals that this is clearly realized in the Eastern European debate.

Contrary to what is the common Western impression of Eastern European social scientific Third World writings, Elisabeth Kridl Valkenier and other "Sovietologists" have convincingly demonstrated that the academic discussions are neither stereotyped, nor unaffected by ideologically nonconforming developments in the Third World (Valkenier 1983). "Partijnost" is beginning to yield to science, both in terms of methodological refinements and empirical analysis, which often leads to open-ended conclusions. What seems to be at issue is a serious attempt to come to grips with political and economic restructuring processes in an increasingly complex and interdependent environment. On the other hand, there is a clear limit to the similarities between Soviet and Western (or, say, Hungarian) social science. Let us have a closer look at Eastern European perceptions of global processes and the policy conclusions derived from them.

Generally, the CMEA foreign economic thrust of the 1970s has, on the theoretical level, been accompanied by the introduction of a near-interdependent world perception, in contrast to the Stalinist dogma of the two, mutually isolated antagonist camps. Maksimova, who introduced the new perception in 1974, stressed the abolition of autarky in the world socialist economic exchange system and pointed, instead, to the existence of a "world economy," of a global system, and thus, by implication, urged socialist cooperative participation in the solution of the global problems (Maksimova 1974, 3-20).[9] Authors Zagladin and Frolov (1981) dwell on the "explosiveness" of world population, food, development and pollution problems, together with global raw material and energy supply problems. It is undoubtedly premature to term the Soviet world view interdependent in the sense in which Keohane and Nye (1977) use the term, but it is worth remembering that this controversial concept has outlived even the recent revival of Cold War rhetoric.

An important feature of the less doctrinaire Soviet world perception is the trend toward perceiving global developments and problems not solely as manifestations of capitalist diseases, but more and more as the result of endogenous processes and internal dynamics. Thus, the abundant Soviet and Eastern European literature on Third World differentiation processes marks a theoretical development that bears much resemblance to the showdown with dogmatic *dependencia* perceptions among Western Marxists and the revival of structuralist approaches focusing on class and state relations. A good case in point are Soviet writings on Latin American "intermediate" or "national" capitalism, where Davidov (1979) states that "*dependencia* has developed into a genuinely internal factor of development." Instead of the previous focus on the "national liberation movement," Soviet scholars now draw attention to the struggle of local bourgeoisies to manifest their power vis-à-vis the developed West and the MNCs.

A debate has evolved around the whole issue of neocolonialism, which has resulted in a certain reevaluation of the "capitalist road of development." Historically, these new interpretations and assessments are a result of the oil crisis of 1973-74, where OPEC countries showed themselves capable of "exerting far greater influence than in the past on the world capitalist economy" (Primakov 1982, 28, 33). Accordingly, Primakov (a prominent expert on the Middle East) has termed the oil crisis "a breach into neocolonialism." Analysts now devote themselves to the contradictory character of present neocolonialism and point, *inter alia,* to the actual development contribution of TNC investments. Though in no way uncritical about capitalist overseas investments, Soviet scholars recognize that the necessary developmental dynamism cannot be brought about by dissociation from the world capitalist economy so, instead, they stress the *progressive* character of LDC integration into the world economy. They argue that "foreign capital is being forced to cooperate with local capital" (Kurzanov 1978, 190). They therefore deem it "absolutely necessary" to study specifically the capitalist model, as "capitalism still disposes of some reserves for its survival as a societal system" (Andreasyan and Ozoling 1983, 674).

Soviet Third World taxonomies are now centered around economic rather than political indicators, reflecting a recognition that new power centers are growing out of LDC economic differentiation. For instance, one Soviet author expects the Middle East and Latin America to develop to the Western European level of the 1950s by the year 2000 (Reisner 1979, 208). Another introduces the following distinction between Third World capitalism, on the one hand, "the mass democratic capitalism from below" and, on the other, "the dependent capitalism" (Kim 1981, 32-3). There are many contributions on the foreign economic activity of the prosperous and aggressive LDCs and, where the focus was previously on Arab, Indian, and Latin American (e.g., Brazilian) expansion and interrelations, there are signs now of a growing interest in the Asian NICs, as well as in NIC-OECD competition in the field of industrial goods (Karagodin 1983; Kapitsa 1982). But policy recommendations concerning CMEA itself are rare or vague.

There is more to these theoretical revisions than the mere reappraisal of the role of the external environment. Beyond lies the more fundamental issue of the character and possibility of Third World development, particularly the question of whether there is any "specific," endogenous Third World development. This controversy is inspired by Lenin's statements about the "diversity" of future peripheral revolutions and can therefore be seen as an offshoot of the old controversy about the "Asian mode of production."[10] Via deliberations on the role of the state in LDCs (where the Soviets appear to be on a par with Poulantzas in the stressing of "the relative autonomy of the state") and specific LDC mixtures of modes of production (Russian *uklady*) theoreticians have developed the concept of the "multistructural society" (Russian *mnogoukladnoe obshchestvo* or *mnogouklad-*

nost). Orientologists like Levkovsky argue that the problems of nation-building and consolidation of socialist orientation in LDCs boil down to the lack of hegemonic structures and, hence, lack of hegemonic classes. The debate among the more innovative orientologists and the "doctrinaires" (among whom are many Africanists) on *mnogoukladnost* is therefore an esoteric debate on the possibility of a "socialist-oriented way of development."

In the 1970s, when Africa particularly was in the midst of a sweeping radicalization, Soviet development theory grew almost sanguine about progressive socialist prospects. But hopes were soon to be replaced by hangovers because of the complexity of development problems and the difficulty in creating an unequivocal socialist development. Soviet frustrations over the acute backwardness of socialist-oriented countries in contrast to the more prosperous capitalist ones are frequent, as is criticism of trends of "bureaucratization" and capitalist degeneration in the state sector of progressive LDCs (Trotsky 1979, 91-3). Socialist orientation is no longer deemed "irreversible," but may be subject to turmoil or even coups d'etat. Soviet policy recommendations to LDCs express a rather soft line on both local and global capitalism, recognizing the suicidal character of excessive revolutionary zeal. Irritation is also perceptible in Novopashin's remark that socialist-oriented countries "disregard . . . the extent to which socialist states are able to provide them with aid" (Novopashin 1982, 13). The boldest explicitly criticize CMEA aid policies: "If we persist in preaching that industrialization is imperative, that private and small-scale production are to be liquidated, we'll play into the hands of the class enemy, of the USA and the whole West" (Dashichev 1981, 174). Dashichev, an influential scholar at the Institute of the Economy of the World Socialist System ("the CMEA Institute") specifically calls for "intensification of our links with such LDCs as Indonesia [and] Argentina, who stand on the threshold of developed capitalism" (1981, 175). This appeal for intensified cooperation with NICs and other capitalist-oriented LDCs is repeated in the new CPSU program.

In other words, Soviet authors have serious doubts not only concerning the expediency of sweeping industrialization, nationalization and collectivization measures in socialist-oriented LDCs and the efficiency of CMEA aid contributions, they have, in fact, doubts about the expediency of socialist orientation per se; the performance of the existing socialist-oriented LDCs has not been impressive, especially not from a global balance-of-power perspective. Therefore, the attention of Soviet scholars has been attracted by NICs. Inherent in these painful new insights lies also the recognition that the power, influence and potential of "real socialism" are limited. Insofar as these new trends in the Soviet scholarly world perceptions penetrate to higher party and government echelons, it will influence the formation of foreign policy. Clearly, CMEA relations with socialist-oriented LDCs have entered a stage of mutual frustrations, notably with respect to Angola and Mozambique.

In contrast to this, NICs are often perceived as powerful counterweights to the industrialized West, so policy recommendations focus on the need to develop closer ties with these LDCs in order to back their independent stance. Socialist relations with NICs fall within the category of "peaceful coexistence," i.e., are placed on a par with relations with the industrialized West; but, Soviet sources insist that relations with NICs are "more mutually advantageous" and even contain elements of "international solidarity" (Diplomatiya Sotsializma, Moscow 1973, 105). In concrete political terms, this solidarity has been coined in the Soviet hesitation to condemn Argentina's occupation of the Falklands and her de facto siding with the Argentinians in the subsequent war. The stable and profound character of Soviet-Indian relations also shows a willingness to give capitalist-oriented LDCs preferential treatment. With a few exceptions, the Soviets are curiously silent on NIC competition with CMEA, and prefer to dwell on cooperative aspects.[11] Specifically they stress CMEA's technology-transfer potential, as well as the promising outlook for Soviet purchases of food and fodder from NICs (Dyakova and Fedotova 1978, 12).

If we then turn to the small CMEA states, the CMEA Six, we see Soviet approaches and evaluations most clearly repeated in the East German debate.[12] Nevertheless, the CMEA Six appear to have nearly the opposite view of NICs than have the Soviets; the Hungarians and, to a lesser degree, the Poles, stand out in stark contrast to the Soviets. Interdependence is common parlance in Hungarian analyses, but in Hungary this concept is directly linked to the global crisis. Thus, the prestigious Hungarian economist Simai reproaches Keohane and Nye (1977) for underestimating aspects of conflict and asymmetrical power relationships in their work on interdependence. Simai maintains that interdependence is "especially influenced by international power relations" (Simai 1981, 21-1). To the Western reader, Simai's criticism of Keohane and Nye may seem unfair but, what is more important, is that Simai is referring to Keohane and Nye in order to throw into relief the specific Eastern European experience with interdependence. So Simai's small-state approach to interdependence should be viewed in the context of Hungary's uncomfortable position of equal economic dependency on the USSR and all other partners, combined with Soviet domination in the sphere of foreign policy. Hungarian contributions are devoted to coming to grips with interdependence as manifested in the present global crisis, as this crisis—or "the major epochal change" as Joszef Bognar terms it—seriously affects Hungary.

In remarkable contrast to the Soviets, Hungarians stress the growing competition from NICs and dwell on the offensive economic strategy of these countries, which, in the words of one economist, raises the prospect of Hungary's "sliding back among the developing countries within a foreseeable time and . . . losing ground within the world economy" (Kadar 1982, 94). Bognar admits that NIC integration into the world economy is "economically justified," but is worried that NICs gain ground at the expense of CMEA countries and points to their "extremely quick" adaption to new techniques, the low wage level in NICs, and their use of capitalist trade and tariff preferences as factors providing a competitive edge over CMEA. He concludes in a pessimistic vein:

> Of course, an intelligent and active trade policy might turn potential competitors into constructive partners; it is, however, questionable how the Hungarian economy can find forms of organization and cooperation which provide adequate protection against the consequences of transitory political tension and cyclical change." (Bognar 1981)

Admittedly, these pessimistic evaluations of the entry of Third World nations into the industrial age could and should also be interpreted as contributions within the internal Eastern European debate on economic reforms, as the above-quoted authors are explicitly advocating further liberalization and export orientation. However, it is clear that the advent of NIDL via NIC industrialization has shocked the CMEA Six and further stressed the urgency of vitalizing CMEA economies.

Although fear and envy are probably the most common and significant Eastern European reaction to NICs, more constructive approaches are also traceable. Thus, other economists have developed a specific version of "If you can't beat them, join them," namely the proposal of redeployment of certain labor-intensive productions to advanced LDCs, i.e., industrial cooperation based on subsequent CMEA import of jointly produced goods. At the 24th Joint Conference of Foreign Trade and Economic Research Institutes of CMEA countries one paper argued:

> In our relations with LDCs a forward-looking approach should not only mean looking for alternative supply sources to cover our future raw material demands. When formulating our strategy on the inevitable industrial restructuring, we must take into consideration the possibility of giving up production of certain goods and import them instead. (Bogo 1983, 9)

As relevant items for this type of LDC cooperation, the author pointed to spare parts and components (i.e., relatively sophisticated products), which in case the proposal was realized, would actually mean the establishment of a NIDL between CMEA and LDCs. In an interview with the author of the paper, she has emphasized that her ideas were met with enthusiasm, even on the part of Soviet economists and, in more recent contributions, she has developed her argument from the perspective of comparative advantages and levels of economic development (Bogo 1984; Bogo 1980). Other contributions focus on light industrial areas of productions, such as textiles, garment, underwear, shoes and leather products, and sports articles and point to certain examples of this type of CMEA industrial redeployment to Egypt, India, and Pakistan (UNCTAD document, 1980). The scope, the number and overall economic significance of such arrangements seem extremely limited at present[13] and have not been used in relation to either Latin American or Asian NICs, and it remains highly doubtful if they would actually welcome the idea. The material on this type of East-South cooperation is sparse, one is left with the impression that CMEA insists on keeping more advanced areas of productions for itself, which would collide with NIC ambitions. So, though the actual experience from this new approach is too fragmented to speak of a new CMEA policy, it nevertheless deserves mention as it signifies an attempt to combine socialist and LDC industrialization efforts, based on a sheer economic argument.

In conclusion, it could be said that whereas the CMEA Six tend to view the NIC process in negative terms as something that exacerbates Eastern Europe's awkward, highly interdependent position in the world economy, the Soviets tend to view the NIC process positively—namely from a global balance-of-power perspective. The Soviets tend to see both political and economic benefits in cooperation with certain NICs (notably Latin American NICs), whereas the East Europeans are only in the process of developing an economic argument for enhancing cooperation with advanced LDCs. On balance, it would seem that the Eastern European industrial redeployment approach would be of a greater, general significance to the East-South relationship, if realized on the level of concrete economic relations. But here one is certainly speaking of the future and, indeed, it may well be that such a NIDL scenario will never unfold.

CONCLUSION

The central purpose of this paper has been to analyze the effect of the emergence of NIDL between developing and developed countries on CMEA, and more specifically on East-South relations. The analysis showed the NIDL has tended to clash with CMEA's own attempt at foreign economic expansion toward the West, following intense CMEA technology imports from that region. In particular, the small Eastern European states are in fact giving priority to many of the industrial fields typical of NICs and other industrializing LDCs. On balance, NICs appear to have a decisive comparative edge over CMEA on the world market. This is due not only to political and institutional factors (the disadvantage inherent in the entry of centrally planned economies on the world capitalist market), but also to technical factors such as the backward technological level of CMEA, particularly in comparison with the Asian NICS.

So, the establishment of NIDL has certainly been felt in the CMEA region, which can also be seen from the Eastern European economic literature, where the emergence of NICs is used as an argument to advocate further radical economic reform. The Soviet Union, which is to a far lesser extent competing directly with NICs on the West European market, welcomes NICs as something like a potential counterbalance to the industrialized West. This de facto *volte-face,* in the Soviet view of capitalist development, was explained with references to the strikingly ambivalent Soviet attitude toward socialist-oriented countries. Thus, the relatively tolerant Soviet position toward NIDL and NICs can be understood partly as a mere balance-of-power approach in line with the Soviet traditional dualistic world view and partly as an analytical development away from advancing socialist delinking strategies for LDCs toward advocating an economically rational approach to development, of which the NICs are the obvious case. This pragmatic theoretical development runs parallel to developments in the overall CMEA analytical approach to CMEA's position in the world economy and to integration. CMEA economists have more or less accepted interdependence as the fundamental condition, which implies recognition of CMEA's vulnerability to external economic developments. Autarky is viewed as an unviable strategy, a fiction in the era of "advanced socialism." In other words, the advent of NIDL and the following crisis in East-West economic relations has demonstrated CMEA economic vulnerability, an overlooked addendum to the often described foreign policy dependency. This, I think, is the real background for the increasing pragmatism among theoreticians from the CMEA region, and not so much political degeneration, as held by some Western Marxists.[14]

Concerning the effects of NIDL and the NIC process on East-South relations, this chapter identified fuel, minerals, food and fodder as the most relevant import items for CMEA countries from LDCs, which in a situation of greatly limited economic freedom of maneuver for CMEA economies, will mean a low import inclination concerning manufactures. Accordingly, NICs will not come to view CMEA countries as ideal partners for them in their industrial strategy and vice versa. This does not necessarily mean the CMEA economists rule out any future exchange of industrial goods between CMEA and LDCs. Although it is difficult to determine the influence of the Hungarian economists' advancing industrial redeployment and coproduction with LDCs on a joint venture basis, the argument as such is perfectly logical from a CMEA point of view. Thus, demographic trends in the CMEA indicate a sharp reduction in the labor force in the years to come, which in turn will necessitate industrial restructuring away from labor-intensive toward capital- and technology-intensive production. From this it follows that the otherwise highly conventional division of labor between CMEA and LDCs may be somewhat modified in the future, namely with respect to certain advanced

LDCs such as India, whereas it is doubtful if this scenario will apply to CMEA relations with NICs. For the moment, CMEA and NICs show little interest for each other's industrial potential, and competition prevails in relation to third countries.

Contrary to what seems to be the widespread assumption concerning Soviet and Eastern European policies toward the Third World, it would appear the CMEA approaches LDCs from a rather defensive position. CMEA's complex, or indeed ambivalent attitude to LDCs has most clearly been revealed at UNCTAD forums in recent years—e.g., on the issue of a New International Economic Order.[15] In conclusion, there seems to be a decisive asymmetry between the politico-military and the economic level in CMEA's Third World relations, an observation that requires methodological consequences. In other words, we should drop the isolated study of either politico-military or economic relations, and attempt a more comprehensive approach.

NOTES

This chapter is a revised and updated version of a paper originally prepared for the Joint Sessions of Workshops of the European Consortium of Political Research (ECPR), Salzburg, April 1984.

1. There is no consensus among either political scientists or international organizations concerning which countries should be termed NICs. The OECD list includes some of the countries mentioned in the following, plus some Southern European OECD members. In this article we adhere to a demarcation proposed by the Hungarian economist, Istvan Dobozi—i.e., Argentina, Brazil, Mexico, Hong Kong, Taiwan, South Korea, Singapore, Malaysia, Thailand, and the Philippines. The Soviets have no "authoritative" lists of NICs, but can be assumed generally to accept the list quoted here.

2. The "authoritative" work on NIDL is F. Fröbel, J. Heinrichs, and O. Kreye, *Die neue internationale Arbeitsteilung, Strukturelle Arbeitslosigkeit in den Industrieländern und Industrialisierung der Entwicklungslañder* (Hamburg: Reinbek Rowolt, 1977).

3. The Soviet Union, Poland, German Democratic Republic (GDR), Czechoslovakia, Hungary, Romania, and Bulgaria.

4. The most thorough investigation of CMEA levels of technology is found in *The Technological Level of Soviet Industry,* eds. R. Amann, J. Cooper, and R. W. Davies (New Haven: Yale University Press, 1977).

5. The plea for export vitalization has, of course, been particularly strong among the small Eastern European countries, whose dependence on foreign trade is far greater than the Soviet Union's. Soviet writings on the urgency of enhanced exports can be cited, see e.g., A. V. Engibarov, *Nyekotorie voprosy povysheniya efektivnosti eksporta* (Moscow, 1983).

6. CMEA debt to Western banks, including debt of CMEA banks to the West, amounted to $64.5 billion by 1983, which is far below the debt level of Latin American countries. Mexico alone had a debt of $85 billion by April 1983. Debt levels vary among CMEA countries. The Soviet debt was $7.9 billion.

7. Various Soviet authors have stressed the expediency of LDC agricultural imports, not least after the introduction of the Food Program in May 1982—see, e.g., *Sotrudnichestvo stran-chlenov SEV s razvivayushchimisya gosudarstvami v reshenii prodolvolstvennoy problemy* (Moscow, 1983). Following the abortive grain embargo by President Carter, Latin American countries, notably Argentina, have been prominent suppliers of wheat to the Soviet Union. Argentina is now the number-two Soviet LDC partner.

8. A good illustration of that is Soviet trade with India, as 78 percent of Soviet exports to this country consisted of oil by 1982, and where Soviet sources have estimated a 60 percent share of manufactures in Soviet purchases from India. See Kiselev and Drozdov, "USSR and India: Trade and Cooperation," *Foreign Trade* 8 (1983): 10.

9. Op. cit. Engibarov boldly states that Soviet and CMEA participation in the global division of labor is "irreversible."

10. See V. Maksimenko's review of A. Levkovsky, *Sotsial'naya struktura razvivayushikhsya stran* (Moscow: 1978) in *Narody Azii i Afriki* 1(1979):109-10. Lenin's original deliberations on these themes can be found in his *Collected Works,* Russian ed., vol. 45, 381.

11. See for example, A. Samoilov, *Ekonomicheskoe sotrudnichestvo blizhnevostochnykh neftedobyvayushchikhsya stran s gosudarstvami Yuzhnoy Azii* (Ph.D. diss., Moscow, 1982); and M. Volkov, "Problemy industrializatsii razvivayushchikhsya stran" *Voprosy ekonomiki,* 8 (1979):110, where the author points exactly to those fields of NIC industrialization that potentially threaten the Soviet Union, e.g., metallurgy.

12. Like their Soviet counterparts, East German Third World specialists are deeply concerned over the lack of deeper, structural consolidation of socialist orientation. See C. Mahrdel, "Soziale Dimensionen nationaler Befreiung in Asien und Afrika," *Asien und Afrika und Lateinamerika,* 5(1983):833.

13. Grosser and Tuitz's investigation of CMEA restructuring within manufactures contains no mentioning of redeployment strategies—see UNIDO paper ID/WG.357/5.

14. The most famous contribution in this vein is probably an essay by a veteran among dependencia theoreticians, A. G. Frank, "Long Live Transideological Enterprise! The Socialist Economies in the Capitalist Division of Labor," revised and enlarged version in *Crisis in the World Economy* (New York, 1980):178-262. Following Frank's logic, foreign trade in itself is the evil, which also leads him to overrule all of the existing socialist countries and strategies as being compromised!

15. Generally, CMEA economists deny or explain away the crisis in East-South relations. A rare exception from this pattern is L. Zurawicki, "The New International Economic Order: A View from the Socialist Corner" in *Intereconomics* (March-April 1982):91-6.

6

Richard Higgott

The Dilemmas of Interdependence: Australia and the International Division of Labor in the Asia-Pacific Region

Even more so than their colleagues in North America, scholars of international relations in Australia have, for a long time, relegated the study of international political economy (IPE) to a secondary position, behind the primary issues of "war, peace, power and influence" (Holsti 1985, 1). Of late, however, IPE has undergone something of a growth of recognition in its own right, rather than as a residual category in a broader discipline (see *inter alia* Hollist and Tullis 1985; Strange 1985; Staniland 1985, especially chapter 5).

Within the study of IPE a number of key issue areas have attracted the attention of scholars working at both theoretical and empirical levels. One of these, the evolution of a new international division of labor (NIDL), is the organizing concept for this chapter. NIDL, in brief and at the risk of caricature at this stage, can be seen as the internationalization (and often disaggregation) of the production process brought about by advances in technology and the ability of capital to relocate to those areas of the globe where high and often more immediate returns on investment are to be had (Higgott 1984; Fröbel et al. 1980).

The outcome of the evolution of the NIDL is a redefinition of the location of various sectors of the international political economy, according to the degree to which states are incorporated into, or marginalized from, the NIDL. We are thus in a position to distinguish sharply between the nature of incorporation of states, such as some of those of Asia (Hofheinz and Calder 1983; Hamilton 1983; Higgott and Robison 1985) on the one hand, or the "marginalization" of many of the states of sub-Saharan Africa on the other (Higgott 1986a). Such analytical insights that are provided by the concept of a new international division of labor also allow us to understand, in part, the processes of deindustrialization, which some analysts tell us is the lot of earlier industrial powers such as Great Britain (Bellini 1981; Blackaby 1979; Gamble 1981).

One state that represents a particularly interesting, if not unique, challenge to students of the new international division of labor is Australia; there are many reasons for this that will be explored in this chapter. At the outset, we should perhaps note that even though it is ostensibly one of the world's richest developed countries, Australia nevertheless has an economic profile akin to that of many developing countries. It is strongly dependent on the export of primary produce and raw materials on the one had, and the import of manufactured goods, technology and capital on the other. The importance of such economic factors for Australia's international relations has not always been recognized in the scholarly literature. Unfortunately, the analysis of Australia's position in world affairs has traditionally been the preserve of political scientists and economists operating in isolation from one another and with a "never the twain shall meet" mentality.[1] The first group, located almost exclusively in a "realist" tradition of international relations thought, have focused on the politico-diplomatic and strategic aspects of Australia's global position (see, for example, Millar 1977). The economists, on the other hand, have tended to focus on Australia's position in the global economic order; however, they have proved to be less homogeneous than the political scientists.

Two major schools of thought can be discerned: the neoclassical economists and, for want of a better expression, what we may call the neo-Marxist political economists.[2] The intellectual debate over the last decade or so has been dominated, not surprisingly, given its predominance in the Australian community of economists, by the neoclassical perspective. That the neo-Marxist perspective has been of relatively minor importance in the debate over Australia's location in the international economic order has been due to a variety of factors, not the least of which is the deleterious effect on their case of the often polemical manner in which they put their argument. This state of affairs has been unfortunate, to say the least; it has caused students of Australian foreign policy to neglect many of the important questions raised (if not necessarily answered) by the more radical perspectives in the course of their analysis. Accompanying a dismissive attitude to the perspective of the neo-Marxists has been a more general discounting of the very notion of "an international political economy," irrespective of ideological persuasion.

The 1980s, however, have seen some change in this state of affairs. This change has come about not only because it is no longer possible to ignore the relationship between politics and markets in international affairs (Spero 1985; Almond and Genco 1977), but also because of the increasing number of studies of Australia emanating from what we might call "a political economy perspective" (see, *inter alia,* Catley 1984; Head 1983; Alexander 1983;

McMichael 1981). The essence of such studies is not necessarily a common ideological perspective—indeed the search for one would often prove elusive. Rather, such analyses are united by the broad range of questions they ask about Australia in the international economic order—particularly questions of a structuralist nature concerning the globalization of production set out below.

We have moved in the 1980s to a situation where the position of Australia in the international political economy is recognized as important a focus for study as is the position of Australia in the *international system of states.* It is not to challenge the existence of the international system of states in urging the appropriateness of the international political economy as a unit of analysis; rather it is to reaffirm that the global nature of production in the international division of labor is every bit as significant in the last quarter of the twentieth century as is interstate diplomacy in a system of states. Australia in the 1980s is a good example of a state that conducts its foreign policy in a manner in which the search for economic welfare in the international economic order is every bit as significant as the search for national security.

In contrast to a position that much neoclassical or mercantilist economic theory would have us accept, Australia's freedom of maneuver in the international economic order is highly circumscribed by colonial heritage, geopolitics, and its pattern of incorporation into the economic order. One does not, however, have to accept the extremes of a structuralist analysis, of a Wallersteinian variant for example, to accept the reality of the limits on Australian behavior.

It is the purpose of this chapter to suggest that Australia's position in the new international division of labor, and indeed the NIDL itself, is neither as economically determinist as the dependency theorist would have it, nor as politically voluntarist as the neoclassical economists would have us believe.[3] Put another way, NIDL's grip is neither ironclad nor are its opportunities boundless. This chapter aims to make a small contribution to the ongoing analysis of the new international division of labor and to an understanding of Australia's position in it, specifically at the regional Asian-Pacific level.

There are four broad sections: (a) an introduction to the concept of the new international division of labor and the kinds of issues it raises for a state such as Australia; (b) a brief résumé of the process of Australia's incorporation into the political and economic order in the twentieth century; (c) an analysis of Australia's position in its regional economic environments broadly at the level of the Asian-Pacific region and more narrowly in the Southeast Asian context; and (d) government responses, with particular reference to the policies of the current Hawke Labor government in its attempts to consolidate Australia's position in its current regional economic environments.

THE NEW INTERNATIONAL DIVISION OF LABOR AND AUSTRALIA: AN INTRODUCTORY APPROACH

There is now a substantial body of literature that recognizes the emergence of a new international division of labor qualitatively different from the division of labor that prevailed approximately up to the end of the 1960s; the existence of this new stage in the global political economy is recognized by scholars operating across a variety of intellectual paradigms. There is also a body of literature that attempts to locate various parts of the global political economy within NIDL and suggests the degree to which they have been favorably or unfavorably incorporated (Higgott 1984, 1986a). Most attention to date has been on the position of the newly industrializing countries (NICs) in NIDL and particularly the extent to which the processes of industrialization have been fostered by it (Leaver 1985). Given its location as what one scholar called the "misplaced continent" (Grant 1983)—a white, Christian, sometime ailing capitalist "middle" power located at the center of the world's most rapidly developing economic region, but a region with different historical, cultural, and economic impulses—Australia represents a unique case study. Further, the Asian-Pacific region in which Australia is located has been central to the evolution of NIDL.

This chapter need not, indeed could not, replicate Caporaso's exegesis on the international division of labor in this volume; rather, it needs to pick out those characteristics of the division that are appropriate for this discussion of Australia. At its simplest, the evolution of NIDL represents a qualitively distinct stage in the process of international capital accumulation. This somewhat bold assertion may be justified, albeit briefly, in a number of ways. First, capitalism at the end of the twentieth century—expectations of theorists of the crisis of "late capitalism" and its imminent demise notwithstanding—appears to be alive and well, albeit in those areas of the world that Marx himself would find difficult to imagine. Second, its impact on social structure seems essentially "vertical" rather than "horizontal." This would appear to be the case, whether we recognize the emergence of "situses" rather than classes, as foretold by Daniel Bell (1973) or the emergence of a segmented labor market (as opposed to dual economies) cogently outlined by Caporaso in Chapter 1.

The third distinct feature of the evolution of a new international division of labor lies in some of its implications for political arrangements, particularly with regards to relationships between state and capital. Although only in the infancy of conceptualization at this stage, this issue has received considerably more treatment of late. This analysis, especially concerning the relationship between the evolution of NIDL and the emergence of "corporatist" political structures, has been carried out in European (Katzenstein 1983, 1985), Latin American (Collier 1979), African (Shaw 1982; Higgott 1985,

1986a), Asian (Feith 1980; Higgott and Robison 1985), and theoretical contexts (Higgott 1983; Evans, Rueschmeyer, and Skocpol 1985). The issue with regard to Australia is explored briefly in the last section of this chapter.

Industrialization of the NICs of Australia's Asia-Pacific region has, to a large extent, been facilitated by (indeed is characterized by) the internationalization of production, a process which has involved the relocation of industrial activities, especially component manufacture and assembly, from industrialized to developing countries. This relocation has been enhanced by technological innovation providing for the disaggregation of the production process, so that labor-intensive aspects of the production of complex products can be carried out in countries providing cheap and largely unskilled and semiskilled labor (Fröbel et al. 1978).

This stage in international capital accumulation constitutes a tendency toward redefining not only the position of developing countries, but also the already industrialized ones. The essence of the new division is greater specialization in the production process and the ensuing facility for location and relocation of productive activity. The process of refinement still continues with investors now drawing the distinction between varying categories of developing countries. For example, some labor-intensive industrial activities are nowadays being moved from Hong Kong and Singapore into countries of even lower wage costs, such as Malaysia or, more recently, Sri Lanka. The increasing sophistication of this international specialization has depended very much on a continuing supply of new entrants to the cause of export-oriented industrialization (EOI) to compensate for the rising production costs in already established production sites (Rodan 1985a). Whereas this is still a strong trend, there is some evidence to suggest that the process is not exhaustive. In a recent analysis of South Korea, S.K. Cho (1985) has suggested that there are limits to export-led industrialization; this is being brought about by advances in automated production, diminishing cheap labor in the NICs, and an accompanying decline in the power of organized labor in some developed countries—making them, once again, more attractive propositions for international capital than some NICs or LDCs.

In either scenario, one thing is quite clear: production is a global, not national, process in the last quarter of the twentieth century. We must, therefore, treat the international political economy as a whole for the purposes of analysis. Different parts of the productive process interact with one another and change in response to one another; they do not remain geographically distinct or separate. To urge a recognition of this process of increasing complexity and fragmentation is not the same as suggesting that the nation-state is no longer the major unit of identity in the international arena. Rather, it is to suggest that it is no longer the only one, particularly if our methodological concerns are with the international political economy instead of with a highly undefined international system. Within the context of the recent international political economy, we do, however, have to recognize what we might call the "dedomiciling" (Leaver 1985) of international capital or, in less jargon-ridden fashion, the ability of international capital to relocate itself in those areas of the world capable of providing the greatest returns. In this context, we have seen the advanced industrial countries undergo a process of divestment of the more labor-intensive manufacturing processes to the Third World as a response to profitability considerations, although these tendencies have been offset, in part, by the concentration of capital and technology-intensive industries in high-wage countries (Adams 1971, 1972; Sharpston 1975; Plaschke 1975).

Australia's economic profile exhibits a "mix and match" of characteristics of both developed and less developed countries. Its consequent "location" within the NIDL is conditioned by this profile—by the fact that it is neither LDC or NIC on the one hand, nor one of the world's major industrial powers on the other. Similarly, it cannot satisfactorily be compared with the small but highly developed industrial states of Europe, given its Pacific location and its predominantly raw-material, primary-produce orientation in the structure of its economy. Like the "small states" (Vital 1967; Katzenstein 1983) of Western Europe, it has high levels of urbanization, high wage rates, and a four-level sectoral distribution of its economy (primary through quaternary). However, as can be seen from table 6.1, the bulk of Australia's exports, in contrast to other advanced industrial states, were and (despite a drop in the twenty-year period between 1960 and 1980) still are generated in the primary sector. In addition, imports traditionally show a higher proportion of manufactured goods than is typical for the other advanced industrial states (table 6.2).

In clarifying the utility of the notion of Australia as a "small state," we should note—notwithstanding the fact that it is a nation-continent (smaller in size only than the USSR, Canada, the USA, China, and Brazil) and that its

Table 6.1

Exports of Primary Produce and Raw Materials as a Percentage of Total Exports

	1960	1981
Australia	92	72
Industrial market economies	34	27

Source: World Development Report (1984): Table II, 238-9.

Table 6.2

Imports of Manufactures as a

Percentage of Total Imports

	1960	1981
Australia	68	77
Industrial market economies	43	51

Source: World Development Report (1984): Table II, 238-9.

gross domestic product in 1982 was, at U.S. $164,210 million, the eleventh largest in the world—it does suffer many of the vicissitudes of a "small" economy in the contemporary division of labor. In particular, Australia needs to "comply with the demands of the global economy with all the *reactive* decision-making processes and rationalization necessary to guarantee the continuing processes of national development" (Katzenstein 1983, 92). Indeed, apart from times of acute national crisis such as war, trade policy (as a factor in economic policy, for example) can be considerably more important on a day-to-day basis than problems of security.

It is the growing recognition of the importance of the evolving division of labor in the Asia-Pacific Region that is applying a corrective to this traditional neglect of the economic imperative in the study of Australia's international relations. Concern with the issues of the international political economy, as opposed to the system of states, is essentially a phenomenon of the post-colonial world that has arisen from a recognition by the new states of the grossly asymmetrical position they hold in the international economic order. Size and newness are thus important spurs to an emphasis on the economic dimension of foreign relations. As Maurice East notes in an important paper:

> The importance of economic factors in small state foreign policies is demonstrated. The involvement of economic bureaucracies and the utilization of economic techniques of statecraft are more frequent in the foreign policy of small states than that in large states. (East 1973, 576)

Historically this has been the case in Australia. Indeed, in the past, the Australian Treasury and the Department of Trade, which preceded an Australian Foreign Service, always played a very important role in international relations (Edwards 1983). As further sections of this chapter will suggest, the economic dimension of Australian regional relations is paramount.

As suggested, Australia has a somewhat mixed profile, compared to

LDCs on the one hand and developed countries on the other. Not surprisingly, therefore, this is reflected in its relationship to the global political economy. Australia will be shown to have a greater dependence on world markets than larger developed countries, but more autonomy than the majority of LDCs. In many ways, Australia is caught in the middle of any stand-off between North and South in debates over the future evolution of the international economic order. Attempts at policy formulation throughout the 1970s reflected this dilemma (see, for example, Lim 1985; Souter 1983; *Australia and the Third World,* 1979; *Australia and the NIEO,* 1980). Current government strategies to confront this dilemma are the focus of the last section of the chapter.

In formulating strategy, Katzenstein suggests that a state (such as Australia) "whose position is slipping in the international division of labor," can learn a lesson from the responses of the small developed European states to this problem, namely "a dual strategy of international liberalization and domestic compensation based on corporatist political structures" (Katzenstein 1983, 93). In this context, corporatism needs to be seen less as an ideological phenomenon, of either a left- or right-wing variety, than as the "pursuit of strategies that differ from those of either liberalism or socialism" (Katzenstein 1983, 94). He argues that it is the openness and vulnerabilities of these states to the international political economy (to a degree greater than large industrial states) that has given rise to this tendency. Section four of this chapter shows that, while openness and vulnerability are also the order of the day for Australia, the nature of these weaknesses is different; the final section demonstrates how government policy in contemporary Australia reflects the dual emphasis of the small European states, as outlined by Katzenstein.

In general terms, at this stage we can see that Australia's vulnerability is generated by a variety of fairly self-evident factors. First, of course, Australia (with a population of only 15.5 million) is unable to make the economies of scale necessary for the efficient performance of an array of industrial activities deemed central to Western developed societies. Analysis in table 6.3 of Australia's imports and exports by commodity group demonstrates the degree of Australia's dependence on the international economy for manufactured goods; particularly important among these are goods of an industrial and technological nature, such as cars and electronic goods, mostly of course from the USA and Japan (see table 6.5 and the later discussion on the direction of Australian trade). Second, this smallness has meant a specialization in export trade in order to attain market efficiency. Yet, unlike the small European states, this specialization has been in primary produce and raw materials—products highly susceptible to global market prices. Australia is thus, at one and the same time, open and vulnerable because of this lack of diversification, which has as an inevitable outcome a degree of dependence and "openness towards the influences of the international economy much greater than that of large countries" (Katzenstein 1983, 96). Again, tables 6.1 and 6.3 give an indication of the preponderance of primary produce and, of late, raw materials in Australia's export trade. (The nature and implications of this trade are also discussed later.) By contrast, the response of the small European states has been the specialized production of high-value-added goods for the international market, in a manner that Australia has, to date, never even seriously considered.

In another area it is again appropriate to cite at length Katzenstein's study, given the lessons it holds for Australia:

> Dependence on the import of investment goods and the export of consumer goods creates, within the context of openness and vulnerability towards developments in international markets, tendencies that reinforce imbalances in the economic structures of small European states. Their economic specialization leaves different sectors of the economy less integrated than those in large countries." (1983, 98)

Along both sectoral and spatial axes, Australia exhibits considerable asymmetries and conflicts of the kinds alluded to by Katzenstein. While a major asymmetry within Australia is between the varying states of the Federation, this is as much a conflict between different sectors of capital as it is a spatial conflict. Conflicts between the geographically remote and sparsely populated states of the Federation (Western Australia, Queensland, and the Northern Territories) and the smaller, more populous states of the southeastern corner (New South Wales, Victoria, and, to a lesser extent, South Australia) reflect the different priorities of the preponderantly primary-product/raw-material exporting peripheral states—nowadays aggressively oriented towards free-trade policies—and what Head (1983, 9) calls the "manufacturing states" of the southeastern corner. It is these manufacturing states that have, for so long, been the beneficiaries of Australia's highly protective national tariff policies. These conflicts have become particularly acute since the "mining boom" of the early 1970s.

This was not the first mining boom in Australia's history; mining exceeded 15 percent of gross domestic product in 1861, and remained at about 10 percent in the early 1900s. Yet, for a forty year period between 1921 and 1961, mining averaged less than 3 percent of gross domestic product only and, in the twenty years since 1961, it rose above 6 percent of gross domestic product (Helliwell 1984, 89). Mineral exports are, however, unlikely again to match their high point of the mid-1860s, and most of the talk in the 1970s of the new high point of 10 percent of gross domestic product by the end of the 1980s has been off the agenda for five or six years (Helliwell 1984, 90). More important for this discussion is the degree to which a dramatic expansion in the mining sector is thought to be deleterious to other sectors of the economy.

Table 6.3
Distribution of Exports and Imports, by Commodity Group, 1950-80 (Annual Average, Percent)

Type of Trade and Commodity	1950-51 to 1954-55	1955-56 to 1959-60	1960-61 to 1964-65	1965-66 to 1969-70	1970-71 to 1974-75	1975-76 to 1979-80
Imports[a]						
Food, drink, and tobacco	6.7	6.3	5.4	4.9	5.0	5.1
Minerals, fuels, and other basic materials[b]	19.7	21.1	18.5	14.3	11.6	14.6
Manufactured goods[c]	68.9	67.7	70.9	75.6	79.2	77.6
Other	4.7	4.9	5.2	5.2	4.2	2.7
Exports						
Meat	6.2	8.2	9.2	9.5	10.3	9.0
Cereals	12.8	9.9	15.6	12.4	12.1	12.1
Wool	50.7	43.2	33.9	24.3	13.8	10.3
Other rural	12.1	13.9	13.3	11.7	11.0	10.0
Unprocessed and processed minerals[d]	----	----	----	----	15.9	18.7
Coal	0.1	0.4	1.3	3.1	5.6	10.8
Metals	5.3	7.1	7.1	9.8	10.0	9.8
Simply transformed manufactures[d]	----	----	----	----	9.1	9.0
Elaborately transformed manufactures[d]	----	----	----	----	13.9	10.4

Sources: Caves and Krause (1984, 279). Norton, Garmston, and Brodie, Australian Economic Statistics: 1949-50 to 1980-81, 5-8; Department of Trade and Resources, Pattern of Australian Imports, 23-36.

[a] After 1965-66 the classification of imports was changed from the statistical classification of imports to the Australian import-commodity classification. See notes b and c.

[b] Data from 1950-51 through 1964-1965 include basic materials, fuels, and lubricants. Data after 1965-66 include crude materials (inedible), mineral fuels, and lubricants.

[c] Data from 1950-51 through 1964-65 include textiles, base metals, motor vehicles, electrical machinery and equipment, other machines and machinery, and other manufactures. Data after 1965-66 include chemicals, manufactured material, machinery (electric and otherwise), transport equipment, and miscellaneous manufactured articles.

[d] Data begin in 1970-71.

Bob Gregory, an economist at the Australian National University, has attempted to outline the manner in which a continued increase of the position of mining in the Australian economy might undermine the efficiency and competitiveness of other sectors (Gregory 1976, 1982; Johns and McLeod 1977; McQueen 1982). At the risk of oversimplification, Gregory argued that the boom of the 1970s brought not only significant increases in mineral output, but also long-term implications likely to prove disruptive to the sectoral balance of the economy. The crux of Gregory's argument was that the more successful the mineral export boom (fostered by the energy-conscious world of the 1970s), the less competitive other sectors would be. Indeed, he argued that increased mineral exports could have a greater impact on the other importing and exporting sectors of the economy than a general reduction in tariffs of around 25 percent (Gregory 1976, 71-91).

The impact of these sectoral distortions, and several other consequences of the evolution of the new international division of labor outlined, form the central focus for the rest of this chapter. Particularly, it will examine the nature of Australian openness and vulnerability to the international division of labor, especially in its broad Asian-Pacific regional context, before going on to suggest an emerging pattern of political behavior characteristic of the type of corporatism described by Katzenstein. Before moving to the contemporary situation, however, a brief introduction to the process of Australia's incorporation into the global political and economic environment in the twentieth century is in order.

AUSTRALIA AND THE EMERGENT INTERNATIONAL POLITICAL ECONOMY IN THE TWENTIETH CENTURY

There are two facets to the global incorporation of Australia from the time of Federation in 1901 and its gradual emergence from British colonial suzerainty. The first is its integration into the global capitalist system, the second is the taking of a position as an actor in the international system of states and the formulation of a national foreign policy reflecting a loosening (not severing) of the colonial bonds.

If we consider the economic process, then this too can be bifurcated. The key to the change from the first phase to the second phase is similar however, for the political as well as the economic process. It is, of course, represented in the changing global hegemonic fortunes of Britain and America. World War II saw the United States relieve Great Britain as Australia's major security partner, and the postwar period saw the United States also become one of Australia's major economic partners, to be joined in the late 1950s by Japan and, over the last decade, by the other rapidly developing members of the Asian-Pacific region. This last phase is the most important for the purposes of this chapter and receives full treatment in the next sections. Yet several factors from the first phase are major legacies for the contemporary situation and should be noted. Particularly important is the degree to which the period of colonialism created a nationalistic, inward-looking, and highly defensive state structure that protected Australia, as best it could, from the influences of a growing world economy.

Throughout the twentieth century, Australia's historical experience has been that of a highly protectionist state, erecting barriers and providing government subsidy to secure the growth of labor-intensive manufacturing industries that would have failed to develop in the face of external competition. Given Australia's origins as a small, white outpost of the British empire, subject to the "tyranny of distance" and obsessed by a "populate or perish" mentality, protectionism as a means of attempting to create a self-sustainable supply of manufactured goods made excellent sense—as a report on the state of the Australian economy for the Brookings Institute recently acknowledged (Caves and Krause 1984, 1). Further, in the aftermath of World War II, indeed as late as the mid-1960s, it was, as McMichael notes, "precisely the protectionist character of Australian industrialization which attracted foreign capital investment." This process, at the height of the U.S. hegemony of the world economy, fostered Australia's incorporation into the global economy. Protected by tariff walls and supplied by migrant labor "TNCs established a pattern of investment in industrial production" (McMichael 1981, 49).

The changes that came about in the international division of labor in the mid-1960s, however, saw a concomitant change in the role of Australia in that division. The newly industrializing countries of the world, given the benefits of changes in technology, provided a plentiful and cheap supply of labor, leading to rapid growth—especially in the wider Asian-Pacific region. It has been this rapid regional growth that has led to the challenge of Australian manufacturing. Even though the Australian manufacturing sector may never have been large or highly competitive, it did have a ready-made market behind its tariff walls. As will be demonstrated, where increasing industrialization has made the majority of countries more open and dependent on world trade, this has not been the case to date for Australia—certainly not as far as trade in manufactures is concerned. Rather, Australia has become most attractive as a provider of minerals and especially energy supplies.

It is in the context of the nature of their exports that the comparison between Australia and the small, European developed states breaks down. While both share an openness and vulnerability, the Europeans are involved in relatively high-level technological activities, and have a different export pattern and a different pattern of foreign investment in their countries, especially if we look at the high rate of foreign capital invested in the Australian mining sector (Head 1983, 5). It remains only to emphasize that these economic changes did not take place in a political vacuum.

Australia was tied up in the dramatic political processes that evolved out of World War II. Australia has come a long way from the 1940s, when its role in world affairs was seen merely as an appendage of the British empire and when its foreign policies were a mirror image of Britain's world view. After World War II, the United States was inevitably the major influence on Australia's foreign and defense policies and, notwithstanding the efforts of Robert Menzies to arrest the process, many other aspects of Australia's international relations turned away from Europe.

With the benefit of hindsight, many of the changes seemed inevitable (see Millar 1977 for an overview of the period), perhaps none more so than Australia's evolving relationship with Asia following the Japanese occupation of Singapore in World War II (Hamill 1981), Australia's involvement in both the wars in Korea (McCormack 1983) and Vietnam (King 1982) and, more recently, the arrival of the "boat people" refugees and the whole debate over Asian immigration to Australia. I will not discuss in detail the way in which a region that was once regarded as peripheral (when it was not seen as a threat) to Australia's cultural ideology and economic interests has become central—although, as the last section of the chapter will suggest, the process is far from universally understood, accepted, or complete. To be sure, such changes have been a long time in the making. Since the early 1970s, Gough Whitlam and Malcolm Fraser set great store in improving links with Australia's regional neighbors, and regionalism (although not under that name) had been on the agenda of Australian foreign policy since the days of Sir Garfield Barwick's tenure at External Affairs, as it was then known. Since his election in March 1983, Bob Hawke, his government in general, and his foreign minister in particular, have championed regionalism with both a rhetorical and practical vigor.

AUSTRALIA AND THE ASIA-PACIFIC REGION

So far, this chapter has, avoiding attempts at definition, referred only loosely to the notion of an Asia-Pacific Region. It should be noted that it is Australia's regional economic environment that is under consideration. Exact geographical definition is neither desirable nor appropriate; the important factor is to appreciate the regional influences on Australia in the international political economy, as opposed to global influences on Australia in the international system of states. Globalism and regionalism need not be seen as mutually exclusive orbits of the international political economy or system in which Australia operates. Rather, they are two arenas in which the different activities pursued can be fairly well defined.

Briefly, at the global level in the political system, Australia's primary interests are political, diplomatic, and strategic, although factors in the political economy are significant too. This is particularly so with regard to the role Australia plays, or is deemed to play, in support of the United States formally (through its membership in ANZUS) and less formally (through the less clearly defined Australian-U.S. alliance) in the superpower contest. It should, of course, be noted that an important element in the alliance is the role Australia plays in regional security. In another arena are the various regions in which Australia has to "live" on a day-to-day basis. At these levels different factors come into play, and it is much more useful (again, not in any exclusivist fashion) to give primacy to the political economy rather than the political system.

The criteria for defining Australia's region cannot be entirely conventional. Australia is not part of a region in which it shares common historical and cultural links with its neighbors, nor does it have common current institutional links with them; similarly, its "political culture" is different than that of the majority of its neighbors. We need to look instead to other factors, such as economic impacts on Australia, to provide the parameters of Australia's regional environments. As such, there are at least three levels for the analysis of Australia's regional position. At its widest, there is the Pacific region (a geographical, not an institutional arena) containing East Asia (North and South), Japan, and the western seaboard of the Americas. For the purposes of this analysis, East Asia and Japan are the key areas. Second, there is the immediate Southeast Asia region, consisting of Australia and its ASEAN neighbors: Indonesia, Malaysia, the Philippines, Singapore, and Thailand (the newest member of ASEAN, Brunei, is not relevant to this chapter). Finally, there is the Southwest Pacific region, in which Australia, along with New Zealand, has something akin to regional superpower status vis-à-vis the small, island microstates of the Pacific and its former colonial territory of Papua New Guinea. The following discussion is concerned only with the first two levels. Needless to say, important political and strategic questions are to be found at all three levels, but when we focus on an examination of Australia in the international division of labor, politico-economic factors at the levels of the Pacific and ASEAN become the most important. As a final point of clarification, it should be noted that not all states of the East Asian rim are under consideration here. For example, Vietnam is crucial to any discussion of Australia's regional political, strategic, and diplomatic relations, but it is of little import for an analysis of the political economy of Australia's regional relations. Similarly, to ignore India, Burma, and several other states is not to deny their "Asianness" in regional terms, but rather their significance for a study of Australia's political economy. Indeed, it is the *aggregate* impact of the Asia-Pacific region on Australia's political economy, rather than specific bilateral relations, with the exception of Japan, that is under scrutiny here.

Australia and the Pacific Region

The process of dynamic economic growth in the Pacific Basin in the post-World War II era is now sufficiently well known for it simply to be asserted here with the support of a few relevant statistics. Data are drawn from a variety of readily available secondary sources, the importance of which for this paper is the *comparative* nature of Australia's position in this regional context.

Nowadays, it is almost a cliché to talk of a "shift in the world's center of economic gravity" (Madigan 1984, 13). For the first time in 1982, for example, U.S.-Asian trade surpassed U.S. trade with Europe. Japan is clearly the major factor in Pacific growth; its gross domestic product climbed from less than one-eleventh to over one-third of that of the United States between 1960 and 1982 (see table 6.4). But, also during that time, Asia's share of total world gross domestic product grew from 8 to 19 percent, while North America's dropped from 48 to 31 percent. Extrapolation to 1990 sees Asia anticipated to produce 25 percent of world gross domestic product, and the Pacific Basin, as a whole, 50 percent of total world gross domestic product (Drysdale 1984, 1; but also see Hofheinz and Calder 1982 and Uchida et al. 1983). Similar growth patterns have been recorded in Asia's shares of world trade with a growth from 9.5 percent of total in 1960 to 14.4 in 1980 and an expected 22.4 percent at the end of the millenium (Madigan 1984, 31b).

A further dimension to such raw data must be the relative health of Asian growth when compared to that of the rest of the world in the second half of the 1970s, particularly the extent to which the percentage of gross domestic product made up from trade has increased. Peter Drysdale, a longtime student of the Pacific Basin economy (Drysdale 1986, forthcoming), has estimated that the percentages of gross domestic product exported from Northeast Asia and Southeast Asia have grown from 48 percent to 61 percent and from 20 percent to 30 percent respectively, throughout the 1970s (Drysdale 1984, 2). In addition, much of this growth, Drysdale notes, has come about through the growth of interregional trade within the Pacific to the extent that, in the 1980s, more than half of the Asian-Pacific trade is of an interregional nature.

Japan's gross domestic product, as a quick calculation from table 6.4 demonstrates, was at U.S. $44 billion in 1960, only slightly larger than that of Australia (U.S. $16.3 billion) and the five ASEAN states (U.S. $20.9 billion) combined. By 1982, the Japanese economy (U.S. $1,082 billion) had grown to be three times as large as that of ASEAN and Australia (U.S. $370 billion) combined. The real impact of this Japanese growth, moreover, has had an impact on ASEAN (see, for example, Robinson 1985) and Australia as significant as the figures imply—as this chapter will show.

As dramatic as these figures are, we need to keep some sense of perspective. The Pacific Basin has not overwhelmed the other previously developed

Table 6.4
Australia and the Asia Pacific Region: Some Selected Comparative Data[a]

	Total Population (Millions)	Area (Thousands of Square Kilometers)	Gross Domestic Product (Millions of U.S. $)		Gross National Product (Per Capita, U.S. $)	Gross Domestic Production (Average Annual Growth, %)		Exports as a Share of Gross Domestic Product (%)		Gross Domestic Investment as a Share of Gross Domestic Product (%)		Gross Domestic Investment (Average Annual Growth, %)	
	Mid-1982		1960	1982	1982	1960-70	1970-82	1960	1982	1960	1982	1960-70	1970-82
Australia	15.2	7,687	16,370	164,210	11,140	5.6	3.1	15	15	28	22	6.7	1.1
Indonesia	156.2	1,919	8,670	90,160	580	3.9	7.7	13	22	8	23	4.6	13.7
Malaysia	14.5	330	2,290	25,870	1,860	6.5	7.7	54	51	14	34	7.5	11.4
Philippines	50.7	300	6,960	39,850	820	5.1	6.0	11	16	16	29	8.2	9.3
Singapore	2.5	1	700	14,650	5,910	8.8	8.5	163	196	11	46	20.5	8.7
Thailand	48.5	514	2,250	36,790	790	8.4	7.1	17	25	16	21	15. 8	6.4
China	1,008.0	9,561	42,770	260,400	-----	5.2	5.6	---	28[b]	23	28	9.8	6.4
Hong Kong	5.2	1	950	24,440	5,340	----	----	82	100	18	29	6.9	13.6
Japan	118.4	372	44,000	1,081,920	10,080	10.4	4.6	11	15	33	30	14.6	3.3
South Korea	39.3	98	3,810	68,420	1,910	8.6	8.6	3	39	11	26	23.6	11.0
United States	231.5	9,363	505,300	3,009,600	13,160	4.3	2.7	5	9	19	16	5.0	1.3
New Zealand	3.2	269	3,940	23,820	7,920	3.6	1.8	22	29	23	25	3.2	-0.1

Source: World Development Report (1984): Tables 1-5, 218-227

[a] Not all states of the geographical region are included. The socialist states of East Asia are ignored, as are the small states of the Southwest Pacific; Australia's former colony (Papua New Guinea); and the newest but smallest member of ASEAN, Brunei. Those included in the table are Australia's major economic partners of the Asia-Pacific region.

[b] Estimate.

regions of the global political economy. Rather it has joined Europe and North America as a third, fairly clearly defined region of economic activity. In ASEAN, Australia's immediate regional neighbors, growth has been a much more recent phenomenon—largely a process of the last ten or fifteen years. Given their proximity to Australia, their long-term importance is, however, paramount.

Currently, Australia preserves a rough, but rapidly dwindling, parity with ASEAN by virtue of the relative size of its gross domestic product. Australian gross domestic product in 1982 was U.S. $164 billion, compared to the combined gross domestic product of the then five ASEAN states of U.S. $208 billion. Australia's population of just over 15 million in 1982 is dwarfed, however, by an ASEAN population in excess of 270 million. As can be seen from the extrapolations in table 6.5, however, 1970-82 growth rates repeated over the twenty-five years to 2007 and fifty years to 2032 will give Australia gross domestic products of U.S. $352 and U.S. $755 billion (U.S. dollars at 1982 constant prices) respectively and, in sharp contrast, projected gross domestic products of U.S. $1,234 billion and U.S. $7,499 billion for ASEAN. Australia's expected population in the year 2000 is only 21 million in con-

Table 6.5

Growth Projections for ASEAN and Australia, 1982-2032

	Gross Domestic Product (U.S. $ Billions) 1982	Average Annual Growth Rate (%) 1970-82	Projected Gross Domestic Product in 25 Years (U.S. $ Billions)	Projected Gross Domestic Product in 50 Years[a] (U.S. $ Billions)
Australia	164	3.1	352	755
Indonesia	90	7.7	575	3,673
Malaysia	26	7.7	166	1,061
Philippines	40	6.0	172	737
Singapore	15	8.5	115	886
Thailand	37	7.1	206	1,142
ASEAN total	208		1,234	7,499

Source: For columns 1 and 2 is table 6.4.

[a] Projected value = present value $(1 + \underline{i})^n$
Where $\underline{i}$ = annual growth rate
$\underline{n}$ = number of years

trast to an expected population of 377 million for ASEAN (*World Development Report* 1984, 254-5).

Australia's decline as an economic power has been a fairly long-term process. From a position in 1870, when its gross domestic product per capita as a ratio of that of the USA was 173 percent, it had, by 1980, dropped to 80 percent (Caves and Krause 1984, 4). Since World War II, per capita growth has been among the slowest in the developed world, notwithstanding a reasonable rate of population growth. It has, however, taken Australia quite a long time to wake up to this erosion; the somnambulant period of the 1950s and 1960s (the "Menzies era") saw Australia generally quite satisfied with its performance. To be sure, for a long time Australia was fairly well sheltered from the exigencies of the global political economy behind its tariff barriers. The evolution of the new international division of labor has, however, brought major changes in this situation. External factors (especially post-1973) are extremely influential on the Australian political economy. Since the resource boom of the early 1970s, something like 80 percent of Australian exports have been raw materials and primary produce (see table 6.1); these exports account for approximately 15 percent of gross domestic product. Given their subjection to price-setting on world markets, this means, of course, that changes in the size of Australia's gross domestic product (despite the relatively small share of gross domestic product occupied by trade compared to other developed countries) have been profoundly affected by changes in export values (Caves and Krause 1984, 8). Australia is similarly integrated into the world's capital markets, and thus exhibits exactly the kinds of vulnerabilities of "small open economies" alluded to earlier in this chapter.

Turning specifically to Australia's trading position in the post-World War II period, four broad major changes have come about. First, and most obvious, has been the change in the direction of Australia's trade. As can be seen from table 6.6, Europe in general, and the United Kingdom in particular, have declined in importance as partners in almost direct proportion to which the Pacific in general, and Japan in particular, have risen in importance. Initially, Pacific trade saw Japan grow rapidly, while the growth in importance of other Pacific states such as Hong Kong, Taiwan, and Singapore has been a phenomenon of the last ten to fifteen years. Australia's ASEAN neighbors, at this stage, are waiting to catch the next wave, but are expected to be significant in the future (Ho Kwon Ping n.d.).

It is in the context of the increasing importance of the Pacific in world trade, generally, that Australia's trade with the Western Pacific has increased threefold over the thirty or so years up to the early 1980s. Thirty percent of Australia's imports come from Japan and Asia (not to mention in excess of 20 percent coming from the United States) and over 43 percent of Australia's exports go to Japan and the Pacific Basin (see notes to table 6.6 for explana-

Table 6.6

Share of Australian Exports To and Imports From

Selected Trading Partners, 1949-81

(Annual, Average %)

Item and Country	1949-50 to 1953-54	1954-55 to 1958-59	1959-60 to 1963-64	1964-65 to 1968-69	1969-70 to 1973-74	1974-75 to 1978-79	1979-80 to 1980-81
Imports							
United Kingdom	46.9	41.8	31.1	23.9	19.3	12.3	9.3
European Community[a]	8.8	10.1	11.2	12.2	13.4	14.1	12.6
Japan	1.9	2.7	5.8	10.1	15.5	18.8	17.4
South and Southeast Asia[b]	13.1	12.0	9.7	7.2	7.0	9.6	12.4
United States	11.1	12.9	20.0	24.9	23.0	21.2	22.1
Exports							
United Kingdom	35.9	31.3	21.3	15.4	9.7	4.4	4.4
European Community[a]	21.7	21.4	16.2	13.2	9.9	10.5	8.9
Japan	6.7	11.6	16.4	19.8	28.5	31.2	27.1
Pacific Basin[c]	8.7	9.6	9.0	11.8	12.9	14.2	16.0
United States	9.6	6.8	9.6	12.3	12.2	10.3	11.0
Canada[d]	1.5	1.5	1.7	1.7	2.7	2.5	2.1
New Zealand[d]	3.5	5.7	6.0	5.7	5.4	5.2	4.7

Sources: (Krause 1984, 287.) Norton, Garmston, and Brodie, Australian Economic Statistics: 1949-50 to 1980-81, 6, 9; and Department of Trade and Resources, Economic Policy Division, Pattern of Australian Exports, 1970-71 to 1980-81, International Information Paper (April 1983): 19-22, for Canada and New Zealand before 1974-75, see International Monetary Fund, International Financial Statistics, Yearbook 1979, vol. 32; and International Monetary Fund, Direction of Trade Statistics, computer tapes.

[a] The European Community excludes the United Kingdom, Ireland, and Denmark; they are included beginning in 1973-74.

[b] South and Southeast Asia include Bangladesh, Brunei, Burma, Hong Kong, India, Indonesia, Kampuchea, Laos, Macao, Malaysia, Maldive Islands, Pakistan, Philippines, Singapore, Sri Lanka, Taiwan, Thailand, and Vietnam.

[c] The Pacific Basin includes Taiwan, Hong Kong, the Republic of Korea, Indonesia, Malaysia, the Philippines, Singapore, Thailand, and Papua New Guinea from 1970-71. Before 1970-71, countries included are those listed in note b above.

[d] Data for Canada and New Zealand before 1974-75 are in calendar years beginning 1949.

Table 6.7

Exports as a Share of Gross Domestic Product for Selected Industrial Countries, 1960-1982 (%)

Country	1960	1982
Australia	15	15
Canada	18	27
France	15	21
Germany	19	31
Sweden	23	33
United States	5	9

Source: *World Development Report* (1984):227.

tion). Yet this absolute growth of Australian trade with the region contrasts sharply with an actual decline in Australia's degree of penetration of Asian-Pacific markets.

The second major feature of Australian trade history is the degree to which exports as a share of gross domestic product have declined from a high point of about 40 percent at the time of the Korean War commodity boom of the 1950s to just under 14 percent in 1982. As we can see from table 6.7, the currently static nature of Australian exports as a share of gross domestic product contrasts with the more dynamic pattern of other developed countries. In 1981, exports as a proportion of gross domestic product were smaller in Australia than in any OECD countries, other than the two most economically powerful—the United States and Japan—and the four most economically weak—Greece, Portugal, Spain, and Turkey (Helliwell 1984, 91). That the share of exports in gross domestic product did not decline between 1960 and 1982 was due to the offsetting effect of the growth of services, in contrast to the decline of goods as proportions of Australian trade. Explaining the static nature of Australian exports as a proportion of gross domestic product is difficult. But the range of explanations lies with the third and fourth characteristics of Australia's post-World War II trade history, namely the nature of commodity concentration and its comparative position in world trade generally.

The chief feature of Australian exports throughout the twentieth century has been the preponderance of natural resources in these exports. With a proportion varying between two-thirds and four-fifths of total exports, Australia has a profile unique among developed countries, no others of which have such a specialization in the export of natural resources. This degree of specialization has varied over the years, of course, depending on the nature of world market demand, climatic conditions, and technological innovation. Even though the mix of the exports may have undergone significant change, the basic structural pattern has changed little. The most notable change has been in the dramatic decline of wool exports (from nearly 50 percent of total exports in the 1950s to 10 percent in the early 1980s) and a sharp rise in the export of minerals and metals (from about 6 percent in the early 1950s to close to 40 percent in the late 1970s). Manufactures as a share of exports remained fairly static in this period (see table 6.3).

The fourth factor to note is the comparative one that Australian trade has grown more slowly than world trade generally. Between 1970 and 1980, the volume of world trade grew at 5.6 percent per annum, while Australian trade increased by only 3.6 percent per annum (Krause 1984, 278); Australian trade over the period 1939-1975 dropped from 2.5 percent to 1.25 percent of world trade (see Johnson 1984, 69b). In short, Australia has failed to hold its own share of world trade in an era when growth through trade has been the order of the day for many countries—developed and developing.

From the Australian point of view, the reasons for this in the context of the new international division of labor are somewhat alarming. In contrast to those rapidly growing NICs that are being incorporated into NIDL, but in common with many of the poorer LDCs, especially those in Africa (Higgott 1986a), Australia is undergoing a process of "marginalization" through its unfortunate specialization in export commodities with a low-value-added component, which are unable to hold their share of overall world trade. To add to this, Australia appears unable to hold its own overall. For example, while world agricultural production between 1971 and 1981 grew at the rate of 4.2 percent per annum, Australian agriculture only managed an average annual increase of 0.8 percent. The figures for manufacturing over the same period were 6.7 percent and 2.2 percent respectively. Only in mining was the trend reversed, with Australia growing at an annual rate of 7.6 percent, in contrast to world growth of 1.4 percent (Krause 1984, 281).

The evolution of NIDL exposed the weaknesses in Australia's long-held pursuit of inward-looking manufacturing strategies behind high tariff walls. Such strategies remained largely unquestioned in Australia until the late 1960s, and it was not until Gough Whitlam's 1972 across-the-board, 25-percent reduction that tariffs had been lowered since Federation in 1901. Notwithstanding this 1972 reduction, table 6.8 illustrates the degree to which Australia is a high tariff country.

The progressive slide in the efficiency of Australian manufactures would indicate that protectionism has not worked efficiently for a long time. Inward-looking strategies and the nature of assistance to industry to support production for the home market of goods in which Australia has no comparative advantage (real or engineered) have proved detrimental to a forceful approach toward production for export. In the context of the NIDL, this contrasts markedly with the recent history of Japan and the NICs of the Pacific. In these states, we have seen greater innovation in the use of new technologies, greater economic flexibility (especially in the pursuit of outward-oriented strategies) and, perhaps most importantly, the role of the state has been geared for intervention, but intervention to enhance export competitiveness, in ruthless fashion if necessary (see, for example, Hofheinz and Calder 1982; Rodan 1985a and b; Robison 1985). The existence of these factors is harder to identify in the Australian context of the growth period of the 1960s and 1970s.

The importance of trade to Australia at the level of rhetoric always outstripped the facts of post-World War II performance, as Australia actually, at one level, became less of a trading nation. That Australia's trade grew in volume was in large part due to a pull effect from the new industrializers in the region demanding Australia's raw materials—first and foremost, of course, being Japan. It has been growth in the Asian-Pacific region, both absolutely and relatively vis-à-vis other regions of the world, that has helped Australia's exports maintain their purchasing power against imports, despite the fact that its share of world trade has declined. In a relative sense, however, the low-value-added nature of Australia's principal exports has contributed to a decline in the purchasing power of Australia's exports, relative to many of the other nations of its region (see Johnson 1984). Without the resource boom, the balance of export purchasing against imports would not have

Table 6.8

Dutiable Items, 1978

(Tariff Level, %)

	General	Manufactured Goods
United States	9	9.5
EEC	9	9
Japan	11	12.5
Canada	14	14.2
Australia	18	23

Source: Warr (1983):30.

been maintained. The reason for this is well documented; while the value of goods exported between 1950 and 1981 has, in fact, exceeded the value of goods imported for all but eight of those years, the value of services exported has *always* been exceeded by the value of services imported. Thus even though a surplus in visible traded goods has been achieved, a deficit has been the order of the day in invisible trade. This has meant in practice that in all but four years between 1961 and 1982, Australia has run a deficit on its current account (Crough and Wheelwright 1982, 166; Dornbusch and Fischer 1984, 32). The significance of this position becomes clear when we contrast Australia with the small European states in Katzenstein's study, which tend to run a balance-of-payments deficit on traded goods that they offset with a surplus on their trade invisibles. Australia, on the other hand, has the reverse profile. Without its resource wealth, Australia would have had severe problems. Its resources helped it share in Japan's dramatic growth. Indeed Japanese growth was the agent of Australian export growth. From 1949-54 to 1979-81, Australian exports to Japan grew from 6.7 percent of total to 27 percent of total, while Japanese exports to Australia in the same period grew from 2 percent to in excess of 17 percent (see table 6.6). Japan's role as Australia's major partner did, however, peak in the mid-1970s. Further, between 1972 and 1980 Australia's share of Japanese imports declined from 9.4 percent to 5 percent of total.

This pattern is repeated at the wider level in Asia. Whereas Asian trade is increasingly important for Australia, the converse is not the case. This is because Asian trade, in direct contrast to Australian trade, is growing faster than world trade overall. This disparity in the rates of Asian growth and Australian growth is more important than barriers that protect Australian markets from Asian manufactures. The implication of this pattern of growth is quite clear; there is a growing asymmetry of need between Australia and its regional neighbors. Much more important to the growing economies of the Asian region than a healthy relation with Australia, with a market of only 15.5 million people, is an increased trading relationship with the faster growing markets of Europe and North America. Prime Minister Lee of Singapore, for example, has shown a noticeable lack of reticence in pointing out Australia's increasing irrelevance to Asian countries in the formulation of their economic and trading policies.

In the past, Australia was cushioned by its income from resource exports but will, in the long run, need to restructure the "mix" of its exports if it is to get a greater share of world trade. This is easier said than done. As it is widely acknowledged in all sectors of the policy-making community in Australia, the country has a poor track record when it comes to the possession of an efficient outward-oriented manufacturing sector quick to innovate and adjust to changes in market requirements in international trade. Yet it has been those states of the Asian-Pacific region that have been successful in the process of export-oriented industrialization that have fared best in NIDL. Australia, as the figures suggest, has undergone a process of gradual "marginalization."

Another manifestation of this marginalization is reflected in the nature of capital investment in Australia. In the current phase, it seems unlikely that Australia will see a sufficiently large relocation of capital into those sectors of the economy which will produce, along with the necessary technological innovation, high-value-added goods for export. Australia's capital import pattern is, in fact, quite well established. Prior to the mid-1960s, Britain and the United States were the major investors, primarily in the Australian manufacturing sector; they were spurred on by the self-contained and protected nature of the Australian market. Since that time, however, the pattern has been one of a sharp move away from investment in manufacturing towards multinational investment in Australia's mining and resource industries. This general analysis is accepted by both neoclassical analysts of the Australian economy (see Kasper et al. 1980) and analysts of a dependencia perspective on Australia's position in the global economy (Crouch and Wheelwright 1982, 102-9). What is contested is the size of foreign investment in Australia and its impact on the Australian economy and national sovereignty. These broader issues cannot be canvassed fully here, save to say that the dependency theorists are the ones whose figures tend to be on the high side, while on the other hand, for example, the figures in the Brookings report are somewhat lower. Yet even if we utilize the more moderate figures, and the analytical insights that Brookings draws from them, we still find support for an interpretation of the new international division of labor that sees capital locating to specific sectors of national economies, conditioned by a logic of accumulation that is global rather than national. According to the Brookings survey, up to 60 percent of the Australian mining industry is under foreign control, while the level of foreign equity in Australian manufacturing currently stands at about 40 percent of total (Krause 1984, 302). Perhaps more significantly, the increase of foreign direct investment (FDI) in the Australian mining industry came at a time when FDI was decreasing from about 16-18 percent of domestic investment in the late 1960s to 10-11 percent at the end of the 1970s. At the risk of overgeneralizing, Australia's attractiveness to international capital was in the resources it had to offer, rather than in areas of activity with higher-value-added and technological requirements.

The nature of investment in Australia has changed not only sectorally, but also in terms of the origins of investment, albeit at a slower pace. While we must not underestimate the continuing importance of Australia's traditional sources of capital in Europe and North America, it is interesting to note that for the June quarter of 1984, ASEAN was the source of the largest investments in Australia, supplying 583 million out of a total of 1,187 million dollars. The important factor is the pattern, rather than the amount. Asian investment in Australia has been, give or take fluctuations, on the rise for the last decade.

Australia and Japan

Turning from the broad Pacific region, there are two specific relationships that are important for Australia, namely those with Japan and ASEAN. Enough has been written about the evolution of the relationship with Japan not to warrant discussion here (see, *inter alia,* Stockwin 1972; Drysdale and Kitaoji 1981; Whitlam 1981, 79-94; and Rix 1982). Several points are of importance, however. Japan's rise to the position of the world's second largest market economy was the major influence on the volume and pattern of Australia's trade throughout the 1960s and 1970s. After nearly three decades of close economic relations (Australia granted Japan most favored nation status in 1957), the elements of a strong economic dependency by Australia on Japan are firmly in place.

Japan, in the first instance, has by far the strongest hand in the trading relationship, notwithstanding that Australia is the possessor of the raw materials and primary produce. Japan is quite successfully diversifying its sources of supply for coal and iron ore, and Australia is forced more and more to compete with other producers for its share in the Japanese market. This is not, of course, to say that Australia's importance to Japan is insignificant. The trade relationship between the two still ranks as one of the strongest bilateral trading partnerships in the world, although it has undergone a process of decline from its peak in the mid-1970s. In 1972, Australian exports to Japan represented nearly 10 percent of Japan's total imports; by 1980, that figure had slumped to 5 percent. This decline has been due not only to Japan's abilities to diversify sources of supply, but also because of its move into less energy-intensive, higher-technology industries. This decline has been offset to a degree by the growth of South Korea and Taiwan as steel producers and the increase in Australia's provision of raw materials to them. China too is playing an increasingly important role in this respect (*Far Eastern Economic Review,* 19 January 1984, 86; and Hayden 1984). In addition, Japan has in Australia a highly lucrative secondary market for its manufactured goods—especially high-value-added consumer durables such as cars and electronics.

From Japan's perspective, the current relationship is very suitable. Things have changed considerably from the 1950s and early 1970s when Japan was exhorting Australia to produce all the coal and iron it could. Now Japan has a variety of sources, and Australia has been forced to adjust prices accordingly over the last few years in an attempt to maintain its proportion in providing for Japan's iron and coal needs. Policy today is geared to the preservation of Australia's "market share" of Japanese imports, but Japan steadfastly refuses to be drawn on such a commitment. The Japanese communiqué, issued following Prime Minister Hawke's visit to Tokyo in early 1984, said "the *position* of Australia as a supplier of primary products, including minerals, will not decline so long as these Australian products *maintain their competitiveness and their stable supply is assured*" (emphasis added).

In his visit to Australia in January 1985, Prime Minister Nakasone reaffirmed this position, placing particular emphasis on Australia's ability to be a stable, reliable deliverer of raw materials (just as a strike broke out on the railways!). In particular, the visit did nothing to allay the fears of a likely diminution of Australia's market share of beef exports to Japan in the face of pressure for an increased market share from the more politically powerful United States, armed with a $40 billion deficit in trade with Japan with which to bargain (Byrnes 1984, 13). Australia's share fell from 75 percent to 60 percent in 1984, despite "assurances" Bob Hawke insisted he had earlier received in Tokyo; there is nothing to prevent a similar drift happening with the market shares of coal and iron ore. Japan is under pressure from the United States not only to take more beef, but also to buy West Coast coal.

Problems in the Australia-Japan relationship are also as much a matter of style as substance; there is a qualitative asymmetry in the relationship as well as a quantitative one. Australia has never pushed itself as a trading nation; rather, it has been content to be pulled along, or trade only with the "easy countries" (Ramsey 1985, 33). Australian policy has been a "no risk" or "safety first" policy of doing what it is used to, rather than grasping innovative nettles.

> Australians, in Japanese eyes, (for example) for the most part are regarded as farmers and, more recently petitioners in the technology stakes . . . this helps drain what little clout Australia might have in the Tokyo market place. (Byrnes 1984, 13)

Australia's bilateral relationship with Japan is of the utmost importance, but it needs to be seen in a three-way sense as well. The following discussion of Australian-ASEAN relations only makes sense if we appreciate the importance of Japan's role as an economic actor, second to none in the Southeast Asian region. Japan is the predominant economic actor in all the major states but the Philippines, where the former colonial power still holds the position as the major external economic influence. In contrast to Australia, Japan, along with the United States and Europe, holds its share of the ASEAN market. Currently, Japan accounts for 21 percent of ASEAN trade, as opposed to 15 percent for the United States, 13 percent for Europe, and only 2 percent for Australia. Comparable levels of importance can be found in Japanese and Australian investment in ASEAN. Japan's average of 25 to 30 percent of total investment in the region (save Singapore) contrasts with an Australian average of less than 3 percent (*Australia and ASEAN* 1984, 127). Australia's role in the ASEAN-Japan-Australia triangle is one of increasing dependence on, but increasingly less importance to, the other parties.

There are, of course, alternative scenarios to the ones of increasing asymmetry that have been outlined. The changing pattern of Japan's industrial and economic growth in the context of the regional division of labor is going to have a strong and continuing impact. Although Japan's major involvement is in the other rapidly developing states of the western Pacific region, these states are close to creating a market comparable in size to that of Japan. These regions should, according to Peter Drysdale, for example, provide opportunities for Australia comparable to that of Japan in the 1960s and 1970s. China, particularly, could be an important new source for Australia's raw materials. As Drysdale goes on to say: "Australia's trade could more than double over a decade if it maintains its overall share of regional trade" (1984, 8-12). While foodstuffs and raw materials will form the lion's share of this trade, Drysdale does hope for increased exports of value-added goods such as processed commodities and services.

Such projections must be seen at this stage, however, as possibilities rather than probabilities. Australia has not shown the capability to maintain its regional market share in the context of overall growth over the last two decades, as Drysdale himself has noted. And up to the advent of the Hawke Labor government in March 1983, Australia had done little to convince observers of the prospects for the necessary adjustment to the structure of industry that suggests an inroad of any magnitude being made into regional export markets for manufactured goods, of either a labor- or technologically intensive nature (on Australian prospects see Tisdell 1985).

The status, shape, and prospects for economic cooperation in the Pacific Basin are sufficiently ambiguous for us not to automatically assume the emergence of a complementary regional division of labor from which *all* states will inevitably benefit—as some of the more optimistic would hope (see, for example, Duncan 1983). Pacific Basin cooperation, on the other hand, however, has not developed to the degree of conspiratorial sophistication some critics of "Pacific Rim strategies" would have us believe (see Crough and Wheelwright 1982, 58-84). The current status of Pacific unity is, in fact, much more fluid than either of these two positions would suggest. Certainly Japan, strongly supported by the United States, would like to see some degree of institutionalization of cooperation; and, given its predominance in the region's economic growth, it would benefit from this.

ASEAN, as a group and as individual states, on the other hand, are much less wedded to greater institutionalization of economic cooperation at the wider Pacific level. They are currently more concerned with increasing economic activity and cooperation much closer to home (Garnaut 1980). Greater Pacific cooperation, it is felt, especially in some of the less developed states of the region (e.g., Indonesia), would tie them more firmly than they would like into the predominantly lower levels of industrial activity of the regional division of labor (Sung-Joo 1983). ASEAN states are not, however, above suggesting a specific role for Australia in the regional division of labor as a provider of raw materials for their available labor forces. Malaysian Prime Minister Dr. Mahathir is, for example, an advocate of three-way cooperation between his state, Australia, and Japan in which Australia would provide the raw materials and Malaysia would provide the secondary processing of these raw materials en route to Japan for use in high technology activities (*Australia and ASEAN* 1984, 131-2). As attractive as this may appear to Malaysia, giving it the opportunity to maximize its comparative advantage in cheap labor, it does nothing to overcome Australia's problems as a supplier of low-value-added raw materials for international (or in this context, regional) markets.

Australia and ASEAN

> While Australia will be affected by developments in other regions of the world, and by the global interests of the superpowers, no other part of the world promises to be of more consistent importance to Australia than the region of East and Southeast Asia. (*Australia and ASEAN,* 1984:x)

Thus argues a recent high-level parliamentary report on Australian-ASEAN relations. Subtitled "Constraints and Opportunities," the report reflects the near obsession that has been reached in policy-making circles over the management of Australia's relations with its immediate regional neighbors. If we accept the extremely small base from which the partnership began, then the growth in the trading relationship has not been insignificant. An 8 percent growth rate per annum saw the volume of Australian trade with ASEAN grow from $487 million (Australian) in 1972-73 to $3.43 billion in 1983-84. More important, Australian exports to ASEAN have grown at a faster rate than Australian exports overall—15 percent per annum as opposed to 11.4 percent per annum between 1978-79 and 1983-84. During the same period, ASEAN's exports to Australia grew at 14 percent per annum. Currently, ASEAN (as a group albeit most trade takes place at a bilateral level) is now Australia's fourth largest trading partner, providing just over 5 percent of Australian imports and taking about 9 percent of Australia's exports (*Australia and ASEAN* 1984, 133).

When we look at the relationship from the other side of the glass, a somewhat different picture emerges. Australia's importance to ASEAN is marginal: it is a market for only 2.6 percent of ASEAN exports and a provider of only 3 percent of ASEAN's imports. These figures, recorded for 1981, have undergone a decline in the short term. The figures for 1983 are 1.7 and 2.5 respectively (*Australia and ASEAN* 1984, 133).

Notwithstanding the fact that the economic relationship with ASEAN is essentially a sixfold bilateral relationship, there would appear to be little dispute over the asymmetry of need in the relationship being biased heavily against Australia. Furthermore, while the economic relationships are primarily bilateral, the individual members are nevertheless able to mobilize the organization's support in the face of a major economic dispute with a third party. The prime example to date of ASEAN acting as a bloc in international economic issues was the International Civil Aviation Dispute at the end of the 1970s, when ASEAN collectively supported Singapore International Airlines in its dispute with Australia (Lawe-Davis 1981).

A second area in which ASEAN often criticizes Australia is over the trade surpluses that run heavily in Australia's favor. These, however, can turn into deficits for Australia when invisibles are taken into account. In 1981-82, for example, a $180 million dollar (Australian) surplus, when a $545 million flow of invisibles was taken into account, turned into a deficit for Australia of $365 million. The three major reasons for this deficit on invisibles was profit repatriation in ASEAN, widespread Australian travel in ASEAN countries, but above all, the high cost of freight for Australian goods using non-Australian shipping services (*Australia and ASEAN* 1984, 134). This deficit is unlikely to change in the foreseeable future, given Australia's reliance on foreign shipping to move its low-value-to-weight-ratio bulk commodities.

Services such as transport, travel, tourism, insurance, and other commercial and technical services now make up over a quarter of world trade and are increasing rapidly. Australia has been fairly slow in recognizing this growth area and, indeed, only in the last couple of years has its potential been given closer scrutiny (see *Review of the Committee on Australia's Overseas Aid* 1984; Scutt 1985; and Higgott 1986b). Australia is not, however, expanding services as a section of its exports as quickly as some of its regional neighbors. Its 15 percent service export, as a percentage of total exports, is larger than Indonesia's (7 percent), the same as Malaysia's (15 percent), but smaller than Thailand's (27 percent) and the Philippines and Singapore (both 35 percent) (*Australia and ASEAN* 1984, 143).

We must not lose sight of the fact that ASEAN has to be disaggregated. Australia's dealings are still primarily of a bilateral nature and some, quite clearly, are more difficult to manage than others. Australia's neighbors also differ in their levels of development: Indonesia, the largest, nearest, and potentially most powerful neighbor, is still in character an LDC, as opposed to Singapore, which is one of the world's most successful NICs. Singapore's move into the second wave of industrialization in high technology (Rodan 1985b), high-value-added production contrasts with Indonesia's emphasis on more rudimentary labor-intensive activities reminiscent of Singapore a decade ago.

These different levels of development and, by consequence, different degrees of integration into the global division of labor condition the nature of Australia's regional bilateral relations. So too, of course, do political and security factors, which go beyond the scope of this paper, save only to acknowledge the degree to which the political and economic relationships are not mutually exclusive (but see, *inter alia,* Lim 1985 and 1980; Nicholas 1983; Frost 1982; Mackie 1981; and Brown 1980).

THE ROLE OF GOVERNMENT IN ADJUSTING TO THE EVOLVING REGIONAL POLITICAL ECONOMY

Discussion, so far, has suggested a variety of structural factors to explain Australia's "location" in the emerging division of labor in the Asia-Pacific region. This is not the same, however, as implying a total determinism of such constraints. To do so would be to ignore the complicating dimensions of governmental "will" and "capacity" in the face of trends in both the global and regional political economy.

It was suggested earlier, following Katzenstein's analysis of small European states, that there were a variety of political correlates to a perceived position of openness and vulnerability in the international division of labor, particularly tendencies towards corporatist forms of policy making. Nothing has yet been written on Australia that approaches the analytic specificity and quality of Katzenstein's study of the small European states in the international economy.[4] As he suggests, in what one hopes might prove a useful working definition for future analysis of the political responses of Australian government policy toward incorporation into the regional division of labor: "In the areas of economic policy, corporatism can be viewed as a response to openness to, and dependence on, the world economy." In elaborating on this definition, Katzenstein goes on to highlight some of the central components of his corporatist model:

> [It has] the voluntary, cooperative regulation of conflicts over economic and social issues through highly structured and interpenetrated sets of political relationships by business, the unions and the state, augmented at times by political parties. . . . Alternatively, corporatism may be viewed as a particular institutional mechanism concentrating power in the attempt to manage dependence. (Katzenstein 1983, 116 and 128)

Whatever nomenclature one chooses, the election of an Australian Labor government, led by Bob Hawke in 1983, has given rise to a rhetoric of "consensus politics" (Katzenstein talks of "social relationship"). There is the utilization of the "politics of summitry," leading to the *accord* between major groups in the economy, as well as the establishment of bodies such as the Economic Planning Advisory Committee (EPAC) and the Advisory Committee on Prices and Incomes (ACPI), and it signaled the beginning of an

Industry Policy in the reestablishment of the Australian Manufacturing Council (AMC). These initiatives, and the establishment of several other ancillary bodies, place an emphasis on the cooperation of state, capital, and labor unprecedented in Australian history (Dow 1984).

This is not the place to analyze such initiatives, but rather to note that they are, along with a variety of other initiatives at both federal and state levels in Australia, geared to one major end—stemming the process of national decline that is widely believed to be taking place. Two main elements in this process are perceived as essential to success: first, and central to this chapter, is the necessity of finding a proper and prosperous niche in the regional political economy; second, and the success of the first element depends on this, is the intention to bring about a process of structural adjustment of the domestic economy.

Structural Adjustment: Problems and Prospects

Central to discussion of the Australian political economy over the last four years (largely irrespective of ideological perspective) has been the notion that Australia must adjust if it is to reverse, or even at best arrest, that process of decline down the list of affluent states. The Hawke Labour government has been much more circumspect than the previous Labour administration of Gough Whitlam (1973-75), but much more aware of the issues than the immediate Liberal-National Party administrations of Malcolm Fraser (1975-83).

By the time the Hawke government had come to power, it was evident that the supposed resource boom of the 1970s was not going to provide compensatory employment opportunities for jobs lost in Australia's secondary manufacturing industries. There has been neither a flow-on of growth in the service sector nor vast injections of capital into technologically innovative industries, as anticipated at the outset of the mining boom. Jobs lost in the secondary sector to date have not been dramatically replaced in a tertiary sector, which has been unable to match competition from more dynamic regional neighbors (Bowring 1984, 79).

Further, the need to restructure dramatically is not universally accepted across the economic spectrum in Australia. While there is no question in government circles of the absolute need to restructure industry and ultimately reduce tariffs, there are objections from at least two quarters that make unlikely allies. The government position is aptly stated in the words of the foreign minister, Mr. Hayden:

> While structural change will not be easy or painless, it is going to happen. The real question is to what extent it will be foisted upon us, and to what extent we can shape it to maximize benefits and minimize negative aspects. We can seek to delay change but only at the cost of a decline in Australia's

> living standards, relative to those of countries which adjust more rapidly. (*Australia and ASEAN* 1984, 171)

And again in the words of the minister for Industry and Commerce, Senator Button:

> We cannot, in general, increase our protective walls. That will lead to stagnation and withdrawal. . . . There are sound international imperatives why we should become more closely integrated with the region, not insulate ourselves from it. (*Australia and ASEAN* 1984, 171)

Ironically, the opposing view is articulated most clearly by the other arm of the Labor movement, the Australian Council of Trade Unions, which argues that, while Australian industry has to undergo change, "neither current nor foreseeable future economic conditions justify a reduction in protection levels" (*Australia and ASEAN* 1984, 171). This view, again ironically, but perhaps not surprisingly, is strongly supported by those sectors of the Australian manufacturing industry that get most benefit from the country's existing tariff structure. While the ACTU is quite correct to say that Australia's tariff barriers are highly visible, in contrast to some of the many devices its regional partners use to protect and foster their own nascent industries (on Singapore for example, see Rodan 1985a), the fact nevertheless remains that even those most protected of industries (textiles, clothing, and footwear) have shed many thousands of workers over the last decade. Indeed, between 1974 and 1984, the general manufacturing sector's share of total employment fell by 14.8 percent to a figure of 17.7 percent in 1984. This would not, of course, be so drastic if a dramatic process of job-generating restructuring had occurred in other sectors of the economy. For example, although employment in the mining industry grew by 26.3 percent in the same period, in 1984 it only represented 1.4 percent of total employment. While there was growth in other sectors of the work force too, these were essentially nonwealth-generating areas such as community services, which grew by 52.5 percent to represent 17.6 percent of the total work force in 1984—that is, the same proportion as manufacturing. Rapid growth in finance, property, and business services (44 percent over a ten-year period) brought it to just slightly under 10 percent of the total work force (Mulvey and Norris 1985, 21).

The importance of these data for this study can only really be gleaned in comparative perspective. Comparing Australia with its major Pacific partner, Japan, is extremely instructive in this regard. As can be seen from table 6.4, both countries had considerably reduced growth rates throughout the 1970s and early 1980s, when compared with the 1960s: Japan's growth rate declined from 10.4 percent per annum during 1960-70 to 4.6 percent during 1970-82, and Australia's declined from 5.6 percent to 3.1 percent over the same period. In Australia, however, this decline in growth was accompanied by a decline of almost 70 percent in the growth rate in employment, compared with a decline of only 37 percent in Japan. In 1983, Australia's unemployment level (in excess of 9 percent) contrasted sharply with Japan's, which was only slightly over 2 percent (for a discussion of these issues see Henderson 1985). A variety of factors explains the discrepancies between Australia and Japan: wage flexibility (contrast Japan's very free system with Australia's centralized and indexed process of wage determination); the flexibility of labor-market institutions (contrast Japan's lower rate of unionization to that of Australia's—30 percent of the work force, mostly in company-based unions in Japan, 55 percent in Australia, in some hundred or so trade-based unions); and the role of government and the structure of trade. All are important, but the last two are particularly germane to this discussion.

There is broad agreement in both Australia and Japan of the linkage between wages, employment and international competitiveness. That the impact of this linkage is greater in Japan undoubtedly relates to the structure of Japan's trade. Manufactured goods account for 95 percent of Japanese exports in the period 1971-82, while the figure for Australia in the same period was only 27 percent. This preponderance of manufactures in exports, the export consciousness and competitiveness of Japanese industry, especially vis-à-vis the growing competition from the other Asian NICs and the lack of competition from imports into Japan (most of which are agricultural produce and raw materials) have all contributed to keep the Japanese wage structure flexible. Australia, by contrast, sees manufactured goods constituting about three-quarters of its imports—a good deal of which compete with locally produced goods. The lack of competitiveness of local goods had the effect of unifying both capital and labor, in the affected industries, in seeking government support to protect wage levels and market shares. This relationship over the last 15 or so years has insulated Australian manufacturing from the realities of the global market place, and has been the major block to restructuring in Australian manufacturing industries, in the long run probably to no avail. The policy has been described by one author "as attempting to guard a block of ice on a hot day" (Dick 1984, 46).

The issue of restructuring is, however, a lot more complex than some of its most vehement advocates would suggest. This is especially the case with neoclassical advocates, who see it as rational, sensible, and therefore inevitable. The major deficiency in their analysis tends to be with regard to the role of government. Always keen to point to the success of Australia's rapidly developing regional neighbors, whom they perceive as advocates of some kind of late-twentieth-century "laissez faire," they ignore the very crucial role government has played in the development of these states. If tariffs, they argue, are abolished and market principles are allowed to apply, then "comparative advantage" will do the rest (Keegan 1983, 2). Such a position, articulated in a variety of forms, ignores a variety of important factors.

In the first instance, there is no guarantee that the abolition of protection will inevitably see capital that has been traditionally wasted on inefficient industries redirected into new, more competitive sectors of Australian industry (Robison and Rodan 1983, 2-5). Secondly, it is by no means clear in which industries, other than the exploration of raw materials and the production of primary produce, Australia has a comparative advantage. Could Australia compete in the computer industry against Japan, or in the production of automobiles against West Germany? This question was even recently acknowledged, in albeit somewhat different manner, in the recent *Australia and ASEAN* report (1984, 175):

> The Committee would not limit any "comparative advantage" approach to an unimaginative fatalistic assessment of Australia's opportunities in the ASEAN region; otherwise Australia's main economic role in the region might be seen as very much limited to that of efficient primary producer and raw material supplier.

It is also possible that the removal of protective barriers on some manufactures may simply exacerbate an already existing tendency for other nations to dump their more highly subsidized products on exposed Australian markets. The success of many of Australia's regional neighbors in pursuing outward-looking strategies has not been due to any "natural" comparative advantage they may have had, but rather to a comparative advantage created by government through the implementation of long-term government financed and directed strategies. In many of the success stories of Asian development in the postwar world, the relationship between state and capital has been the crucial element in the creation of any comparative advantage (see, for example, Rodan 1985a and b on Singapore; Haggard and Moon 1983; and Cho 1985 on South Korea). This state involvement in support of the creation of comparative advantage also engages in activities of a less savory nature in some of the regional NICs; for example, in the suppression of organized labor or the failure to implement environmental and safety legislation.

The vital point that advocates of wholesale tariff abolition, in the cause of restructuring, invariably fail to comprehend is the degree to which the state has provided vast amounts of support to nascent industries in the rapidly developing countries of the region. Governments build infrastructures that corporations would otherwise have to build themselves; they provide long-term credits and tax incentives; they often help subsidize the restructuring of entire industries; but, *above all,* they provide long-term planning in the pursuit of growth. As Hofheinz and Calder note in their study of East Asia:

> The essence of a growth promoting political environment is neither the presence nor absence of state intervention. It is predictability—predictability of both leadership and commercial policy. . . . A predictable political en-

> vironment has been especially crucial for developing capital intensive basic industries such as steel and petrochemicals, where investments are so massive and complex that executives will not venture on them if the future seems cloudy and uncertain. (Hofheinz and Calder 1982, 25-6)

The very predictability and order of many of Australia's neighbors in the Asia-Pacific region contrasts sharply with the political volatility and lack of direction and purpose of Australian governments prior to the advent of the Labor government in 1983. This is not to suggest that Australia has "turned the corner," despite a somewhat improved economic performance over the last two years. Australia is still not sure of where its comparative advantage may be found in other than primary produce and raw-material exploration. Similarly there is no consensus, despite government rhetoric, as to the role government should play in supporting the process of restructuring, although there is now an acknowledgement that any discussion of why Australia's regional neighbors are outperforming it in the regional and global economic order has to take the role of government in coordinating development strategies into very serious account. What is currently prevalent in the Australian political environment is a recognition that, if Australia does not grasp the adjustment nettle now, it may soon be too late—as Lee Kuan Yew frequently tells Australia. Populist rapportage abounds with horror stories of Australia's "Latin American Future" (*The Australian,* 2 December 1985, p. 2). More important, however, for students of international political economy is the growth of some very serious long-range historical analyses of Australia and, for example, Argentine parallels (see, for example, Duncan and Fogarty 1984; Gerardi 1985; and Denoon 1983).

That the major burden of this adjustment will fall to those sections of the work force whose jobs are "restructured away" is in little doubt. It is in this context, the context of educating sectors of the labor movement to acknowledge and to accept the inevitability of job loss in the process of restructuring, that the position of a "centrist" and "national" leader like Hawke sitting above the party fray is supposedly important. The role of government was to be twofold in the kind of process Katzenstein describes in his case studies. First, government would bring the population along in the spirit of "social partnership" and also provide assistance in such things as retraining those who become the casualties of the adjustment process. Second, government would provide the ground rules for restructuring, in a manner similar to the role played by MITI in Japan and its equivalents in states such as Taiwan, South Korea, and Singapore. It is still too early to pass judgment on whether the "will" and "capacity" of the current Labor government will match the degree of commitment present in its rhetoric. What is worth considering, by way of conclusion to this section, are the constraints that would still exist and the opportunities that would be opened to an Australian economy undergoing a process of restructuring.

The nature of Australia's regional future is, at one and the same time, fairly straightforward, yet extremely complex. It is straightforward to the extent that a starting point for analysis can be pinpointed; it is complex inasmuch as how it evolves will depend on a whole array of government policy choices over the short- to mid-term future. Australia's position in the regional environment is neither pivotal on the one hand nor fixed for all time on the other. As Grant (1983) has noted: "Asia neither threatens nor beckons Australia, but it is there, offering Australia a chance to respond to its presence as one nation among many rather than as an alien outpost." Similar themes are echoed extensively around Australia's immediate regional neighborhood (Sopiee 1984). A widely held perception of the secondary nature of Australia's economic and political role in the region is a starting point for more measured analysis. This is not merely a populist point; it is of analytical importance too. The inability of Australian governments and scholars to recognize, until recently, the dramatic changes taking place in the region has undoubtedly been a factor, albeit an unquantifiable one, in Australia's declining position (McCawley 1983).

This section has suggested that there are prospects for improvement in Australia's regional economic position, if Australia can learn the lessons of the past and adjust its production patterns in a manner that allows it to be integrated into the region, other than as a producer of raw materials and primary produce. Further, while the international division of labor should in no way be seen as deterministic of Australia's (or any state's) future position, it does provide a strong structural influence that requires both governmental will and capacity to combat it.

Particularly, Australia requires the creation of a much stronger export and trading ethic which, for historical reasons outlined earlier, has traditionally been lacking. Given the trade-oriented nature of growth in the region, Australia's living standards seem destined to relative decline in the absence of both a quantitative and qualitative leap in Australian export performance. For this to happen, a variety of problems would appear to be in need of remedy: for example, the creation of an industrial economic base geared toward optimizing export activity, rather than just serving a domestic market, is required. Similarly, the removal of an "industrial-cultural cringe" mentality, which has traditionally led Australian manufacturers not to consider exporting as a vital activity, must be overcome (see *Lifting Australia's Performance,* 1985). If Australia's economic position is to be maintained and, consequently, what political influence it has is not to be lost, then it has no choice but to adopt more outward-looking strategies towards the region. Australia's traditional inward-looking posture is still associated in the minds of its regional neighbors with its Europocentric past. That there is a recognition of major change in Australia's current position (although some sections of the community would resist it if they could) is a sign not only of national maturation, but perhaps more importantly, of an acknowledgement of geo-political reality.

CONCLUSION

The aim of this chapter has been threefold: at a conceptual level, it has argued the analytic utility of the concept of new international division of labor; at an empirical level, it has attempted to locate Australia within this division of labor; and, at an academic/scholarly level, it has attempted to establish the need for an "international political economy of Australian foreign policy" to complement the existing, and preponderantly traditional, approaches to the study of Australia in the international arena. All three tasks have been pursued in somewhat scant manner and await full integrated treatment in a book-length study. If the emphasis in this chapter has been on the conceptual *cum* political economy dimensions, rather than either the historical or the politico-strategic dimensions of Australia's position in the regional and international environments, it has been because the conceptual and political economy dimensions are the ones that have received less scholarly attention to date.

In its "location" of Australia in the international division of labor in the post-World War II period, this chapter has suggested that the evolving division has provided the major structural constraint on Australian economic development. It has, however, been at pains to stress that, as crucial as a NIDL may be in "structuring" Australia's regional economic order, Australia's position is not "determined" by it alone.

Other factors have been, and are, of major importance. Particularly significant has been Australia's colonial heritage and its contemporary political culture. The major aspects of this political culture, again, received only scant treatment, but several important variables in any future analysis of Australia's location in the international political economy emerged, most notably the degree to which Australian governments can, or cannot, exercise both will and capacity to adjust to regional and, indeed, global economic imperatives.

In this regard, the success of Australian government policy, since the change of government in March 1983, has been mixed. Rhetoric and activity have certainly set regional neighbors to thinking very closely about the bona fides of Australia's desire to be "of the region" as well as simply "in the region"—particularly to the extent that Australia can, and wants to, participate in regional growth. This recognition of the economic facts of life has put relations on a more realistic footing than prior to the advent of Labor. Labor has signaled a commitment to carry out policies of structural adjustment noticeably absent during the days of the Fraser administration, when Australian policy toward the region reflected more Fraser's priorities with the "high politics" of Soviet expansionism and the degree to which ASEAN could be a check to it in Australia's neighborhood, regardless of Fraser's rhetoric of free trade (Brown 1980). Such a shift of emphasis notwithstanding, it is still recognized in policy-making circles that Australia's economic prospects in the region will be conditioned by the degree to which its regional neighbors, especially at the immediate level of Southeast Asia, perceive Australia as being sympathetic toward, and its policies in tune with, their interests—as the recent report on *Australia and ASEAN* was keen to point out (1984, 263).

A final important theme pursued in this chapter has been the acknowledgement of a perceived need for a better analysis of Australia's position in the international environment. For the purpose of manageability, this chapter has in fact suggested that it is possible to isolate global and regional, and political and economic, imperatives from each other. Yet this, it needs to be stressed, has been a heuristic device utilized in the interests of *analysis.* Policy making is a much more complex process in which global and regional *interests* cannot be separated and in which they are subject to the two-way pull of conflicting domestic and international political and/or economic priorities. Such is the nature of contemporary international interdependence and dependence where economies, and societies, are incorporated into the global political economy and the international system of states.[5]

By way of conclusion, it should be noted that the nature of Australia's incorporation into the global political economy as described in this chapter, particularly the nature of its contemporary openness and vulnerability, is as important a component of the total picture of Australia's foreign relations as is a comprehension of Australia's position as a member of the international system of states. It is a signpost to the advances in the study of Australia's international relationships that such an assertion is unlikely to meet with the degree of objection today that would almost certainly have been its fate a decade ago.

NOTES

1. There are a few honorable exceptions to this criticism. See, for example, some of the works of Professors Harris (1982, 1986) and J. D. B. Miller (1980, 1982).

2. For authors analyzing Australia from a dependency perspective, see Crough and Wheelwright (1982) and Hyde (1978). From the neoclassical perspective, see Hughes (1983, 1985), Corden (1983), and Perkins (1979).

3. Ruggie (1983), especially the introduction, is an excellent discussion of these two positions.

4. The analysis of corporatism as a potential model for examining aspects of political behavior in Australia is still extremely rudimentary. For a somewhat skeptical view of its utility, see Loveday (1985).

5. Nothing of late better illustrates this point than the implications for Australia of that complex set of issues that have been thrown up by New Zealand's change of policy towards its major ANZUS partner, the United States. The collapse, or serious deterioration, of ANZUS would have not only global and strategic implications for Australia, it would also have implications for Australia's political and economic position in the Asia-Pacific region.

7

James A. Caporaso

Labor in the Global Political Economy

The "struggle for the world product" is not only a struggle to capture final commodities and value contained therein. It is also, more fundamentally, the struggle for work, industry, the control over science and technology, and, ultimately, control of the processes of surplus-extraction and accumulation. From a domestic vantage point, this struggle is not new. The ability to engage in productive work, to achieve access to productive capital, to bargain for a wage or profit, and to reproduce and advance productive capital are familiar activities. But the playing out of these epochal themes at the global level provides at the very least a new theater, a new cast of actors, operating on a grander scale and a partially rewritten script—not in the sense of a novel *telos,* but in the sense of modified rules for conforming to the same, uniform logic of accumulation that has guided economic behavior for hundreds of years.

The events of the last three decades have lent a poignancy to the process of competitive capital accumulation. The sharply increasing level of interdependence among countries, with respect to both trade and capital flows, is now widely accepted. Production and consumption are no longer exclusively, or in some cases even predominantly, domestic processes. The resources and capital used in productive labor may be as foreign as the destination of the produced commodities. Indeed, in the case of export-processing zones, this separation of work from input materials and market destinations is carried to its conclusion. Capital flows in the world have now vastly exceeded flows of commodities. One commentator puts this figure at about $20 to $30 trillion (Garten 1985, 543), a quantity so large as to suggest broad implications for economic, social, and political processes normally thought about only in domestic terms.

The important forces operating in the contemporary global political economy are not limited to interdependence, at least to the extent that this is thought of as the intensification of commodity and capital flows across national borders. Of equal significance are the narrowing of production costs among countries of the advanced capitalist world (Cooper 1968); the migration of first- and second-generation industrial capital from Western Europe, Japan, and the United States to various parts of the Third World; and the growing differentiation among less-developed countries (LDCs); all resulting in resource-rich LDCs, two waves of newly industrializing countries (NICs), and many very poor (still mainly agricultural) countries.

The sharpening of these forces has led to what some authors call a "new international division of labor" (Ernst 1980; Fröbel et al. 1980). For now, I use this term to refer to the complex of changes above. The new international division of labor is an ongoing process and it opens up for us new, uncharted territories. A number of questions seem especially relevant. First, how will the evolving division of labor affect the distribution of the world's jobs? Who (meaning which people in which countries, with what skill levels and wage returns) will have the jobs? What will be the place of core and peripheral countries in this search for productive work, of women and men, young and old, minorities and majorities, and city versus rural workers? Will technological change provide the solvent necessary for accommodating the inevitably conflicting interests by opening "room at the top"? That is, will the discovery and deployment of new technologies allow presently advanced societies to gracefully relinquish light manufacturing (e.g., textiles, apparel) and heavy manufacturing (e.g., consumer durables, automobiles) and move easily to microelectronics, biotechnology, and services, thus allowing a constantly expanding industrial space for new industrial aspirants?

Second, and related to the first question, what is likely to be the future course and limit to the industrial and postindustrial evolution of advanced capitalist societies? We have already seen a relative decline in industrial employment in some advanced capitalist societies (Ginsberg and Voija 1981) and, especially when scrutinized at the margins, a growth of the service sector in relation to industrial employment. There can be little doubt that countries such as the United States and West Germany are "shedding" certain industries, apparel being the most prominent. How far will this process extend? Will it be limited to the labor-intensive, technologically unsophisticated sectors or will it extend up the technological ladder? What limits of both a political and economic sort are there likely to be? Can an advanced society reduce its industrial output indefinitely, in both absolute and relative terms, without affecting its real wealth-producing capacity?

Third, has the state, ironically just when arguments about its autonomy are cresting, been reduced to the role of "helper" or "facilitator" of global capital? Is it, because of the immersion of domestic economies in the competitive global marketplace, bound to abide by a universal logic of capital:

that is, to search for "economies" at all stages of production and distribution; to provide a guarantee for the safe operation of capital abroad; and, to yield to "global wage pressure"? (By the latter I mean bringing domestic wages into line with foreign wages or abandoning production in those sectors, and providing for the social overhead costs of production, including science and technology, as well as basic education, transportation and communications.)

These processes are not qualitatively new, and they now transpire more intensely and on a broader scale. One can't help but think that a certain amount of irreversible momentum toward economic globalism has occurred; and, because of trade liberalization and the expansion of foreign capital, it is unlikely that the economic clock will be turned back. There are too many entrenched interests—not just "special" ones—that stand to lose. All of these questions are worth asking and they implicitly affect subsequent analysis. However, the main purpose of this chapter is to provide a more detailed descriptive examination of the major trends in the international division of labor.

FIVE TRENDS IN THE GLOBAL DIVISION OF LABOR

The Migration of Industrial Capital from Core to Periphery

One dramatic trend of the 1970s and 1980s is the migration of industrial capital from the core regions of the advanced capitalist world to peripheral regions within both the LDCs and core countries. In Europe, the movement was first from north to south, second from west to east. It went from England, Germany, France, Holland, and northern Italy, to Portugal, Spain, Ireland, and southern Italy, then pushed farther southward to Algeria and Morocco.

In North America, capital migrated first from the United States to Mexico, then to Brazil, Chile, Argentina, Venezuela, and other parts of Latin America. In the Far East, it went from Japan to Taiwan, South Korea, Singapore, and then to the Philippines and Malaysia. Despite obvious differences in the movement of capital in these three great epicenters of economic activity, there are also underlying similarities. At least the overall patterns were similar. In the United States, northwestern Europe, and Japan, capital moved initially to the closest places: Mexico, Spain and Portugal, Taiwan and South Korea. After the initial phase of offshore migration, there was a more dramatic movement over long distances—to Latin America rather than Central America, North Africa rather than Southern Europe, the Pacific Basin rather than just Taiwan and South Korea.

In some important respects, the movement of capital in those decades was quite different from the dominant shifts that took place during the 1950s and 1960s. During this period, capital shifted mostly from one advanced capitalist country to another, concentrated in high-technology sectors, and displayed a strong "oligopolistic rivalry" character (Hymer 1979; Gereffi 1983). The more recent wave was in sharp contrast to the earlier one. Industrial-sector characteristics included industries of small scale and low sunk costs; they were competitive rather than concentrated, relied on low and fixed technologies, embodied very small shares of research and development costs, and utilized cheap and unskilled labor. And, as one might expect, this syndrome of properties was found most often, but as I will argue later not exclusively, in the peripheral countries.

Why was there the dramatic movement of capital out of the core during the 1970s and 1980s? There are many reasons and they interact in complicated ways. One could focus on changes within advanced capitalist societies themselves, changes that made for an environment less hospitable for capital's long-term tenure. The rise of wages in Western Europe in the late 1960s and in the U.S., Canada, and Japan during the 1970s was part of the picture (McCracken 1977, 49-50). The Vietnam War and the postwar inflation, the formal or informal indexing of wages to inflation, and the "fixed" nature of benefits led many observers to believe that advanced economies had become rigid and had lost the fluidity that allowed for the Schumpeterian processes of "creative destruction" to occur.

On the other hand, the repulsion of capital from the core was matched by an equally strong attraction from some of the economies of LDCs. The primary pull exerted by these countries stems from their supply of cheap labor in low-technology industries—the labor cost differences between LDCs and advanced capitalist countries are huge. Martin Landsberg, using data from the U.S. Tariff Commission, informs us that the "net Far East labor cost for electronic assembly works out to be only eight percent of that in the U.S." (Landsberg 1979, 57-8). Similarly, a seamstress in Belgium made $160 a week during the late 1970s while the same worker in Hong Kong made $55 and a Sri Lankan worker $5 (Terkl 1978). The technology in the apparel industry is "standard," i.e., it does not vary greatly over time and across countries. When this cheap labor is coupled with the logic of export platforms and free production zones, the attraction it exerts on core capital to move is difficult to resist (Fröbel et al. 1980; Robinson 1979).

In short, the migration of industrial capital from core to periphery both builds upon and further develops the pool of cheap labor from the Third World and the southern periphery of Europe. Internal (i.e., domestic) migrations from rural to urban areas help to create this Third World proletariat, as the deposits of foreign capital in urban areas ease the process and increase the probability that a job awaits the migrant at the end of the journey. Even in Spain these patterns hold: in 1950, about half of the economically active population was engaged in farming, but by 1970, the figure had dropped to

21 percent. Over the same time period, the industrial work force grew from 2.5 to 4 million (Linz 1979, 176). Similar shifts from rural to urban areas were occurring in North Africa, East Asia, and Latin America.

The above material presents the aerial view. It describes the varied experiences of the industrializing less-developed countries (LDCs) in very general terms. At the broadest level, this pattern of peripheral industrialization combines a comparative advantage in cheap labor with foreign capital and technology along with outward-looking trade policies. By the early 1960s, Taiwan and South Korea had finished their "easy" phase of import-substitution and had adopted more liberal, export-oriented policies (Balassa 1979, 27); Brazil's transition to greater reliance on exports dates from 1966, and Mexico's from 1965 (Donges and Riedel 1975, 61). The stimulation of the export sector was not limited to the liberalization of commercial policies narrowly conceived. The establishment of export-processing zones, subsidies to the export sector, tariff exemptions on the import of raw materials and capital goods, preferential interest rates for exporting industries, and accelerated depreciation allowances for capital equipment used for export production are exemplary of the broad range of policy instruments applied.

Despite important variations from country to country, the combination of cheap labor, foreign capital, and liberal trade policies proved to be a powerful chemistry in promoting economic growth. From 1960 to 1964, annual average growth rates for newly industrializing countries (NICs) were impressive, ranging from a low of 4.6 percent in Argentina to a high of 9.6 percent in the Republic of Korea. Table 7.1 presents these data for nine countries.

The growth rates for the manufacturing sector are higher still. From 1960 to 1974 South Korea grew at an annual average rate of 18.5 percent in manufacturing output, Singapore at 13.7 percent, and Brazil at 8 percent. Once again, table 7.2 presents the relevant figures for a larger group of countries.

However, as Cumings (1984) correctly reminds us with special reference to South Korea and Taiwan, economic growth is not simply a product of the 1960s and a turn to the external market; the foundations for growth in manufacturing output had been laid long before then. The Japanese colonial period in Taiwan left a legacy of a strong bureaucracy, and the Chinese mainlanders were instrumental in carrying out a significant land reform (Cumings 1984, 22). Similarly, in South Korea, the Korean War from 1950-53 and the three-month occupation by the North, paved the way for land reform on the Taiwanese model (Cumings 1974, 23). These factors, coupled with the consolidation of the Cold War and the advent of the U.S. defense umbrella to parts of the region, set the stage for economic growth.

It is important to avoid the twin errors of interpreting growth among

Table 7.1
Annual Rates of Growth at Constant Prices (% GDP)

	1961	1962	1963	1964	1965	1966	1967	1968	1969	1970	1971	1972	1973	1974	1960-1974
Argentina	7.1	-1.6	-2.4	10.3	9.2	0.6	2.6	4.4	8.5	5.4	4.8	3.1	6.1	6.5	4.6
Mexico	4.9	4.7	8.0	11.7	6.5	6.9	6.3	8.1	6.3	6.9	3.4	7.3	7.4	5.9	6.9
Korea (Republic of)	5.1	3.0	8.8	8.6	6.0	12.0	7.3	12.8	15.2	8.6	9.8	7.3	16.9	8.7	9.6
Singapore	8.4	7.0	10.0	-3.5	7.5	11.1	11.8	13.9	13.7	-1.7	12.5	13.4	11.5	6.3	8.8
Portugal	5.5	6.7	5.9	6.6	7.5	4.1	7.5	9.7	2.1	7.8	5.7	8.7	11.0	4.3	6.6
Brazil	10.5	4.6	1.3	4.0	2.8	4.7	4.6	9.0	9.6	a	a	a	a	a	4.8
Hong Kong	a	10.2	10.3	9.1	18.1	6.6	8.6	3.7	14.2	6.2	3.1	7.3	12.6	-0.0	8.5
Philippines	5.4	5.0	6.8	3.1	5.2	4.9	6.1	5.6	5.3	6.0	5.9	4.7	9.2	a	5.5
Spain	11.8	9.3	8.8	6.2	7.2	8.3	4.3	5.7	7.8	6.0	4.3	9.6	7.4	5.4	6.9

Source: National Account Statistics. New York: United Nations, 1976.

Note: Data in each column represent the growth rate for that year and the preceding year.
Data in last column represent the average, annual growth rate for all years.
[a] Data not available.

Table 7.2
Annual Rates of Growth in Manufacturing at Constant Prices (%)

	1961	1962	1963	1964	1965	1966	1967	1968	1969	1970	1971	1972	1973	1974	1960-1974
Argentina	10.0	-5.5	-4.1	18.9	13.8	0.7	1.5	6.9	10.4	6.3	9.7	6.0	6.4	6.8	6.3
Mexico	5.5	4.6	9.2	17.4	9.5	9.4	6.8	10.1	8.1	8.7	3.1	8.3	8.9	7.4	8.6
Philippines	3.4	5.1	6.8	2.9	4.4	6.5	9.3	6.9	5.3	6.2	7.6	6.0	11.3	4.1	6.3
Singapore	5.8	8.5	16.8	3.7	13.4	14.3	20.1	20.7	22.5	-1.9	18.7	16.8	16.3	3.8	13.7
Portugal	6.6	6.4	7.0	15.2	10.2	6.9	7.6	12.5	5.9	9.4	7.9	12.4	14.6	2.6	9.2
Brazil	6.6	6.2	5.8	5.1	-4.7	12.3	2.4	15.9	10.8	11.0	11.3	14.1	15.8	a	8.0
Korea (Republic of)	3.1	13.2	17.3	6.5	20.0	17.1	22.8	27.0	21.4	18.4	17.7	15.7	30.9	17.5	18.5

Source: National Account Statistics. New York: United Nations, 1976.

Note: Data in each column represent the growth rate for that year and the preceding year.
Data in last column represent the average, annual growth rate for all years.

semiperipheral countries as either a consequence of the technical virtuosity of economic policy makers or as due, in a simple sense, to structural position occupied in the global system. Policies were important, as was proximity to Japan and location on the outer reaches of the U.S. defense perimeter. However, the ability to understand, to anticipate, and to exploit the eternal movements of the product cycle may have been (and continue to be) important in explaining the upswings of South Korea and Taiwan. In simplest terms, the product cycle theory (Vernon 1966) suggests that each product has a natural cycle, from birth through growth, maturation, and decline. The "natural" global distribution of productive factors suggests that products should originate in certain countries and gradually spread to others. Innovation would be followed by production for the domestic mass market and for export abroad. As the product matures, other countries acquire the technology and compete with the innovator in both foreign and domestic markets. In response to these trends, the innovating firm exports its capital to foreign countries to take advantage of the cheap labor costs and access to local markets (Caporaso 1981, 369-70).

The above description of the product cycle is fairly mechanical, and it implicity assumes that the sources of the cyclical movements in question reside in a combination of properties intrinsic to the products themselves and to spatial diffusion processes. What this focus leaves out, and what Cumings's article on the Northeast Asian political economy captures so well, are the dynamic political aspects of the product cycle. To be sure, South Korea and Taiwan have, to a limited extent, been passive beneficiaries of downswings in Japan's economic cycles, with the Japanese willingly exporting capital in declining industrial sectors; but this is far from a mechanical process. Both South Korea and Taiwan have also been sensitive to the economic growth potential of entering the product cycle at the right moment, of utilizing state power to protect young industries, and of anticipating and exploiting an international environment of very fluid and shifting comparative advantages (Cumings 1984, 2). While many dependency theorists overly emphasize the static and unchanging aspects of the international political economy, world systems analysis recognizes such changes but trivializes them by seeing them as largely relative. However, it is difficult to ignore the far-reaching changes that have already occurred, even though the long-term consequences of these changes still elude us.

There is, of course, a dark side to these processes of rapid economic growth—the turn to authoritarian regimes in Latin America during the 1960s is an example. During this decade, alliances between the military and technocrats emerged in Brazil (1964), Argentina (1966), Peru (1968) and Chile (1973) (Perlmutter 1981, 152). What does this turn to authoritarianism involve? According to prominent scholars (O'Donnell 1975; Collier 1979; Cardoso and Faletto 1978), this "new authoritarianism" or "bureaucratic authoritarianism," as O'Donnell has labeled it, is characterized by a "self-avowedly technocratic, bureaucratic, nonpersonalistic approach to policy making and problem solving" (Collier 1979, 400). These regimes are exclusionary in terms of political participation, technocratic in style, and oriented toward economic growth for legitimation; and they thrive, therefore, on a mixture of political apathy and economic mobilization.

In addition to the authoritarian character of regimes undergoing dependent industrialization, these same countries have public sectors in which the state is heavily involved in economic activities, not just indirectly through providing loans, infrastructure, and the right "economic climate" for business. Rather, the state directly enters the production process either as a partner with private capital or as a wholly owned state enterprise. Cardoso and Faletto point out that in Brazil, Chile, Columbia, Peru, Mexico, and Venezuela the public sector contributes more than 50 percent to capital formation (1978, 203). Indeed, the literature on "the state as entrepreneur" has mushroomed (Bennett and Sharpe 1980; Baer, Newfarmer, and Trebat 1977; Duvall and Freeman 1983), and perceptive, as well as careful studies of the interrelationships among state capital, foreign capital, and local private capital have been carried out (Evans 1979).

While the shift to authoritarian governments was pronounced in Latin America, especially to the extent that it occurred on the heels of populist governments attempting to broaden the base of political participation, the intensification of authoritarian rule in East Asia presents a more complex picture. To be sure, the transition from import-substitution policies of the 1950s to export-oriented industrialization (EOI) policies of the 1960s was accompanied by a repression of labor. The stimulation of manufactured exports based on cheap labor and the simultaneous restructuring of the economy away from agriculture toward light manufacturing and later toward heavier industries have been centerpieces in the economic strategies of South Korea, Singapore, Taiwan, and, to a lesser extent, the Philippines and Malaysia. This change of economic strategy was accompanied by controls on labor and with a decrease, rather than growth, in the power of organized labor (Deyo 1984, 268). In both South Korea and Singapore "the EOI initiative was accompanied by imposition of drastic controls over labor, in both cases including deregistration of unions, jailing of labor militants, and enactment of major legislative restrictions on collective action" (Deyo 1984, 277).

In the same article, Deyo also demonstrated that low levels of unionization were not the result of declining levels of organization in established industries, but rather of weak labor organization in the new ascending export industries such as electronics, plastics, and garment manufacturing (Deyo 1984, 28). Thus when changes in the labor force are viewed at the margins, rather than for the economy as a whole, the negative link between manufacturing growth and union strength becomes quite pronounced.

Other weaknesses could be mentioned, even though they cannot be examined in a detailed way in this chapter. The effects of rapid growth on internal income inequality, the possibilities of creating massive sectoral imbalances, economic disintegration among sectors, and massive displacement of workers from rural farm households to urban centers are all important phenomena. But the superficial empirical record is far from unequivocal. South Korea and Taiwan have much less inequality than would exist under a tradeoff-pessimist model of "the more growth the less equality," while perhaps Brazil and Mexico have more. The point in this section is not to draw up a balance sheet of costs and benefits of peripheral industrialization, but to sensitize ourselves to the complexity involved and to point to areas where future research is needed.

The relocation of capital in peripheral regions of the world had, and continues to have, profound consequences. One important consequence concerns the creation of jobs in low-technology manufacturing sectors of the periphery and attendant, though not necessarily offsetting, loss of jobs in the core. Bluestone and Harrison report on extensive job losses and plant closings in the United States in steel, machines, automobiles, apparel, and electronics (1982, 25, 27), and Aho and Rousslang demonstrate job losses associated with trade-sensitive sectors of the U.S. economy (1979).

The movement of the industrial capital from core to peripheral countries is already part of the historical record, but the long-term consequences are not well understood. Does the pattern of limited, dependent industrialization signal a new era for LDCs, and does it foretell a fundamental break with the old international division of labor? Are the LDCs on the verge of a long technological ascent of which the newly industrializing countries provide only the first phase? The opportunities for economic restructuring within the advanced capitalist world, the transition from industry to services (in terms of employment if not output), and the enthusiasm with which core capital moves to the periphery all suggest more of the same. On the other hand, job losses in the core, the possibilities of a labor backlash, the economic nationalism (of which trade protection is only a part) which has already taken root, and the intensification of automation and robotization (Junne 1984) are forces working in the other direction.

The Rise of Global Production-Sharing

At the most general level, global production-sharing refers to the increasing integration or articulation of production processes across national lines. The term "sharing" may be misleading and is not intended to convey the idea of symmetry of interests, rewards, and bargaining power. It does, however, indicate a process of industrial integration or mutual engagement of productive forces and, possibly, an extension of the idea of economic rationality to a global level. At a more specific level, global production-sharing may mean the actual joint ownership of productive facilities and coproduction agreements, vertical integration of firms and industries, or subcontracting processes.

Coproduction arrangements. Although the dominant form in which international capital has operated has been through wholly owned subsidiaries, joint-ownership schemes are becoming increasingly popular. As Bluestone and O'Cleireacain point out (1984, 384-5), cooperative ventures have been undertaken in industrial sectors such as commercial aircraft, automobiles, electronics, and telecommunications. The much publicized agreement between General Motors and Toyota to produce a subcompact in Fremont, California, is but one example. U.S. workers will gain jobs, the corporate structure of GM will gain about $1 billion in design savings, and Toyota will circumvent possible import quotas and local content requirements (Bluestone and O'Cleireacain 1984, 384-5). Japanese automobile workers are, of course, the losers.

Joint production arrangements are becoming increasingly popular as a way of bringing about "superior trades" in the utilization of cross-national cost advantages in design, capital sourcing, management skills, technological differences, labor costs, and tax differences, just to mention a few categories where important cross-national differences may exist. A second rationale is one of reducing economic nationalism which, it is hoped, occurs by creating crosscutting ties. Pluralism and the logic of multiple, crosscutting loyalties and interests are transferred to the global scale. A third rationale is that while firms may prefer to operate with wholly owned subsidiaries, they may have little choice but to join forces with host-country capital. If LDCs require joint ownership as a condition for access, foreign firms will have to comply, or lose their market shares to competitors.

There are numerous forces making global production sharing an increasingly frequent phenomenon. Improvements in transportation and communications make it technically possible (Barnet 1980), the rise of economic nationalism in LDCs makes it politically prudent, and the fragmentation of the labor process makes it socially feasible and economically efficient (Fröbel et al. 1980; Levin and Rumberger 1983).

The last factor calls for an additional word. The fragmentation, or specialization, of labor has a long and venerable history within classical political economy. Indeed, it was the subject of Adam Smith's famous chapter 1 of book 1 of the *Wealth of Nations.* To the extent that the labor process can be disaggregated (broken down into finer and finer job tasks), then to that extent the production process is likely to become more efficient and the labor process more deskilled, substitutable, and alienated. As Braverman put it:

> Insofar as the labor process may be disassociated, it may be separated into elements some of which are simpler than others and each of which is simpler than the whole. Translated into market terms, this means that the labor power capable of performing this process may be purchased more cheaply as disassociated elements than as a capacity integrated in a single worker. (1974, 81-2)

Vertical integration. The term vertical integration refers to a form of organization whereby a firm joins together, in one corporate logic and a single organizational unit, many different phases of the production process, potentially covering the sourcing of productive factors and extending to marketing the final products. A firm that operates according to the principles of vertical integration has several distinct advantages. By organizing its factor and product markets and integrating its operations upstream and downstream, a firm creates for itself a kind of protective envelope that cushions it from market forces, locks potentially independent producers into its organizational hierarchy, and provides for itself additional flexibility (in tax practices, for example). Gereffi's (1983) superb analysis of U.S. transnational pharmaceutical corporations in Mexico shows convincingly that these firms benefited from transfer-pricing policies linked to the pharmaceutical firms' vertically integrated structure. In addition, because the TNCs locked Mexican raw material suppliers into downstream operations on which they were ultimately dependent, and because efforts on the part of Mexican suppliers to extend processing operations under their control ran into superior organizational and scientific capabilities of the TNCs, the TNC could maintain ultimate control.

What are the effects of this corporate structure for the LDC? It lessens the LDC's autonomy, takes pricing power away from it, and allows the TNC to create and exploit barriers to entry at certain locations within the overall productive structure—most importantly at the level of the production of science and technology upon which the production and sale of pharmaceuticals depends. By integrating vertically, the TNC can create the conditions under which it may differentially control various aspects of the production process. At the level of raw materials supply and crude processing, transnationals encourage a proliferation of suppliers. At the higher levels of technological sophistication, they limit competition—and these firms have the capacity to do this because of their ability to constantly innovate. They control the innovations through patents and by carefully guarding the scientific knowledge on which they are based. In turn, this ability to control various parts of the production process results in downward pressure on prices at the stages of raw material supply and intermediate products and upward pressure on the technologically sophisticated end of the continuum. Once again, Gereffi's case studies in Mexico demonstrate very nicely the price movements over time for raw materials, intermediate inputs, and finished products (Gereffi 1983, 108).

International subcontracting. In contrast to foreign direct investment, international subcontracting involves very little, if anything, in the way of transfer of physical production facilities, technology, and managerial know-how. It may involve all of these things, but the logic of the process appears to move in the opposite direction: it minimizes the actual transfer of physical capital, reduces "sunk costs," and maximizes the ability of a firm to pick up and move to another location, should the opportunity arise. It is the logic of "footloose" industries and "runaway shops" moving easily around the globe to exploit changing opportunities and constraints.

Subcontracting refers to a process whereby a firm in one part of the world contracts with a producer in another part of the world to produce a product, component, or service, which is then fitted into a more complex production or marketing scheme of the parent country firm. The contractee (usually an LDC firm) produces solely for the purpose of marketing its goods in the advanced country or, if they are marketed in another country, they are marketed with the facilities of the advanced country. Subcontracting processes can take several forms: first, they can be contracted by producer firms who want to fit the component into a larger product; or second, they can be subcontracted by a retail firm that just wants to sell the product. The contracting party may provide production facilities, such as loan capital, physical equipment, or technical assistance. The foreign firm is now assured of a market, but it keeps this assurance only at the price of producing for a particular firm. Again, this locks it into a structure of production and marketing in much the same way that vertical integration operates.

Subcontracting activity has increased tremendously over the years, particularly to the LDCs. In 1969, U.S. imports of subcontracted goods were six times as high as the 1966 level and in 1973 they were twenty-five times as high. What kinds of goods tend to be subcontracted? First of all, they are labor-intensive goods. It is important not only in the LDC, but also in the advanced country, that the goods be produced by labor-intensive means; in fact it is critical that the particular product area resists mechanization in the advanced country. The second point is that the whole product does not have to be labor-intensive. It is only necessary that relevant segments of the production process are so.

What has been the impact of international subcontracting? We know that this form of activity provides jobs and does so with a minimum of dependence on direct foreign investment, the difficult and costly business of identifying foreign markets, advertising in them, and distributing their goods for sale—this is all done by the contracting firm. However, international subcontracting has created a new form of dependency. The LDC firm is tied into a vertically integrated production process and depends upon the parent company to sell its goods. If the firm does not, there is no guarantee that the LDC firm can sell them on its own. Indeed, orders are such that they may be tailor-made for very refined markets, making transfer of them to other markets difficult. In addition, the contracting firm has a great deal of flexibility: it can switch contracts from one firm to another or from one country to another; it is much easier to switch a subcontracting arrangement than it is for a TNC to switch locations. In the latter case, there are huge physical facilities in place and large sunk costs, all of which make it difficult and costly to pull out. Furthermore, many TNCs locate where they do because of access to some raw material or market.

The threat to move, or even a capacity for moving, gives a great bargaining edge to the advanced country; and this, in turn, has stimulated competition among LDCs for access to the contracts and markets of the advanced countries. Competition takes the form of better terms, with respect to tax holidays, infrastructure, subsidies, cheap credit, and control of wages. Upward adjustment can take place, as it has in Hong Kong and Singapore, but, when it does, there simply has to be room above to move into a higher position in the international division of labor.

Peripheralization of Labor in the Core

What may or may not be a trend is not given by brute descriptive facts—it is also, at least, partly a matter of theoretical interpretation. Without theory, it becomes impossible to distinguish short-term discontinuities and cyclical phenomena from the more durable structural effects. This methodological point is most relevant to the third trend, since there is no standard, universally acceptable body of data by which to verify whether this trend exists. No doubt, parts of the labor force in advanced capitalist countries have benefited from changes in the international division of labor. Some occupations have been "bumped" upward in the technological ladder while others have found specialized and, at least momentarily protected, niches. However, in this section I will address myself to labor in general and try to identify patterns.

An analysis of trends concerning labor in advanced capitalist countries requires a clear reference point from the start. It requires a picture of the position of core labor in the international political economy. In the standard world system description, core labor is represented as high-wage, skilled, organizationally strong, protected by a strong state against international labor markets, and benefiting from unequal exchange with products produced in the periphery (Emmanuel 1972). In part, the labor wages in the core countries are high because of the high productivity of labor there, but also in part because of the organizational power of labor and its consequent ability to extract larger "concessions" (i.e., larger shares of their total output) from capital. So quite apart from questions of differentials in labor skills, productivities, etc., core labor is paid better wages because of its historical achievements in class struggle. In the end, the exploitation of labor in the core is less than that of labor in the periphery (Amin 1977, 126).

The issue of differential power (and hence rewards) of labor in core and periphery forms a centerpiece for theories of unequal exchange. Leaving aside for the moment the profound problems that the absence of a well worked-out theory of value poses for such theories, contemporary arguments fall into two categories. On the one hand are those who see the privileged position of core labor deriving from the process of unequal exchange itself (Wallerstein and Prebisch). Because of various factors such as the organizational strength of core labor, its operation in oligopolistic industries, and the protection afforded by strong states, products exported by the core are able to extract higher prices than products imported from peripheral countries. The process allows core capital the opportunity to provide for the reproduction requirements of their workers at a cheaper wage, since the commodity basket of labor is now cheaper. This, in turn, fosters higher rates of accumulation, which allows for higher wages in the long run.

The other viewpoint is that core labor does not so much benefit from the exchange process as that the exchange process incorporates (represents, reflects) inequalities generated by differential rates of exploitation in the domestic system of production. Ross and Trachte (1983, 399) demonstrate that Amin, by starting from different premises, is able to reach different conclusions. Amin (1976) tries to show that the existence of large labor surpluses in many LDCs (surpluses existing because of simultaneous buildups of urban-industrial centers and rural disintegration) exerts continual downward pressure on the price of industrial labor. By contrast, advanced capitalist countries differ strongly in degree, if not in kind. To be sure, the concept of a reserve army of unemployed is applicable, and high rates of unemployed show that there is still substance to this old idea. But the historical supply of workers streaming from the rural sector is now gone, the agricultural work force having approached its minimum in the United States, Canada, and most of Western Europe. Besides, the unemployed are often not quite so destitute, and hence not anxious for "work at any price." They have what some have called a "social wage," a politically guaranteed minimum that makes labor markets "less flexible," as some neoclassical economists put it.

However idealized this picture of strong core labor may be, it forms the starting point for our assessment. In the remainder of this section on the peripheralization of core labor, I want to comment on the historic successes of labor, the responses of capital, and the consequent dimunition of labor's position in core countries.

Historic success of core labor. By comparison with labor in less developed countries, core labor has made enormous historic strides. As Bergquist points out, these gains took place in two arenas, inside the state and the market (1984, 9). Capital was forced to concede a larger share of output to labor while the state brought about "a significant redistribution of wealth and a weakening of the disciplinary power of the capitalist labor market by leaving in place the social welfare institutions won by popular forces during the world crisis" (Bergquist 1984, 9).

The power of labor stemmed from two sources. On the one hand, it became increasingly effective at organizing itself and in transmuting its latent strength into an active organizational weapon. Unionization was itself important, as was the capacity of labor to work through the various political party structures. Perhaps just as important is what Arrighi and Silver call "workplace bargaining power," the ability of workers to exert more pressure on capital right at the point of production, rather than in the state arena (1984, 193-4). The increasing concentration and centralization of capital increased its vulnerability to workers' demands within the workplace. From the historic struggles of the nineteenth century, intensified during the Depression and the post-World War II era, labor and capital reached a compromise; a social contract took shape that rested on a recognition of each other's strengths and limits. To labor went a recognition of its organizational existence and power and its right to strike, as well as higher wages and benefits. At the political level, the state increased its contribution to labor in the form of what Bowles and Gintis call the "citizen wage," "that part of a person's consumption supplied by the state by virtue of his citizenship rather than directly acquired by the sale of labor power. . . ." (Bowles and Gintis 1982, 53). In return, labor gave up a say in price policy, organization of production, and decisions concerning investment (Arrighi and Silver 1984, 202). Questions of ownership and production, workers' control, and accumulation itself were pushed aside in favor of high wages and benefits.

Labor's "Faustian pact" turned out to be short-sighted because it failed to acknowledge the asymmetries of power and flexibility between capital and labor inherent in the structural positions of their own compromise. For a while, it appeared as if the bargain that labor made had paid off: the post-Depression and postwar years saw escalating growth rates and consistent real wage increases. However, these forces masked the rivalry inherent in the capital-labor relationship because foreign investment was predominantly among advanced countries themselves, and differentials in wages did not appear as the crucial issue. But all of this was to change. Labor's increased strength spawned new efforts by capital to circumvent labor's gains, efforts that ultimately led to the removal of some industries' physical capital from core countries.

Capital's response. By the mid- to late-1960s, capital was operating in an environment increasingly inhospitable to its activities. If this was not true in an absolute sense, it was more and more so for the business environment in LDCs: in terms of economics, domestic capital's opportunity costs of staying inside the core increased over time. The high cost of labor—from the private and the citizen wage, the regulation of business, the internalization of external costs of production (e.g., pollution)—contributed to lowering the rate of profits. In this kind of environment, any move to low-wage LDCs was likely to be followed quickly by other industrial rivals, and the cost of not doing so was likely to be a loss of market shares. Therefore, the TNCs, as well as other forms of international capital, were critically important in emancipating capital from its domestic shell and in providing it with a scope, flexibility, and bargaining power far superior to labor's.

Capital pursued strategies on several fronts. As Bergquist points out:

> The multinational corporation evolved as an effort by capital to take advantage of the opportunities for accumulation, and avoid constraints on that process, that were embodied in these various victories of popular forces. In the United States core it served as a vehicle for disinvestment, thus enabling capitalists to elude high and expanding labor and taxation costs at home, yet take advantage of increased domestic demand fostered by those wages and the redistributionist policies of the social welfare regime. (1984, 10)

Other strategies were important too, as Bluestone and Harrison show (1982, 166). For example, avoiding labor unions became increasingly sophisticated, first within a national, and later an international, context. Another strategy, parallel production, involved the establishment of production facilities within the same industry in different national settings. This means that when labor pressure and demands within one setting are too high, duplicate production facilities in other countries can be stimulated, and capital can circumvent (and thus attenuate) labor's position:

> Parallel production is often implemented even when it involves foregoing some economies of scale at the original site. The compensation to the company is that a strike or other form of disruption at the original shop can be met by redirecting more production to the non-union facility. In this way the firm can break a strike without even committing a statutory unfair labor practice. (Bluestone and Harrison 1982, 166)

Of course, the consequences for core labor are serious: loss of jobs, income losses, unemployment among females and minorities, and social and psychological disruption (Nash 1983, 12). Fröbel and coauthors put the job-loss estimates in textiles and apparel alone, in Germany during the 1970s, at over 357,000 (Fröbel et al. 1980), while Bluestone and Harrison (1982) estimate that 32 million jobs were lost in the United States during the decade of the 1970s, due to investments and plant closings. And, while the latter is not a net figure (i.e., it does not deal with jobs created), it nevertheless provides an indication of the magnitude of economic disruptions in society. Quite apart from whether or not people are permanently without work, they are fated to become economic gypsies, in endless pursuit of shifting jobs.

Finally, what are we to make of that elusive quality, *the culture of work*? Here we are confronted with an irony: the "culture of work," or the "work ethic," seems to have evolved in orchestration with a historically antithetical theme—the idea that all work shall be provided (or not provided) by the market. This has put industrial man in a curious position. Work was more and more touted as the centerpiece of meaningful participation in society, at precisely the same time that industrial society committed itself to a technological dynamic that was bound to destroy jobs. Thus, the ideology of industrial capitalism put an accent on work only to eliminate it: it created the moral incentives for work only to continually destroy or shift work's material base. The ethos of industrial capitalism, if there was one, was of technical rationality, efficiency, and progress; this was bound to replace labor with capital, to deskill work, and fragment the production process. And to put the issue of scale into perspective, this ceaseless energy of capitalism—its "need" to accumulate, its constant technical progress and social destruction—is not qualitatively new. But the fact that these processes operate on a global scale means that they respond to global stimuli, and the domestic consequences are more frequent and more intense.

Effects on core labor. In spite of the fact that changes in the global division of labor have profoundly affected labor in the core, some economists are inclined to argue that, in the long run at least, these changes will be for the better. These economists see such changes as part of a process of creative destruction, whereby a healthy economy sheds its old occupational skins and dons new ones for the years ahead. Whereas the substitution of new industries for old ones entails a certain amount of dislocation, such substitution is not without certain progressive effects. Old, less productive industries will die off and new, more productive ones will be added. The newer ones will be cleaner, more efficient, of higher technology, require more education and skills, and provide higher wage returns. Thus, the economies of core countries will advance, in part through a reskilling of extant jobs, in part by the selective accumulation of new job cohorts.

The problem with this scenario is that it does not seem to be supported by the facts. In the remainder of this section I will argue that in addition to the loss of jobs in the core, with the deterioration of permanent income for the reemployed and the decreased bargaining power of labor, core labor has been negatively affected in several ways, sometimes counterintuitively. Further, I will discuss the intensification of labor immigration into some core cities, the reappearance of sweatshops and cheap labor in the core, and the restructuring of the U.S. economy, at least partly, in a downward direction.

Earlier I noted the movement of capital from core areas to the periphery and how this process was used to bypass wage demands and to increase the bargaining power of capital. This exiting of capital, however, has created a partial vacuum in the core, which is being filled in numerous ways. A focus on New York City may help to illustrate some of the patterns.

In a pioneering article, Ross and Trachte (1983) document the severe loss of jobs in the manufacturing sector in New York City. Using data from 1950 to 1981, they show that New York lost more than one-half of all jobs in manufacturing, or 545,000 jobs. When the data are disaggregated, the decline goes from 230,000 to 116,000 in durable goods, 808,000 to 419,000 in nondurable goods, and 341,000 to 140,000 in apparel and textile industries (Ross and Trachte 1983, 408-9). They then argue that the response to manufacturing capital outflow and job loss in the manufacturing sector has occurred on two fronts. On the one front, jobs have been created in the administrative and service sectors, for bank tellers, file clerks, secretaries, janitors, sales clerks, and accountants. On the other, there is a revival of manufacturing (often clandestine) in low-wage, nonunionized areas, often employing immigrant labor. Once again, Ross and Trachte (1983) and Sassen-Koob (1983) provide both insights and important data. In New York City during the 1970s, there were perhaps fewer than 200 garment sweatshops while, by 1983, this figure had grown to between 3,000 and 4,500, employing large numbers of migrants, many illegal, from the Caribbean, Latin America, and the Far East (Ross and Trachte 1983, 416).

Sassen-Koob (1983) documents the new flow of migrant labor from the periphery to core starting from the mid-1960s. She rightly notes the irony attending the simultaneous outflow of capital and inflow of labor, an irony that dissolves only by seeing part of the labor market in core cities as basically peripheral in character. New York City, while dramatic in the way it combines these seemingly antithetical flows, is not unique; the large migrations from the Caribbean Basin and Southeast Asia have been directed to London and Los Angeles (Sassen-Koob 1983, 185-6).

The outflow of industrial capital, along with the inflow of foreign labor, have combined to make the conditions for the operation of capital more attractive in core cities. While the garment industry in New York was one of the most seriously damaged sectors during the 1960s and 1970s, it has been undergoing a revival since the late 1970s, which is concentrated in selected areas. In Chinatown, the garment industry has been thriving, growing from about 180 factories in 1970 to 400 by the end of the decade (Sassen-Koob 1983, 194). As Ross and Trachte say:

> New York sweatshop workers, who typically earn less than $1.75 per hour, receive wages more like those of apparel workers in Singapore and Hong

> Kong than their counterparts in Sweden, the Netherlands, and Belgium. (1983, 416)

Although the picture is far from complete, and despite the existence of contradictory trends, it appears that the peripheralization of labor in New York City is not an isolated case. In a series of papers, Levin and Rumberger (1983, 1984) start to provide an answer to the important question, posed by Sassen-Koob, of where the jobs will come from to employ immigrant labor. Contrary to much opinion about the "high-tech, high-service economy," new jobs are not, and will not be, predominantly in the high-tech sector nor will existing jobs be adjusted upward in their skill requirements (Levin and Rumberger 1983, 2). Using data and growth projections provided by the U.S. Bureau of Labor Statistics, Levin and Rumberger note that employment will increase by 22 million between 1978 and 1990. Included in this 22 million are jobs created in high-technology areas: computer systems analysts, data processing machine mechanics, and computer operators. While these job categories are characterized by high growth rates, they do not account for substantial absolute increases in jobs since the increases proceed from a small base. When absolute numbers are examined, the job increases are accounted for by low-technology industries and unskilled services. Levin and Rumberger provide us with a dramatic result: out of the twenty job categories that are expected to generate the most jobs from 1978 to 1990, not one is high technology (1983, 4). Indeed, the five occupations expected to produce the most jobs are janitors, nurses' aides, sales clerks, cashiers, and waiters and waitresses. Only two of the top twenty categories require a college degree (1983, 5). Insofar as the evidence is available, it simply does not support a transition to a society based on high technology, skilled labor, information and services requiring extremely high levels of education and training.

Female Labor and the Global Political Economy

Despite the historically persistent and geographically pervasive differentiation of labor along gender lines, there has been little systematic attention paid to the place of female labor in political economy. To be sure, there have been feminist writings from well before the twentieth century; in 1640, writers who chose to call themselves "Mary Tattle-Well and Ionne-Hit-Him Home Spinsters," wrote a pamphlet called *The Womens' Sharpe Revenge,* that raised the same issues of work, marriage, and status that preoccupy many writers today. Mary Wollstonecraft's *Vindication of the Rights of Women,* first published in 1792, was one of the first works to question the culture of "female sensibility"—a culture that involved the transition from "goodwife" to "mistress" (George 1973). As prescient as these works were, they did not set forth an analysis of the issues in terms of political economy.

Their aim, understandably enough, was to make society aware of the plight of women, in hopes of opening doors for change. Apart from Engels' *Origins of the Family, Private Property, and the State* (1884), and John Stuart Mill's and Harriet Taylor Mill's *Essays on Sex Equality* (published at different times between 1832 and 1969), there is precious little in the political economy literature that treats the question; and, the writings of Smith, Ricardo and Marx are almost completely lacking in this regard.

The virtue of modern feminist writings is not so much that they present us with a satisfactory theoretical account of the dynamics of women's labor in society, but that these writings hit us squarely with some brute facts. Put in the simplest terms, these facts are as follows: all societies have a gender division of labor (Mackintosh 1981, 1), this division of labor excludes women from certain jobs, it segregates them from status and income categories within broad job classifications, it gives unequal pay for similar jobs, and it has the effect of under-valuing or not valuing (meaning nonpriced rather than unappreciated) women's work in the home (Oakley 1981, 160-3). In addition, studies that have been carried out on the sociology of women's unemployment (Marshall 1984), job segregation (Mackintosh 1981), and the feminization of poverty (Sarvasy and Van Allen 1984) all point to the subsidiary role of women in the political economy.

It is not at all clear that the political system is yet a corrective to women's position in the economy. Nancy Folbre's (1984) examination of government actions in the areas of family policy, labor market policy, and welfare policy all bear out this general thesis, as does Michael Boskin's study showing that "the net effect of the tax system is clearly to drive female labor out of the market into the home . . ." (1974, 256). Finally, the world of political representation is perhaps the most highly stratified of all. Putnam reports that "women are the most underrepresented group in the political elites of the world. . . . In most parliamentary democracies, women constitute about five percent of the national legislature, and a virtually identical ceiling seems to apply to membership in the central committees of the Communist party in such countries as China and Russia" (1976, 32-3).

The transformations of the global political economy, including the changes previously discussed, have been associated with the changing role of women in the labor forces of both core and peripheral countries. The broad patterns include intensified incorporation of women into low-skilled manufacturing and assembly jobs in the Third World, unemployment of women in similar economic sectors within the advanced capitalist world, and apparently increasing employment of female labor in higher-skilled, higher-wage occupations in some parts of the advanced capitalist world. In a sense, the declining industries with a concentrated female work force in the core countries provide a complement to that of the ascending industries in the Third World. As Lim points out:

> The labor-intensive industries in which women manufacturing workers are concentrated in mature capitalist economies are the very industries that are losing their comparative cost advantage to newly industrializing countries. It is likely that these labor-intensive industries maintained their comparative advantage as long as they did because they employed the lowest-paid workers in those countries—women, often women of minority races. (Lim 1983, 78)

Indeed, the conclusion seems inescapable that women in core countries working in low-skilled manufacturing occupations, e.g., apparel, footwear, textiles, or electronics, have been damaged by peripheral industrialization and female workers in the periphery have been provided with many more jobs. Indeed, these two phenomena are cosymptoms of the same underlying process—the migration of industrial capital from core to periphery.

Women are also among the groups in the United States most damaged by foreign trade. In a study done for the U.S. Department of Labor, Aho and Rousslang (1979) provide data showing to just what extent female workers were affected by trade. They isolated forty trade-sensitive industrial sectors; of these, twenty were the most negatively affected by foreign trade and twenty the most positively affected. Women comprised an average of 57.2 percent of the work force in negatively impacted industries and 20 percent in the positively impacted industries. Percentage figures were highest in "apparel made from purchased material," "footwear except rubber," and "watches, clocks, and parts" (Aho and Rousslang 1979, 5).

It is highly likely, however, that women are not uniformly losing in all sectors of the economy. Lawrence has carried out an interesting study for the Brookings Institute, in which he examines the effects of economic dislocations in the U.S. economy on the distribution of income earnings. He found that although the middle class had declined somewhat, the decline was confined exclusively to males. The share of low-income-earning females in every sector of the economy was found to be shrinking, while the proportions of females in the middle- and upper-class categories increased (1984, 4).

The redeployment of capital on the global scale has increased the reliance on female labor in labor-intensive manufacturing industries in the Third World. The transition from import-substitution policies to "outward-oriented industrialization" (export promotion, the construction of free enterprise zones and other policies to attract foreign capital) all intensified the search for cheap labor in low-skilled, nonunionized manufacturing sectors. This labor turned out to be mostly female. Fröbel et al. report that in West German subsidiaries operating in low-wage countries, 43 percent of those employed are younger than twenty and more than 90 percent are female (Fröbel et al. 1980, 18). Similarly, a study of women workers in Mauritius shows that the "majority of women factory workers are under age 25 (70 percent), are single (77 percent) and have completed, or almost completed, primary school (74) percent)" (Hein 1984, 254). And just to provide some idea of the wage gaps, an unskilled worker in 1976 received 55 cents in Hong Kong, 52 cents in South Korea, 32 cents in the Philippines, and 17 cents in Indonesia (Ehrenreich and Fuentes 1981, 54). The incorporation of women into the labor force in the Third World constitutes an important change in the international division of labor, the consequences of which we have barely begun to assess. There are a large number of sources which either claim or provide evidence that females are marked by characteristics that make them more desirable workers. Among these reputed characteristics are docility, dependability, dexterity, conscientiousness, and a disinclination to join unions or engage in strikes (Barnet 1980, 256; Hein 1984, 262; Lim 1983, 78). Whether these traits are in the realm of fact or folklore, we do not know; but what seems clear is that employers believe them to be true—a fact that gives them an independent significance.

The descriptive accuracy of these facts can hardly be disputed. What is more controversial is how to explain them. Theorists of many different persuasions have found the set of issues discussed here most difficult to deal with. Part of the problem is that issues of gender are so interconnected with those of class, status, and familial relations that it is difficult to disentangle them. To what extent is the division of labor in some sense natural, i.e., given by biological differences between men and women? To what extent is this division a socially determined process? If it is a socially determined process, how much of it can be explained by reference to the process of capital accumulated, differential, and perhaps socially constructed, preferences of women and men and by the patriarchal structuring of male-dominance relations?

These are, of course, difficult questions to answer and, besides this, there have been many unhelpful starting points. To view the labor market as one homogeneous pool of labor resources is not a useful way to begin. If we start this way, the striking descriptive differences in women's and men's work become inexplicable, except by appealing to preferences between men and women for different kinds of work. Tautologies aside, it seems preposterous to speak of a woman's special "taste" for housework or for children, the latter sometimes treated as "consumer durables" with a given lifespan in the home. Similarly, the concepts of productive and unproductive labor, as elaborated by Smith in *The Wealth of Nations,* and by Marx in *Theories of Surplus Value,* have not taken us very far, except by providing us with a category within which to situate domestic labor. In attempting to understand the division of labor between men and women, scholars from different traditions have developed the household economy model. As Deere and de Janvry point out, in peasant societies the household is both a unit of production in the economic sense, as well as the chief unit of reproductive activity (1979, 1-2). With the emergence and evolution of industrial capitalism, a bifurcation took place that separated household relations and productive activities. As Secombe put it in an article titled "The Housewife and Her Labour Under Capitalism," the domestic unit became increasingly responsible for the reproduction of labor power for the labor market, while a differentiated industrial sphere assumed a primary role in producing goods and services for the commodity market. This split in the labor process was virtually congruent with the division of labor along gender lines (1974, 6).

This split between household and commodity labor has encouraged an understanding that sees housework and household activities as separate, indeed qualitatively distinct from, economic activities in general. Indeed, some have seen household work as so different that it lies outside the law of value. Olivia Harris (1981) has developed this argument, while not subscribing to it, on the basis of the work of Sahlins (an economic anthropologist) and Chayanov (a Russian economist). Chayanov's basic idea was that the peasant economy was not based on the same calculations as a capitalist firm but was instead oriented toward the consumption needs of the household (Harris 1981, 53). Sahlins, with his "domestic mode of production," argues that there is a difference in the way exchange takes place within, as compared to between, households; intrahousehold relations are characterized by the pooling of resources, and interhousehold relations by more finely calibrated exchange mechanisms (Harris 1981, 54). Although there are, no doubt, substantial differences within and among households, the domestic mode of production elevates these differences into two qualitatively distinct realms, and hence cuts off our understanding of the ways in which the household functions in the general economy.

Whatever the merits or limitations of the domestic mode of production, the evidence is clear that the division of labor is not physiologically determined. There is nothing natural about a division between household and commodity production, just as there is no asocial determination of what is women's and men's work. Boserup's important empirical findings on the cross-cultural diversity of the gender division of labor in agricultural production is striking (Deere 1982, 795). Not only did the content of men's and women's work vary across cultures, but it also changed over time in response to variations in land tenure, type of cultivation, technology and employment (Deere 1982, 795-6). Boserup's systematic findings are supported by more interpretive works. Margaret George's (1973) "From 'Goodwife' to 'Mistress': The Transformation of the Female in Bourgeois Culture" provides insights into the changes in women's role in domestic and societal labor, the withdrawal from commodified labor, and the assumption of domestic tasks.

Perhaps some progress can be made in understanding the division of labor along gender lines through the application of segmented labor market theory. If we start from one of the fundamental premises of segmented labor market theories, that cleavages are important in structuring economic activities, gender differences present themselves as one important source of cleavage. These cleavages may be important in allocating jobs, establishing wage differentials, employment priorities, benefits and the seasonality of work. If gender differences are seen in this light, we may provide ourselves with theoretical leverage in understanding work in both the household and the commodified economies.

The basic segmented labor market model has been set forth in an earlier chapter of this book. The "minimalist idea," as Berger and Piore (1980, 17) put it, is that the economy is composed of two sectors: a primary sector containing high-wage, usually skilled jobs, and a secondary sector containing low-wage, usually unskilled jobs. The second category is disproportionatly staffed by youths, racial and ethnic minorities, and women. This is the most primitive version of the model, but even this version encourages us to frame our analysis in potentially helpful ways.

To take a few simple examples of the role of women in the economy we can start with temporary work, which, according to both Berger and Piore (1980, 39) and Oakley (1981, 159), is carried out predominantly by women. Oakley shows that, in 1976, in Great Britain 40 percent of the employed women worked part time compared to 5 percent of employed men (1981, 159). In addition, there is often a substitution effect between women's unemployment and older workers (Berger and Piore 1980, 39), suggesting that women's jobs compete at the margin with employment opportunities for other peripheral groups. And third, in Italy it has been shown that increases in female employment occur partly in response to progress in the unionization of males (Berger and Piore 1980, 31). What these examples suggest is, at the very least, that women play not only a role very different from men's in the economy but a very definite, perhaps theoretically determinable, one.

The understanding of female work, and the gender divisions of labor in general, has suffered from neglect by both neoclassical economics and Marxian economic theory. Neoclassical economics has found household work uninteresting because it lies outside the pale of price theory, while Marxian economics has tended to neglect household work because it constitutes unproductive labor, producing only use values but no surplus, hence no accumulation. What is exciting, and promising, about recent work in feminism, Marxism, and segmented labor market theories, is the effort to theoretically integrate the functioning of labor markets with the gender division of labor and the process of capital accumulation. Maureen Mackintosh puts the case for this approach very well:

> The method of argument in this approach is to try to show that, because of the existence of the sexual division of labour, capital is able to extract greater profits from its workforce than would otherwise be the case. Within

> the sphere of wage work, for example, women have long formed a cheap labour force, paid less relative to their productivity than men, and the effect of this has been to increase profits both within developed industrial capitalist countries and in the Third World. . . . It has also been suggested that capital benefits from using women as a "reserve army" of labour: a flexible supply of workers who can be absorbed in a phase of expansion, and thrown out—not merely out of work but out of the labour force, back into dependency within the home. (Mackintosh 1981, 5)

Mackintosh's analysis of female labor in the commodified sector provides a picture of the economy that is quite similar to Berger and Piore's dual economy mode. The existence of a large female labor pool that is predominantly unorganized and more willing than men to accept temporary employment, provides a powerful stabilizing element to the economy. Similarly, Mackintosh attempts to incorporate household work into a general theory of the labor process and capital accumulation. Not content with leaving housework at the level of unproductive labor (meaning once again unproductive of a surplus), she points out that:

> Unpaid labour within the home, almost all done by women, raises the standard of living of the working class above that provided by the wage alone, and provides the services of care and socialization of children, that is, of the future labour force. (Mackintosh 1981, 5)

Household work, by providing use values that otherwise would have to be bought as exchange values, can be assessed within an opportunity cost framework. How much would it cost to purchase the goods and services produced by household work on the open market? The existence of commercial dry cleaners, launderers, housecleaning companies, day-care centers, and even food-shopping entrepreneurs provides us with clear price standards by which to calculate the "worth" of housework. And once this worth is calculated, we have a good measure of housework's replacement cost. Seen in this light, it becomes clear that housework plays a major role in lowering the cost of the bundle of commodities consumed by labor, and hence lowers the wage bill. From here, we are but a short step away from the role of household labor in the process of capital accumulation.

The Rise of Industrial Policy

We arrive here at the fifth and last trend to be discussed—the rise of industrial policy. As with the other trends, this one should not be viewed in an isolated way but, rather, as closely connected with the rest. Once again, industrial policy is not a new phenomenon. Alexander Hamilton's *Report on Manufactures* (1792), List's *National System of Political Economy* (1904), and Lloyd George's policy documents, *Britain's Industrial Future* (1928) and *We Can Conquer Unemployment* (1929) display a rich tradition of industrial-policy thinking that spans the eighteenth through the twentieth centuries.

Despite the historical longevity of the practice of industrial policy, the idea goes down with difficulty in many places. In the United States there is something approaching consensus among mainstream (i.e., neoclassical) economists on the undesirability of industrial policy (see the strongly negative views put forward by Charles Schultze, "Industrial Policy: A Dissent," 1983) and, among policy makers, it is viewed as a self-aggrandizing, if not pernicious, attempt at a substitute for sound macroeconomic policies. Industrial policy is viewed as a variation on the mercantilist theme, based on an antiquarian economic philosophy that has not yet absorbed the message of Adam Smith, as well as a thinly veiled guise for the historical processes of state-building or the prevention of economic decline. Indeed, to adopt the organic metaphor, one could argue that there are two phases—the first and the last—of the natural cycle of birth, growth, maturation, and decline in which industrial policy is pronounced: paternalism (the beginning), in which arguments for infant industry are rife, and a senescent protectionism, in which declining sectors clamor for security (the end).

The objection to industrial policy is somewhat understandable. Subsidies to steel industries, tax advantages for export-oriented industries, price supports for farmers, and depletion allowances for oil companies do not constitute a list that smacks of the public interest. In part, industrial policy does pursue the logic of mercantilism, for it is an attempt by special interests to secure monopoly privileges through the channels of state power (Ekelund and Tollison 1981, 5). But, industrial policy can be used to identify leading sectors (those exerting the greatest pull on the rest of the economy), to stimulate research and development, to align the educational system with the changing occupational structure, and to aid in the formulation of an industrially relevant science policy.

The arguments about the strengths and limitations of industrial policy will continue, and those who elevate efficiency above all other values (e.g., community, tradition, security) will almost surely oppose it. But industrial policy efforts are not motivated simply by declining industrial sectors where productivity improvements are responsible for job losses (*Economic Report of the President* 1981, 196); indeed, it is by no means clear that economic sectors where job losses are high show lower growth rates than elsewhere. It may be simply that cheap labor in these sectors in foreign countries causes capital to flow out, because it is in these industries that the comparative cost advantages are greatest between core and periphery, thus causing core industries to decline. In other words, declining industries may be a result, rather than cause, of capital migration. Whatever the merits of the arguments for and against industrial policy, it is fair to say that every country in the world has one, and it is almost unimaginable not to have one. To think of making decisions in a country without affecting the composition and volume of trade, the structure of industrial production, the rate of investment, and the pattern of employment is not plausible. The United States is no exception in this regard, as many scholars have shown (Bluestone and O'Cleireacain 1984; Diebold 1980). However there are large differences among countries in the degree to which industrial policy is conscious, composed, and coherent, rather than simply a label pinned on the industrial consequences of tax laws, energy laws, education policy, and a host of concessions to special interests.

What is industrial policy? Let me begin by defining it broadly as the application of governmental effort toward the shaping of productive and commercial structures of activities. As Miriam Camps has noted, this definition provides a new way of looking at "tariffs, subsidies, and other nontariff barriers (NTBs), environmental controls, special arrangements for particular sectors such as energy or agriculture, company law, regulatory instruments such as antitrust laws, some aspects of foreign investment, [and] some aspects of science technology policy. . . ." (Camps 1975, 23). Although the conscious use of industrial policy is not new, its application in Western Europe underwent a dramatic change in the late 1960s. With the completion of the customs union and free-trade areas by 1 July 1968, the economies of the European Economic Community (EEC) members were vulnerable to international competition and, as a result, were very sensitive to sectoral or macro changes across borders. Slight increases or decreases in exchange rates, transportation costs, wage-output ratios, inflation rates, and profit margins could make the difference between national or foreign firms supplying the domestic market. The importance of these factors was noted by Guido Colonna Di Paliano, the EEC commissioner for industrial policy, when he argued that, from the time of the customs union "it has appeared necessary for the Commission to define a structural policy which takes as its principal objective the creation of an integrated industrial issue. The common market of products being realized, it is now necessary to create a productive mechanism which corresponds to the dimensions of this market" (Di Paliano 1970, 7).

The dramatic reductions in tariffs and quotas did not exhaust the collection of foreign economic policy tools available to the member states. Instead, the challenge of trade barriers to those outside the community stimulated the inflow of foreign direct investment. Thus, as far as economic competition between the EEC and outsiders (particularly the United States) was concerned, 1968 did not mark the end of an era, but rather the transition point from commodity to capital-technological competition. The surge of foreign capital, first from the United States to Western Europe and later the reverse, stimulated a renewed interest in industrial policy. Tensions between the market for commodities, organized at the international level in Europe, and structures of production, organized at the national level, created a pressure for an industrial policy to enlarge the scope of industrial production. The irony of the European situation, as Di Paliano again pointed out, is that to the extent that productive structures in Europe were continental, this was expressed mostly in the conclusion of agreements with third countries, especially the United States (Di Paliano 1970, 8). It was in this way that emerging global triangles (United States, Japan, Western Europe) and, later rectangles (United States, Western Europe, Japan, and newly industrializing countries), prompted interest in industrial policy at the EEC level. Of course, there were industrial policies among member states also, and they were no doubt even more important than the international efforts in Brussels to shape a unified industrial policy.

At the national level, however, there were many differences: France's penchant for national champions, so evident in the electronics industry (Zysman 1977); the aversion of the United Kingdom and West Germany (despite *soziale Marktwirtschaft*) to intervention in specific sectors (although Germany did intervene in coal, electronics, and aerospace); the inertia of the Italian state in forming any national policy because of widespread distrust; and, the historical anxiety in Sweden that labor-intensive manufacturing was going into a "global squeeze" and thus needed to be phased out in favor of higher value-added manufacturing where high wages could be justified. These variations on industrial policy point to the fact that, although global forces have been pushing in a uniform direction, individual national differences are important in determining policy variations, more or less in accord with a process identified by Katzenstein in *Between Power and Plenty* (1978).

With specific regard to the place of labor in advanced capitalist societies, and the policies of governments regarding the complex of issues centering on unemployment, retraining, declining industrial sectors, and global competition, we can detect a mix of commonalities and differences. Sweden provides wage assistance to workers in declining industries and special incentives to move from labor-intensive, low-value-added industries to less labor-intensive, higher-value-added ones. In France, as Bluestone and O'Cleireacain point out (1984, 392), all firms with ten or more employees make an annual contribution to be used to finance retraining: job maintenance subsidies are widely used in France, Germany, and the United Kingdom. On the other hand, the Reagan administration has increasingly moved to the market—at least in nondefense areas—and has attempted to substitute "good macroeconomic policy" for sectoral interventions. Even the limited assistance provided under the Trade Adjustment Assistance program has been dropped (Bluestone and O'Cleireacain 1984, 392).

Although the weight of decisions concerning industrial policy lies at the national level, it is important to recognize the strong pressures emanating from international society that compel some kind of national response. Without a recognition of the "globality" of the stimuli, one falls into the trap of seeing industrial policies as results of purely subjective national preferences: the United States's aversion to sectoral policy, France's preference for indicative planning, and Japan's blending of public and private power in ways that are often mystifying to Westerners. In addition, viewing national economic decisions that concern industrial policy in terms of which products to produce nationally and which to import, is to miss an important fact about the modern global division of labor: production itself has become internationalized—not just distribution.

The vertically integrated structure of the modern firm allows utilization of international production possibilities. Thus, in our emerging division of labor, where cheap labor in some countries combines with flexible technology and the mobile capital of others, the opportunity to export the labor-intensive aspects of production is more and more taken. For instance, West Germany's Agfa has gone to Japan because of the lower cost of labor, reportedly half that of Germany's, while the camera firm Rollei-Werke has established subsidiaries in Singapore (Levinson 1971, 98-9).

These changes in the international division of labor have had political repercussions at the domestic level. They have affected, and will continue to affect, the role of the state in productive enterprises within their own territory. Traditionally, the state has had the role of referee (antitrust policy), "fireman" (saving "endangered" firms), or promoter (paying for the social costs of production, while allowing firms to privatize profits). Now that many tariff barriers have been removed and production has been internationalized, the costs of protecting weak firms have increased. Thus, according to a French authority:

> Though the state in the past had been the last recourse for enterprises in difficulty, it would be obliged henceforth to refuse systematically to aid the feeble, in order that it might devote still more resources to reinforcing the strong. It would be necessary for French enterprises to have international stature and competitiveness, capable of facing up to the multinational giants of the United States or Japan, or other members of the Common Market. (Michelet 1974, 120-1)

To summarize the central theme of this section, one could say that industrial policy is an increasingly important complement, and sometimes competitor, to macroeconomic policies, in attempting to achieve the goals of various interests. In addition, industrial policies have more and more an international dimension, a tendency having much to do with the migration of industrial capital, internationalization of production and the increasingly insecure position of domestic labor in the international division of labor. These trends are likely to continue.

INTERPRETATIONS

This chapter discussed five important trends related to labor in the global political economy; others that are not discussed may be equally important. For example, I could have focused on the increasing automation of the labor process in the northern countries (Junne 1984; Giuliano 1982), the deskilling of labor in the process of mechanization and automation (Bright 1958), the increasingly hostile position of core labor toward new international economic order demands (Stohl 1982), the "partial deproletarianization of labor" (Bowles and Gintis 1982), and the implications of changing demographic trends for jobs in the future (Drucker 1981). All of these topics are important and worthy of attention, but instead I wish to speculate on the five trends that are the foci in this work. I want to suggest some broad interpretations of what they may mean and to highlight questions and themes that may be usefully pursued in future research.

First, to the extent that any single set of factors can account for such far-reaching changes, we can ask what "motivates" the system. This is a question to which I have not tried to provide a direct answer, and perhaps it is impossible to do so. Still, there are some assumptions I have made which, however partially, serve to locate the trends within a theoretical framework. The most important assumptions are that economic activity is organized by firms, that these firms operate in environments that are competitive and increasingly global, and that, as Chase-Dunn put it, the "complicated game of competition in the capitalist world economy is a combination of profitable commodity production with efficient use of geopolitical power" (1984, 86). Further, the consequences of competitive economic activity, and the activities of the state, can at one level be usefully analyzed in terms of the consequences for different class groups.

What does such a framework imply? In part, it implies that the logic of competitive capital accumulation drives the system. Individual, self-regarding firms, at a minimum, try to survive and, at a maximum, try to rapidly accumulate capital. Somewhere in between, they strive to maintain historical market shares—a position that is compatible with either absolute growth or decline.

As with the security dilemma, which constantly haunts the international strategist, the manager of a firm also confronts an uneasy set of choices. To him (or her) what at first appears as a choice between frantic accumulation and steady-state production turns out to be illusory, somewhat (not entirely) akin to the cooperative option in a prisoner's dilemma game. The motives for accumulation are both offensive and defensive, and, as in many other arenas, the best defense (i.e., against competition from other firms) is a good offense. "Accumulate or die," as Marx put it.

Shifting focus from the level of the firm to the global political economy,

I will argue that initial changes in the organization of the international system have led to further changes in the global division of labor—that is, in the distribution of power between labor and capital in the core and periphery and, at least potentially, between core and periphery. The capital, energy, and political effort that went into the rebuilding of Western Europe and Japan after the end of World War II, the economic revival of the advanced capitalist world, the formation of the European Economic Community and the successes of the General Agreement of Tariffs and Trade (GATT) all had long-term consequences. The international economy became liberalized, but it did so at differential speeds both geographically and sectorally—faster within the advanced capitalist world than between it and the Third World and faster in manufactured goods than in agricultural goods—and these differences placed pressures on lagging sectors and regions to catch up. To take one example, the progressive elimination of internal tariffs among EEC countries and the corresponding alignment of their common external tariffs toward nonmembers created unfavorable movements in terms of trade for nonmember countries. So, rather than allowing themselves to be driven out of EEC markets by politically motivated changes in relative prices, firms in various countries moved capital directly into EEC countries, circumventing (or rather "jumping") the tariff wall.

Although changes in the commercial realm provided one motivation for the international movement of capital, and hence for changing the bargaining power between labor and capital, a stronger reason is perhaps provided by a complex of changes in the domestic relationship among capital, labor, and the state. Indeed, the story that currently deals with capital flight, the "runaway shop," and the disciplining of labor in both core and periphery must look for its roots in the emergence and development of a society that was both capitalist and social-democratic, the historic accords between capital and labor in core countries, and the improvement of organized labor's position in the core.

To understand the place of labor and capital in the advanced capitalist world, a definitive conception of these societies is needed. A conception that comes to grips with both the institutional forms of social democracy and capitalism's "private" production relations seems to provide the most useful starting point. In contrast to theorists who see capitalist society as constituting a "real economy," with derivative social, cultural, and political formations, Bowles and Gintis (1982) provide us an alternative. For them, the "advanced capitalist social formation may be better represented as an articulation of the liberal democratic state and capitalist production, in which the dynamics of the whole cannot be reduced to the structure of either" (Bowles and Gintis 1982, 52). According to this formulation, liberal, democratic capitalism is a society with two fundamental realms of activity. One realm is dominated by the logic of commodities, and buying and selling, as well as the wage labor-capital relationship—in short, the logic of markets. The other realm is dominated by a different idiom: here one speaks of human rights and obligations—rather than endowments, property rights, and utilities—terms that suggest matters of principle, rather than buying and selling. The former realm describes the commodified relations among people, and the latter carves out an area of society and attempts to preserve relations in a decommodified form. Rights, as Okun reminds us, differ from the logic of markets in that they are universally distributed, cannot be bought and sold, and are not subject to the laws of comparative advantage and price theory. The two realms, of commodified and decommodified relations, are represented by the market and the welfare state respectively.

The above representation provides us with a picture of a liberal, capitalist society composed of two partly contradictory and partly functional components. The overall movement of this social formation is the result of the relative strength of the two components, whether oppositional or harmonious, and the dynamics of their interaction. In historical terms, two important developments within this social formation involve the historic compromises between capital and labor and the "citizen wage" (Bowles and Gintis 1982, 56). The capital-labor accords and the citizen wage have implications beyond the already described enhanced bargaining power of labor. There is little doubt that labor, during the 1950s and 1960s, increased its share of the economic product (Bowles and Gintis 1982, 53-4) and that the share of the product going to profits declined (Nordhaus, 1974). This may have been greeted by labor's satisfaction in the short run, but in the longer run, the consequences for core labor were serious and, for the most part, negative. While the McCracken Report, issued in 1977, used a vocabulary different from that of Marxian crisis theory, the analysis was, in some fundamental respects, similar: the "wage explosions" of the late 1960s and 1970s, the soaring costs of government and the extent to which regulations absorbed corporate resources occupied central positions. Then there were those "accidents," not to be explained by either economic or political theory: the Vietnam war, the oil price increases, the inflation psychology that manifested itself in second-derivative expectations. All of these forces created an increasingly inhospitable environment for corporations in advanced capitalist countries, at least according to the eminent authors of the McCracken Report (1977).

The benefits extracted by the privileged elements of core labor rested on at least one tacit premise: capital and labor were parties captive to the negotiating table, and neither could get up and leave to find a better deal elsewhere. By the 1960s, and in varying degrees before this, reality had undermined this presumption: third world labor pools, disciplined to the rigors of factory life and carefully monitored by their governments, greatly improved transportation and communication technologies; core area fiscal and tariff legislation strongly encouraged the export of capital. Both made for intensified capital mobility.

Management and capital came to be in a peculiar position. Having acquiesced to the "new social contract" through fifty to sixty years of hard bargaining with labor, and unable to win within the rules of the game instituted by domestic society, capital decided to leave rather than continue the fight on the same turf. Rather abruptly, then, capital began to undo the historically protracted achievements of labor. This movement of capital was not an isolated phenomenon, but part of a general conservative trend: right-wing governments in the United States and the United Kingdom, attacks on the welfare state, the "disciplining" of labor, and attempts to deregulate major aspects of the economy were involved. All of these changes, particularly the movement of capital itself, are now possible because capital is no longer bound by the national straitjackets. It is subject only to the limits of conducting economic transactions over large spaces and the unfamiliarity of "local" conditions. Capital today constitutes "moveable wealth," in Hirschman's sense; it is less and less bound by the local markets in which it operates, or the size of its fixed physical plant, or its proximity to markets. Indeed, the asymmetry between the mobility of labor and capital constitutes the chief source of the increased power of capital in the contemporary world.

To highlight another theme implicit in this analysis, we can ask what is the future of core societies. Will these societies glide effortlessly into postindustrial utopia, free from the resource requirements and polluting effects of industrial production, as well as the tyranny and monotony of the factory as a workplace, into an economy dominated by skilled high-technology producers and education information specialists? Or, are we more likely to see a nation of fast-food enterprises, clerks, custodians, boutiques, and collectors of art, antiques, and land, existing in a *rentier* economy? We are far from a consensus on answers to these questions. Optimists such as Peter Drucker argue that jobs in advanced countries will require more and more education and others, such as Levin and Rumberger (1983) argue, on the basis of their data, that future jobs will require less education.

If one examines recent trends and searches for historical parallels (Spain, the Netherlands, the United Kingdom) one is inclined to discard theories of progress and substitute instead cyclical or organic metaphors. It is tempting to suggest that the product-cycle view has an analog in the life cycle of nations, which looks as follows: countries are born and start to produce at the lower ends of the technological scale (light manufacturing, consumer goods); they move to consumer durables and heavy industry, from there to high-technology production in oligopolistic industries, and finally to services and speculative investments. Chase-Dunn claims to detect a pattern similar to this in the trajectories of hegemonic powers: increasing competitiveness in consumer goods gives way to the export of capital, the final phase of the great powers being lived out as centers of world finance and services (1984, 90). Is this suggestion a misinformed parallel that mistakes a cyclical downturn in the core for a durable secular trend? Is it a modern physiocratic lament about industrial decline, akin to the physiocratic mistake about the implications of agricultural decline? Is there anything to it? The increasing role of services in many advanced industrial economies should at least cause us to reflect on this point.

We come now to that elusive arena of culture, where we are more likely to speak in the idiom of purpose, meaning, and motivating ideas. What are the philosophical foundations, ideas, and world views that underpin movements in the global political economy? How do systems of ideas make sense of these changes? For some countries, particularly the United States, the remarkable idea that politics and economics operate in separate spheres (or on two tracks) has persisted and requires some explanation. To some extent, this ideational separation is due to the creation of a world in which the political and economic did, in fact, operate at least partially in different arenas. The conclusion of World War II saw efforts to create this two-track system—security, alliances, and arms made up "high politics," and questions of production and commerce were "low politics." The two arenas came together in the creation of "rules of the game," i.e., a structure within which economic activity could take place in a depoliticized way, on a day-to-day basis.

However, the separation of politics from economics goes much deeper. It flows naturally from the cosmology spawned by liberalism, which, as Michael Walzer argues, involves "a certain way of drawing the map of the social and political world" (Walzer 1984, 315). According to liberalism, society is not treated as an organic whole or a single functioning reality. Instead, liberalism "drew lines, marked off different realities, and created the sociopolitical map with which we are still familiar. . . . Liberalism is a world of walls, and each one creates a new liberty" (Walzer 1984, 315). He might have added that it "creates a new barrier to understanding."

Marxism, of course, offers an alternative cosmology in which society is treated as an integral whole. As a philosophy, it has never been sympathetic to drawing boundaries. It has tended to turn a suspicious eye toward liberalism's attempt to do so, viewing such attempts as an ideological front for capitalist firms, allowing them to simultaneously avoid government "interference" when it hurts (by taxation, restrictions on mobility of capital, or laws to internalize the external costs of production) and to embrace it when it helps (by regulating strike activity, supporting research and development costs, or paying for the education of the work force) (Walzer 1984, 315).

Marxists do not always appreciate the positive side of liberalism. Walzer's point about walls and freedom has some merit. The abolition of dynastic government (which limited political office to blood lines), and the separation of church from state and state from civil society, have created huge areas of social life where *individuals*—for this term is now appropriate—can strive with their own wits and resources to achieve goals. Indeed, as is so often emphasized, this freedom is also a freedom to fail on both a material and psychological plane; the historical transition from a fixed to a fluid place in society, and identification in terms of "who I am"—based largely on hereditary status that gave way to one based on "what I do"—provided a profound shock to modern society. But it also brought privacy, autonomy, and the possibility of advance.

Although these final comments are speculative, and take us some distance from the central remarks in this chapter, it is necessary to pursue them in order to make sense of the evolution of the modern global political economy. In the final analysis, this political economy is not just a product of technical economic forces, but also of the ideas and political forces that helped give them shape.

NOTES

I would like to thank the following people for their comments on this chapter: Christopher Chase-Dunn, Robert Cox, Edward Greenberg, John Grove, W. Ladd Hollist, Barry Hughes, Gerd Junne, Peter Katzenstein, Robert Keohane, Gregg Kvistad, James Mittelman, LaMond Tullis, Peter Van Ness, and Spencer Wellhofer.

BIBLIOGRAPHY

Acs, Z. J. (1984). "Managing the Decline of the Corporate Sector." *SAIS Review,* 4(2) (Summer-Fall):149-168.

Adams, G. (1971). "New Trends in International Business: World Wide Sourcing and De-domiciling." *Acta Oeconomica,* 7:349-67.

Adams, G. (1972). "Some Implications and Concomitants of World Wide Sourcing." *Acta Oeconomica,* 8:309-23.

Aggarwal, V. (1983). "The Unraveling of the Multi-Fiber Arrangement, 1981: An Examination of International Regime Change." *International Organization,* 37(4) (Autumn):617-646.

Aglietta, M. (1976). *Regulation et crises du capitalisme, l'experience des Etats-Unis.* Paris: Calman-Levy.

Aglietta, M. (1982). "World Capitalism in the Eighties." *New Left Review,* 136 (Nov.-Dec.):5-41.

Aho, M. C., and D. J. Rousslang. (1979). "The Impact of LDC Trade on U.S. Workers: Demographic and Occupational Characteristics of Workers in Trade-Sensitive Industries." Washington, DC: U.S. Department of Labor, Office of Foreign Economic Research, pp. 1-16.

Alexander, M. (1983). "Australia in the Capitalist World Economy." In B. Head (Ed.), *State and Economy in Australia.* Melbourne: Oxford University Press.

Alexander, T. (1984). "Reinventing the Computer." *Fortune,* March 5, pp. 62-70.

Alker, H. R. (1973). "Political Capabilities in a Schedule Sense: Measuring Power, Integration, and Development." In H. R. Alker, K. W. Deutsch, K. W. and A. H. Stoetzel (Eds.), *Mathematical Approaches to Politics,* pp. 307-373. San Francisco, CA: Jossey-Bass.

Almond, G. A., and S. Genco. (1977). "Clouds, Clocks and the Study of Politics." *World Politics,* 29(4):489-522.

Altschuler, A., et al. (1984). *The Future of the Automobile—The Report of MIT's International Automobile Programme.* Cambridge: The MIT Press.

Amin, S. (1977). *Imperialism and Unequal Development.* New York: Monthly Review Press.

Anthony, P. D. (1977). *The Ideology of Work.* London: Tavistock.

Arendt, H. (1958). *The Human Condition.* Chicago and London: University of Chicago Press.

Arnold, W. F. (1984). "The Question: Automate, Emigrate or Evaporate?" *Electronic Business,* (February):178-183.

Arrighi, G., and B. J. Silver. (1984). "Labor Movements and Capital Migration: The United States and Western Europe in World Perspective." In C. Bergquist (Ed.), *Labor in the Capitalist World Economy,* pp. 183-216. Beverly Hills, CA: Sage.

Atkinson, M. (1985). "If You Can't Beat Them: World Product Mandating and Canadian Industrial Policy." In Duncan Cameron and Francois Houle (Eds.), *Canada and the New International Division of Labour,* pp. 125-144. Ottawa: University of Ottawa Press.

Avery, W. P., and D. P. Rapkin (Eds.). (1982). *America in a Changing World Political Economy*. New York: Longman Press.

Baer, W., R. Newfarmer, and T. Trebat. (1977). "On State Capitalism in Brazil: Some New Issues and Questions." *Inter-American Economic Affairs,* 30 (Winter):69-91.

Balassa, B. (1979). "The Changing International Division of Labor in Manufactured Goods." World Bank Staff Working Paper 329. Washington, DC: World Bank.

Balassa, B., and C. Balassa. (1984). "Industrial Protection in the Developed Countries." *The World Economy,* (June):179-196.

Banfield, E. (1958). *The Moral Basis of a Backward Society*. Glencoe, IL: Free Press.

Baran, P. (1958). *The Political Economy of Growth*. New York: Monthly Review Press.

Barnet, R. J. (1980). *The Lean Years: Politics in the Age of Scarcity*. New York: Simon and Schuster.

Baumol, W. J. (1952). *Welfare Economics and the Theory of the State*. Cambridge: Harvard University Press.

Becker, D. (1983). *The New Bourgeoisie and the Limits of Dependency*. Princeton: Princeton University Press.

Behrman, J., and W. Fischer. (1980). *Overseas R & D Activities of Transnational Companies* (Cambridge, MA: Oelgeschlager, Gunn and Hain).

Bell, D. (1973). *The Coming of Post-Industrial Society*. London: Penguin Books.

Bellini, J. (1981). *Rule Brittania: A Progress Report for Doomsday*. London: Jonathan Cape.

Bellon, B. (1983). "La Chimie." In B. Bellon & J. M. Chevalier (Eds.), *L'Industrie en France,* pp. 157-197. Paris: Flammarion.

Bennett, D., and K. Sharpe. (1980). "The State as Banker and Entrepreneur." *Comparative Politics,* 12 (January):165-189.

Berger, S., and M. J. Piore. (1980). *Dualism and Discontinuity in Industrial Societies*. Cambridge: Cambridge University Press.

Bergquist, C. (1984). "Placing Labor at the Center: Introduction." In C. Bergquist (Ed.), *Political Economy of the World-System Annuals: Vol. 7. Labor in the Capitalist World Economy* pp. 7-19. Beverly Hills, CA: Sage.

Bertrand, O. (1982). "Das flexible Fertigungssystem im Werk Bouthéon von Renault Véhicules Industriels (R.V.I.)." In B. Lutz and R. Schultz-Wild (Eds.), *Flexible Fertigungssystem und Personalwirtschaft. Erfahrungen aus Frankreich, Japan, USA und der Bundesrepublik Deutschland,* pp. 41-55. Frankfurt: Campus.

Bickerstaffe, G. (1984). "Convergence of Technologies Sparks Growing Number of Corporate Tie-ups." *International Management,* (December):41-47.

Blackaby, F. (1979). *De-Industrialisation*. London: Heineman.

Block, F. (1977). *The Origins of International Economic Disorder*. Berkeley and Los Angeles: University of California.

Bluestone, B., and B. Harrison. (1982). *The Deindustrialization of America*. New York: Basic Books.

Bluestone, B., and S. O'Cleireacain. (1984). "Industrial Policy Priorities in the Trade Jungle." *World Policy Journal,* 1 (Winter):377-395.

Boeke, J. N. (1961). "Dualistic Economics." In *Indonesian Economics: The Concept of Duality in Theory and Policy*. Amsterdam, Netherlands: Royal Tropical Institute.

Boismenu, G., and G. Ducantenzeiler. (1985). "Le Canada dans la circulation internationale de technologie." In Duncan Cameron and Francois Houle (Eds.) *Canada and the New International Division of Labor.* Ottawa: University of Ottawa Press.

Boskin, M. (1974). "The Effects of Government Expenditures and Taxes on Female Labor." *American Economic Review,* 64(2):251-256.

Bowles, S., and H. Gintis. (1982). "The Crises of Liberal Democratic Capitalism: The Case of the United States." *Politics and Society,* 11(1):51-93.

Bowring, P. (1984). "Stop Waltzing Matilda." *Far Eastern Economic Review,* January 19, p. 79.

Braverman, H. (1974). *Labor and Monopoly Capital: The Degradation of Work in the Twentieth Century.* New York: Monthly Review Press.

Brenner, R. 1977. "The Origins of Capitalist Development: A Critique of Neo-Smithian Marxism." *New Left Review,* 104 (July-August):25-92.

Brewer, A. (1982). *Marxist Theories of Imperialism.* London: Routledge & Kegan Paul.

Brewster, H. (1973). "Economic Dependence: A Quantitative Interpretation." *Social and Economic Studies,* 22(1):90-95.

Bright, J. R. (1958). "Does Automation Raise Skill Requirements?" *Harvard Business Review,* 36 (July-August):85-98.

Britton, J., and J. Gilmour. (1978). *The Weakest Link: A Technological Perspective on Canadian Industrial Underdevelopment.* Ottawa: Science Council of Canada, Background Study 43.

Brown, C. (1980). "Australia-ASEAN Relations." *Australia-Asia Papers,* No. 8. Nathan: Griffith University, Centre for the Study of Australian-Asian Relations.

Buchanan, J. M. (1969). *Cost and Choice: An Inquiry in Economic Theory.* Chicago and London: University of Chicago Press.

Buchanan, J. M. (1975). *The Limits of Liberty: Between Anarchy and Leviathan.* Chicago, IL: University of Chicago Press.

Buchanan, J. M., and G. Tullock. (1965). *The Calculus of Consent: Logical Foundation of Constitutional Democracy.* Ann Arbor, MI: University of Michigan Press.

Burnham, W. D. (1982). *The Current Crisis in American Politics.* New York: Oxford University Press.

Business International S. A. (1979). *Europe in the 1980s: Corporate Forecasts and Strategies.* New York: Business International S.A.

Bylinksky, G. (1983). "The Race to the Automated Factory." *Fortune,* February 21, pp. 52-64.

Byrnes, M. (1984). "Japan: The Biggest But Maybe Not the Best." *Australian Financial Review,* August 30, p. 13.

Cain, G. G. (1975). "The Challenge of Dual and Radical Theories of the Labor Market to Orthodox Theory," *American Economic Review,* 65 (May):16-22.

Cain, G. G. (1976). "The Challenge of Segmented Labor Market Theory: A Survey." *Journal of Economic Literature,* 14(4):1215-1257.

Cameron, D. and F. Houle (Eds.). *The New International Division of Labour.* Ottawa: University of Ottawa Press.

Camps, M. (1975). "First World Relationships: The Role of the OECD." *The Atlantic Papers, No. 2.* Paris: The Atlantic Institute for International Affairs.

Canadian Council of Professional Engineers. (1983). *Brief on Research and Development in Canada.* Ottawa: CCPE, Feb.

Caporaso, J. A. (1981). "Industrialization in the Periphery: The Evolving Global Division of Labor." *International Studies Quarterly,* 25(3):347-384.

Cardoso, F. H. (1973). "Associated Dependent Development". In Alfred Stepan (Ed.), *Authoritarian Brazil.* New Haven: Yale University Press.

Cardoso, F. H., and E. Faletto. (1979). *Dependency and Development in Latin America.* Berkeley and Los Angeles: University of California Press.

Carnoy, M. (1984). *The State and Political Theory.* Princeton: Princeton University Press.

Carr, R. (1984). *Puerto Rico: A Colonial Experiment.* New York: Vintage Books.

Catley, R. (1984). "Economic Cycles and Labor Policy: Political Determinism and Economic Determinism." In J. Eastwood, J. Reeves, and J. Ryan (Eds.), *Labor Essays.* Melbourne: Drummond.

Caves, R. (1972). "International Corporations: The Industrial Economics of Foreign Investment." In J. Dunning (Ed.), *International Investment,* pp. 256-301. United Kingdom: Penguin.

Caves, R. (1982). *Multinational Enterprise and Economic Analysis.* Cambridge: Cambridge University Press.

Caves, R., and L. B. Krause (1984). *The Australian Economy: A View from the North.* Sydney: Allen and Unwin for the Brookings Institute.

Centre de prospective et d'evaluation (CPE). (1983a). *Characterisations des cooperations entre sociétés americaines et japonaises dans le domaine des technologies critiques.* Etude realisée sous la direction de Marcel Bayen. Paris: Ministere de la recherche et de l'industrie.

Chase-Dunn, C. K. (1984). "The World System Since 1950: What Has Really Changed?" In C. Bergquist (Ed.), *Labor in the Capitalist World Economy,* pp. 75-103. Beverly Hills, CA: Sage.

Chenery, H. B., and D. B. Keesing. (1979). *The Changing Composition of Developing Country Exports.* World Bank Staff Working Paper 314. Washington, DC: World Bank.

Cho, S. K. (1985). "The Dilemmas of Export-Led Industrialization: South Korea and the World Economy." *Berkeley Journal of Sociology,* 30:65-94.

Coase, R. H. (1960). "The Problem of Social Cost." *Journal of Law and Economics,* 3:1-44.

Coleman, K., and C. Davis. (1983). "Preemptive Reform and the Mexican Working Class." *Latin American Research Review,* 18(1):3-31.

Collier, D. (Ed). (1979). *The New Authoritarianism in Latin America.* Princeton: Princeton University Press.

Cooper, R. N. (1968). *The Economics of Interdependence.* New York: McGraw-Hill Book Co.

Corden, M. (1983). "Australia and the World Economy." In P. Dibb (Ed.), *Australia's External Relations in the 1980s: The Interaction of Economic, Political and Strategic Factors.* Canberra: Croom Helm.

Cornelisen, A. (1976). *Women of the Shadows.* Boston: Little, Brown and Co.

CPE. (1983b). *Le Développement des produits nouveaux au Japon.* Etude realisée par Eurogestion. Paris: Ministère de la recherche et de l'industrie.

Crotty, R. (1979). "Capitalist Colonialism and Peripheralisation: The Irish Case." In Dudley Seers (Ed.), *Underdeveloped Europe.* Atlantic Highlands, NJ: Humanities Press.

Crough, G., and E. Wheelwright. (1982). *Australia: A Client State.* Ringwood, Victoria: Penguin.

Cumings, B. (1984). "The Origins and Development of the Northeast Asian Political Economy: Industrial Sectors, Product Cycles, and Political Consequences." *International Organization,* 38(1):1-40.

Dankbaar, B. (1983). "Is the International Car Industry Moving South? Trade, Foreign Investment and Relocation in the Passenger Car Industry." *Discussion Paper IIM/IP,* 83(5):1-39. Berlin: International Institute of Management.

"Data Networks Shrink Research Frontiers." (1984). *International Management,* (July):31-32.

Deere, C. D. (1985). "Rural Women and State Policy: The Latin American Agrarian Reform Experience." *World Development,* 13(9):1039-1053.

Deere, C. D., and A. DeJanvry. (1979). "A Conceptual Framework for the Empirical Analysis of Peasants." *American Journal of Agricultural Economics,* 61(4): 601-611.

Delapierre, M., and J. B. Zimmerman. (1984). "L'industrie du traitement de l'information." Note de travail pour GEST, Grappe technologique et strategie industrielle. Paris.

Delion, A., and M. Durupty. (1982). *Les Nationalisations 1982.* Paris: Economica.

Denoon, D. (1983). *Settler Capitalism: The Dynamics of Dependent Development in the Southern Hemisphere.* Melbourne: Oxford University Press.

Deyo, F. (1984). "Export Manufacturing and Labor: The Asian Case." In C. Bergquist (Ed.), *Labor in the Capitalist World Economy,* pp. 267-288. Beverly Hills, CA: Sage.

Dibb, P. (Ed.). (1983). *Australia's External Relations in the 1980s: The Interaction of Economic, Political and Strategic Factors.* Canberra: Croom Helm.

Dick, H. (1984). "Restructuring: A Bridge Too Far?" *The National Times,* February 24-March 1, p. 46.

Diebold, W., Jr. (1980). "Adapting Economics to Structural Change: The International Aspect." *International Affairs,* 54 (October):558-573.

Diebold, W. (1980). *Industrial Policy as an International Issue.* New York: McGraw Hill for the Council on Foreign Relations.

Di Paliano, C. (1969). "Industrial Policy: Problems and Outlooks." *Bulletin of the European Communities,* 2(2):5-8.

Di Paliano, G. C. (1970). "Pour une politique industrielle de la communauté." In *Bulletin des communautés européennes.* Brussels: European Community.

Dobb, M. (1973). *Theories of Value and Distribution Since Adam Smith: Ideology and Economic Theory.* Cambridge: Cambridge University Press.

Dobozi. "Intra-CMEA Universal Cooperation: Implications for Trade with OECD and Third World Countries." Paper prepared for IV General Conference EADI, Madrid 1984, Working Group A1 East-South Economic Interaction Mimeo.

Doeringer, P., and M. J. Piore. (1971). *Internal Labor Markets and Manpower Analysis.* MA: Lexington Books.

Dolan, M. (1983). "European Restructuring and Import Policies for a Textile Industry in Crisis." *International Organization,* 37(4) (Autumn):583-616.

Donges, J. B., and J. Riedel. (1975). "The Expansion of Manufactured Exports in Developing Countries: An Empirical Assessment of Supply and Demand Issues." *Weltwirtschaftliches Archiv,* 113(2):58-87.

Dornbusch, R., and S. Fischer. (1984). "The Australian Macroeconomy." In R. E. Caves and L. B. Krause, *The Australian Economy: A View from the North.* Sydney: Allen and Unwin.

Dow, G. (1984). "The Case for Corporatism: A Second Look at the Hawke Government's Tendencies Towards 'Corporatism.'" *Australian Society,* 3(11):22-4.

Dresdner Bank, 1983. "Wächsende Konkurrenzfähigkeit der Schwellenländer." *Wirtschaftsberichte,* XXXV (3):6-7.

Drucker, P. F. (1981). "The Next American Work Force, Demographics & U.S. Economic Policy." *Economic Development Commentary* 5 (October):1-10.

Drysdale, P. (1984). *Pacific Growth and Economic Interdependence.* Perth: Australian Institute of International Affairs, May, mimeo.

Drysdale, P. (1986). *The Economics of International Pluralism: Economic Policy in the Pacific Community.* Sydney: Allen and Unwin for the Australian Institute of International Affairs.

Drysdale, P., and H. Kitoaji (Eds.). (1981). *Japan and Australia: Two Societies and Their Interaction.* Canberra: Australian National University Press.

Duncan, M. (1982). "The Information Technology Industry in 1981." *Capital and Class,* (17) (Summer):78-113.

Duncan, T., and J. Fogarty. (1984). *Australia and Argentina: On Parallel Paths.* Melbourne: Melbourne University Press.

Duncan, W. (1983). "Towards a Pacific Community." *Canberra Times,* May 31, p. 8.

Dunk, W., and C. Beinhorn. (1984). "Making R & D Dollars Work Harder: Global Competition Is Forcing Industry to Develop More Effective R & D Strategies." *High Technology* (April):67-69.

Dunning, J. (1979). "Explaining Changing Patterns of International Production: In Defense of the Eclectic Theory." *Oxford Bulletin of Economics and Statistics,* 41(4) (November):269-296.

Durkam, J. (1978). "The Irish Economy: The Recent Experience and Prospective Future Performance." In Brendan Dowling and Joe Durkan (Eds.), *Irish Economic Policy.* Dublin: Economic and Social Research Institute.

Durkheim, E. (1893, 1933). *The Division of Labor in Society.* New York: Free Press.

Duvall, R. D., and J. R. Freeman. (1983). "The Techno-Bureaucratic Elite and the Entrepreneurial State and Dependent Industrialization." *American Political Science Review,* 77(3):569-587.

East, M. A. (1973). "Size and Foreign Policy Behaviour: A Test of Two Models." *World Politics,* 25(4):556-576.

Edwards, P. G. (1983). *Prime Ministers and Diplomats: The Making of Australian Foreign Policy.* Melbourne: Oxford University Press.

Edwards, R., M. Reich, and D. M. Gordon (Eds.). (1973). *Labor Market Segmentation.* Lexington, MA: D. C. Heath.

Ehrenreich, B., and A. Fuentes. (1981). "Life on the Global Assembly Line." *MS.,* 9(7):53-71.

Ellis, P. Beresford. (1972). *A History of the Irish Working Class.* London: Gollancz.

Ekelund, R. B., Jr., and R. D. Tollison. (1981). *Mercantilism as a Rent-Seeking Society.* College Station, TX: Texas A & M Press.

Elsenhans, H. (1983). "Mass Incomes as a Condition of Capitalist Growth." *International Organization,* 37:1.

Emerson, R. M. (1962). "Power-Dependence Relations." *American Sociological Review,* 27(2):31-41.

Emmanuel, A. (1972). *Unequal Exchange: A Study in the Imperialism of Trade.* New York and London: Monthly Review Press.

Emmerij, L. J. (1980). "Mogelijke gevolgen van micro-electronica voor de internationale arbeidsverdeling." *Economisch-Statistische Berichten,* March 12, pp. 300-305.

English, M. (1984). "The European Information Technology Industry." In A. Jacquemin (Ed.), *European Industry: Public Policy and Corporate Strategy,* pp. 227-273. Oxford: Clarendon Press.

Ernst, D. (1980). *The New International Division of Labour, Technology, and Underdevelopment.* Frankfurt: Campus.

Ernst, D. (1981). "Restructuring World Industry in a Period of Crisis—The Role of Innovation. An Analysis of Recent Developments in the Semiconductor Industry." *UNIDO Working Paper on Structural Change,* prepared by the Global and Conceptual Studies Branch, Division of Industrial Studies, UNIDO/ IS.285, December 17.

Ernst, D. (1984). "The Impact of Microelectronics on the Worldwide Restructuring of the Electronics Industry. Implications for the Third World." To be published in *World Development* (special issue on microelectronics).

Esping-Andersion, G., et al. (1976). "Modes of Class Struggle and the Capitalist State." *Kapitalistate,* (Summer).

Esser, J. (1982). *Gewerkschaften in der Krise.* Frankfurt: Suhrkamp.

Evans, P. B., D. Reuschmeyer, and T. Skocpol (Eds.). (1985). *Bringing the State Back In.* Cambridge: Cambridge University Press.

Evans, P. (1979). *Dependent Development.* Princeton: Princeton University Press.

Evans, P. (1982). "Reinventing the Bourgeoisie." In Michael Burawoy and Theda Skocpol (Eds.), *Marxist Inquiries.* Chicago: University of Chicago Press.

Febre, L. (1948). "Travail: evolution d'un mot et d'une idée." *Journal de Psychologie normale et Pathologique,* XLI(1).

Feith, H. (1980). "Repressive Developmentalist Regimes in Asia: Old Strengths, New Vulnerabilities." *Prisma,* 19 (December):39-55.

Fields, G. S. (1980). *Poverty, Inequality, and Development.* Cambridge: Cambridge University Press.

Folbre, N. (1984). "The Pauperization of Motherhood: Patriarchy and Public Policy in the United States." *Review of Radical Political Economics,* 16(4):72-88.

Foster-Carter, A. (1976). "From Rostow to Gunder Frank." *World Development,* 4:3.

Frank, A. G. (1969). *Capitalism and Underdevelopment in Latin America.* New York: Monthly Review Press.

Frank, A. G. (1983). "What Is To Be Done with Strawmen?" *Development and Change,* 14:4.

Freeman, C. (1974). *The Economics of Industrial Innovation.* Harmondsworth, UK: Penguin.

Freeman, J. R. (1983). "State Entrepreneurship and Dependent Development."

American Journal of Political Science, 26:2.

Freeman, J. R., and R. Duvall. (1984). "International Economic Relations and the Entrepreneurial State." *Economic Development and Cultural Change,* 32(2):373-400.

Frieden, J. (1985). "The Indebted Emerald Isle." Mimeo.

Friedman, E. (Ed.). (1982). *Political Economy of the World-System Annuals: Vol. 5. Ascent and Decline in the World System.* Beverly Hills, CA: Sage.

Friedrichs, G. and A. Schaff (Eds.). (1983). *Microelectronics and Society: A Report to the Club of Rome.* New York: Mentor Books.

Fröbel, F., J. Heinrichs, and O. Kreye. (1977). *Die neue internationale Arbeitsteilung. Strukturelle Arbeitslosigkeit in den Industrieländern und die Industrialisierung der Entwicklungsländer.* Reinbek: Rowohlt.

Fröbel, F., J. Heinrichs, and O. Kreye. (1978). "The New International Division of Labour." *Social Science Information,* 17:123-142.

Fröbel, F., J. Heinrichs, and O. Kreye. (1980). *The New International Division of Labour.* Cambridge: Cambridge University Press.

Frost, F. (1982). "ASEAN and Australia." In A. Broinowski (Ed.), *Understanding ASEAN.* London: Macmillan.

Gallez, A. (1983). "Asia's Newly Industrializing Countries: Recent Problems and Prospects for the Eighties." *Vierteljahresberichte der Friedrich Ebert-Stiftung,* (93):267-283.

Gamble, A. (1981). *Britain in Decline.* London: Macmillan.

Garnaut, R. (Ed.). (1980). *ASEAN in a Changing Pacific and World Economy.* Canberra: Australian National University Press.

Garson, B. (1975). *All the Livelong Day: The Meaning and Demeaning of Routine Work.* United Kingdom: Penguin Books.

Garten, J. E. (1985). "Gunboat Economics." *Foreign Affairs,* 63 (3):538-559.

Garvin, T. (1981). *The Evolution of Irish Nationalism.* Dublin: Gill and Macmillan.

George, M. (1973). "From Goodwife to Mistress: The Transformation of the Female in Bourgeois Culture." *Science and Society,* 37:152-177.

Gerardi, R. E. (1985). *Australia, Argentina and World Capitalism 1930-1945.* Sydney: Transnational Corporations Research Project.

Gereffi, G. (1983). *The Pharmaceutical Industry and Dependency in the Third World.* Princeton: Princeton University Press.

Ginsberg, E., and G. J. Voijta. (1981). "The Service Sector of the U.S. Economy." *Scientific American,* 34(3):48-55.

Giuliano, V. E. (1982). "The Mechanization of Office Work." *Scientific American,* (September):148-164.

Gooding, K. (1984). "A Cultural Revolution at GM." *Financial Times,* November 14.

Goodman, P. (1968). *People or Personnel and Like a Conquered Province.* New York: Random House.

Gordon, D. M., R. Edwards, and M. Reich. (1982). *Segmented Work, Divided Workers.* Cambridge: Cambridge University Press.

Gourevitch, P. (1984). "Breaking with Orthodoxy: The Politics of Economic Responses to the Depression of the 1930s." *International Organization,* 38:1.

Gramsci, A. (1971). *Prison Notebooks.* New York: International.

Grant, B. (1983). *The Australian Dilemma: A New Kind of Western Society.* Sydney: MacDonald Futura.

Gray, H. J. (1983). "Technology's Global Role in Industrial Transition." *High Technology,* (December):12-14.

Greaves, D. (1974). *The Irish Crisis.* New York: International.

Gregory, R. (1976). "Some Implications of the Growth of the Mineral Sector." *The Australian Journal of Agricultural Economics,* 20(2):71-91.

Gregory, R. (1982). "Inter-sectoral Links." In S. Harris and G. Taylor (Eds.), *Resource Development and the Future of Australian Society.* Canberra: Australian National University, CRES Monograph No. 7.

Grieco, J. (1982). "Between Dependency and Autonomy: India's Experience with the International Computer Industry." *International Organization,* 36:3.

Habermas, J. (1975). *Legitimation Crisis.* Boston: Beacon Press.

Haggard, S., and C. Moon. (1983). "The South Korean State in the International Political Economy: Liberal, Dependent or Mercantile?" In J. Ruggie (Ed.), *The Antinomies of Interdependence: National Welfare and the International Division of Labour.* New York: Columbia University Press.

Hamill, I. (1981). *The Strategic Illusion: The Singapore Strategy and the Defence of Australia and New Zealand.* Singapore: Singapore University Press.

Hamilton, C. (1983). "Capitalist Industrialisation in Southeast Asia's Four Little Tigers." In *Journal of Contemporary Asia,* 13(1):35-73.

Hamilton, N. (1981). *The Limits of State Autonomy.* Princeton: Princeton University Press.

Hancock, E. (1983). "Academe Meets Industry: Charting the Bottom Line." *The Johns Hopkins Magazine,* (August):I-IX.

Harris, S. (1982). "The Separation of Economics and Politics: A Luxury We Can No Longer Afford." In C. Bell (Ed.), *Academic Studies and International Politics.* Canberra: Canberra Studies in World Affairs, No. 6.

Harris, S. (1986). "The Linking of Politics and Economics in Foreign Policy." *Australian Outlook: The Australian Journal of International Affairs,* 40(1):1-6.

Harsanyi, J. C. (1965). "Measurement of Social Power, Opportunity Costs, and the Theory of Two-Person Bargaining Games." In J. David Singer (Ed.), *Human Behavior and International Politics,* pp. 378-85. Chicago, IL: Rand McNally.

Hart, K. (1981). "Informal Income Opportunities and Urban Employment in Ghana." In I. Livingstone (Ed.), *Development Economics and Policy: Readings.* London: George Allen and Unwin.

Hayden, W. G. (1984) "Australia and China." *Australian Journal of Chinese Studies,* 1:83-97.

Head, B. (Ed.). (1983). *State and Economy in Australia.* Melbourne: Oxford University Press.

Hechter, M. (1975). *Internal Colonialism: The Celtic Fringe in British National Development, 1536-1966.* Berkeley and Los Angeles: University of California Press.

Heilbroner, R. L. (1980). *The Making of Economic Society.* Englewood Cliffs, NJ: Prentice-Hall.

Hein, C. (1984). "Jobs for the Girls: Export Manufacturing in Mauritius." *International Labor Review,* 123 (March-April):251-265.

Helleiner, G. K. (1981). *Intra-firm Trade and the Developing Countries.* United Kingdom: Macmillan.

Helliwell, J. F. "Natural Resources and the Australian Economy." In R. E. Caves and

L. B. Krause, *The Australian Economy: A View from the North.* Sydney: Allen and Unwin.

Henderson, A. G. (1985). "A Comparison of Australian and Japanese Labour Markets." *Australian Bulletin of Labour,* 12(1):22-45.

Hepburn, A. C., and E. Rumpf. (1977). *Nationalism and Socialism in Twentieth Century Ireland.* New York: Barnes and Noble.

Higgott, R. A. (1983). *Political Development Theory.* New York: St. Martins Press.

Higgott, R. A. (1984). "Export-Oriented Industrialisation, the New International Division of Labour and the Corporate State: An Essay in Conceptual Linkage." *Australian Geographical Studies,* 22: 58-71.

Higgott, R. A. (1985). "The State in Africa: Some Thoughts on the Future Drawn from the Past." In T. Shaw (Ed.), *Africa Projected: From Recession to Renaissance by 2000?* London: Macmillan.

Higgott, R. A. (1986). "Africa and the New International Divison of Labour." In J. Ravenhill (Ed.), *Africa in Economic Crisis.* New York: Columbia University Press.

Higgott, R. A. (1986). "Structural Adjustment and the Jackson Report: The Nexus Between Development Theory and Foreign Policy." In P. Eldridge, D. Forbes, and D. Porter (Eds.), *Australia's Overseas Aid: Future Directions.* Canberra: Croom Helm.

Higgott, R. A., and R. Robison (Eds.). (1985). *Southeast Asia: Essays in the Political Economy of Structural Change.* London: Routledge and Kegan Paul.

Hirschman, A. O. (1945). *National Power and the Structure of Foreign Trade.* Berkeley and Los Angeles, CA: University of California Press.

Hirschman, A. O. (1979). "The Turn to Authoritarianism in Latin America and the Search for its Determinants." In David Collier (Ed.), *The New Authoritarianism in Latin America.* Princeton: Princeton University Press.

Hobday, M. (1984). "The Brazilian Telecommunications Industry: Accumulation of Microelectronic Technology in the Manufacturing and Service Sectors." Sussex, England: Science Policy Research Unit, March.

Hoffman, J., and R. Rush. (1983). *Microelectronics and Clothing: The Impact of Technical Change on a Global Industry.* Geneva: ILO.

Hoffman, K., and H. Rush. (1980). "Microelectronics, Industry, and the Third World." *Futures,* (August):289-302.

Hofheinz, R., and K. Calder. (1983). *The East Asia Edge.* New York: Basic Books.

Hollist, L., and L. Tullis (Eds.). (1985). *An International Political Economy.* Boulder, Colorado: Westview Press.

Holsti, K. J. (1985). "Politics in Command: Foreign Trade as National Security Policy." Mimeo. Washington: ISA Conference, March 5-10.

Hood, N., and S. Young. (1982). *Multinationals in Retreat: The Scottish Experience.* Edinburgh: Edinburgh University Press.

Hughes, H. (1983). "Australia and the World Environment: The Dynamics of International Competition and Wealth Creation." In J. Scott (Ed.), *Poor Nation of the Pacific: Australia's Future?* Sydney: Allen and Unwin.

Hughes, H. (1983). "Global Economic Relations." *Australian Outlook: The Australian Journal of International Affairs,* 37(3):132-37.

Huizinga, J. (1954). *The Waning of the Middle Ages.* New York: Doubleday.

Hunt, E. K. (1979). "The Categories of Productive and Unproductive Labor in Marxist Economic Theory." *Science and Society,* XLIII(3) (Fall):303-325.

Hymer, S. (1975). "The Multinational Corporation and the Law of Uneven Development." In H. Radice (Ed.), *International Firms and Modern Imperialism,* pp. 37-62. Harmondsworth, United Kingdom: Penguin.

Hymer, S. (1976). *The International Operations of National Firms: A Study of Direct Foreign Investment.* Cambridge: The MIT Press.

Hymer, S. (1979). *The Multinational Corporation: A Radical Approach.* R. Cohen et al. (Eds.). Cambridge: Cambridge University Press.

Hymer, S., and R. Rowthorn. (1970). "Multinational Corporations and International Oligopoly: The Non-American Challenge." In C. P. Kindleberger (Ed.), *The International Corporation: A Symposium.* Cambridge: Cambridge University Press.

Inayatullah, N. (1985). "Labor and the Division of Labor: A Critical Analysis of Ambiguities in Political Economy." Manuscript, University of Denver, pp. 1-19.

Jacobsen, J. K. (1978). "Changing Utterly? Irish Development and the Problem of Dependence." *Studies,* 67:268.

Jacobsen, J. K., and C. Hofhansel. (1984). "Safeguards and Profits: Civilian Nuclear Exports, Neo-Marxism, and the Statist Approach." *International Studies Quarterly,* 28:2.

Jacobsen, J. K., and C. Hofhansel. (1987). "The Microchip Dilemma and Macropolicy: On the Political Economy of High Technology." *World Politics,* (forthcoming).

Jenkins, R. (1984). "Divisions Over the International Division of Labour." *Capital and Class,* 22 (Spring):18-57.

Jessop, B. (1982). *The Capitalist State.* New York: New York University Press.

Johns, D. S., and B. Macleod. (1977). "The Gregory Chant." *Australian Quarterly,* 2:92-105.

Johnson, J. T. (1981). *Location and Trade Theory.* Chicago, IL: Department of Geography Research Paper no. 198.

Johnson, M. (1984). "The Search for a New Japanese Locomotive." In R. Catley (Ed.) (1984). *Australia and Asia: Towards New Horizons.* Adelaide: Australian Institute of International Affairs.

Jones, D., and J. Womack. (1984). "Freeway 2000: The Hard Road South: Radical Advances in Car Manufacture Reduce Early Prospects for Third World Producers—But Open a Route to the 1990s." *South,* (November):69-71.

Junne, G. (1984). "Automation in the North: Consequences for Newly Industrializing Countries." University of Amsterdam. Mimeo, pp. 1-26.

Kaplinsky, R. (1980). "Microelectronics and the Third World." *Radical Science Journal,* (10):37-51.

Kaplinsky, R. (1981). "Radical Technical Change and Export-Oriented Industrialisation: The Impact of Microelectronics." *Vierteljahresberichte der Friedrich-Ebert-Stiftung,* (83):81-99.

Kaplinsky, R. (1984). *Automation. The Technology and Society.* Harlow: Longman.

Kaplinsky, R. (1984). "Electronics-Based Automation Technologies and the Onset of Systemofacture: Some Implications for Third World Industrialisation." *World Development* (forthcoming).

Kaplinsky, R. (1984). "The International Context for Industrialisation in the Coming

Decade." *Journal of Development Studies,* 21(1):75-96.

Kasper, W., et al. (1980). *Australia at the Crossroads: Choices to the Year 2000.* Sydney: Harcourt, Brace, Jovanovich.

Katzenstein, P. J. (1978). *Between Power and Plenty: Foreign Economic Policies of Advanced Industrial States.* Madison, WI: University of Wisconsin Press.

Katzenstein, P. (1983). "The Small European States in the International Economy: Economic Dependence and Corporatist Politics." In J. Ruggie (Ed.), *The Antinomies of Interdependence: National Welfare and the International Division of Labour.* New York: Columbia University Press.

Katzenstein, P. (1985). "Small Nations in an Open International Economy: The Converging Balance of State and Society in Switzerland and Austria." In P. B. Evans, D. Reuschmeyer, and T. Skocpol (Eds.), *Bringing the State Back In.* Cambridge: Cambridge University Press.

Kaufman, R. R. (1979). "Industrial Change and Authoritarian Rule in Latin America: A Concrete View of the Bureaucratic-Authoritarian Model." In David Collier (Ed.), *The New Authoritarianism in Latin America.* Princeton: Princeton University Press.

Kaufman, R. R. (1985). "Democratic and Authoritarian Responses to the Debt Crisis: Argentina, Brazil, and Mexico." *International Organization,* 39:3.

Keegan, D. (1983). "Business Delivers the Real Message." *The Australian,* April 12, p. 2.

Kennedy, K., and B. Dowling. (1975). *The Irish Economy Since 1947.* Dublin: Gill and Macmillan.

Keohane, R. O. (1982). "The Demand for International Regimes." *International Organization,* 36(2):325-355.

Keohane, R. O. (1984). *After Hegemony: Cooperation and Discord in the World Political Economy.* Princeton, NJ: Princeton University Press.

Keohane, R. O., and J. S. Nye. (1977). *Power and Interdependence.* Boston, MA: Little, Brown, and Co.

Kindleberger, C. (1979). "The Monopolistic Theory of Direct Foreign Investment." In G. Modelski (Ed.), *Transnational Corporations and World Order: Readings in International Political Economy,* pp. 91-107. San Francisco: Freeman & Company.

King, P. (Ed.). (1982). *Australia's Vietnam.* Sydney: Allen and Unwin.

Knight, F. H. (1924). "Fallacies in the Interpretation of Social Cost." *Quarterly Journal of Economics,* 38:582-606.

Kox, H. (1981). *De personenauto-industrie. Tendenties tot verplaatsing van produktie naar periferielanden.* Onderzoeksrapport IRIS, rapport no. 14. Tilburg: Katholieke Hogeschool, Instituut voor Ontwikkelingsvraagstukken.

Krasner, S. D. (1982). "Structural Causes and Regime Consequences: Regimes as Intervening Variables." *International Organization,* 36(2):185-205.

Krasner, S. D. (1978). *Defending the National Interest.* Princeton: Princeton University Press.

Krause, L. B. (1984). "Australia's Comparative Advantage in International Trade." In R. E. Caves and L. B. Krause (Eds.), *The Australian Economy: A View from the North.* Sydney: Allen and Unwin for the Brookings Institute.

Lall, S. (1975). *A Case Study of the Pharmaceutical Industry: Major Issues in Transfer of Technology to Developing Countries.* Geneva: UNCTAD, Doc. No. TD/B/C.6/4, 8 October.

Landes, D. (1969). *Prometheus Unbound.* Cambridge: Cambridge University Press.

Landsberg, M. (1979). "Export-Led Industrialization in the Third World: Manufacturing Imperialism." *Review of Radical Political Economics,* 11(4):50-63.

Lange, P. (1981). "Consenting to Restraint: The Political Economy of Wage Regulation." Mimeo.

Larue de Tournemine, R. (1983). "Activités publiques dans le secteur telecommunications." In *L'Innovation vers une nouvelle revolution technologique,* pp. 225-238. Paris: La Documentation française.

Laslett, P. (1973). *The World We Have Lost* (2nd ed.). USA: Scribner's Sons.

Lawe-Davies, J. (1981). "The Politics of Protection: Australia-ASEAN Economic Relations 1975 to 1980." *Australia-Asia Papers No. 13.* Nathan: Griffith University, Centre for the Study of Australian-Asian Relations.

Lawrence, R. Z. (1984). "Sectoral Shifts and the Size of the Middle Class." *The Brookings Review,* 3 (Fall):3-11.

Lean, D., J. G. Ogur, and R. Rogers (1982). *Competition and Collusion in Electrical Equipment Markets: An Economic Assessment.* Washington, DC: Federal Trade Commission, Bureau of Economics.

Leaver, R. (1985) "Reformist Capitalist Development and the New International Division of Labour." In R. A. Higgott and R. Robison (Eds.), *Southeast Asia: Essays in the Political Economy of Structural Change.* London: Routledge and Kegan Paul.

Lever-Tracy, C. (1984). "The Paradigm Crisis of Dualism: Decay or Regeneration?" *Politics and Society,* 13(1):59-89.

Levin, H. M., and R. W. Rumberger. (1983). "The Educational Implications of High Technology." Report No. 83-A4 (February). School of Education, Stanford University.

Levine, D. (forthcoming). *Needs, Rights, and Markets.* Denver, CO: manuscript.

Levinson, C. (1971). *Capital, Inflation, and the Multinationals.* London: Allen & Unwin.

Lewis, A. W. (1978). *The Evolution of the International Economic Order.* Princeton: Princeton University Press.

Lewis, J. P., and V. Kallab (Eds.). (1983). *U.S. Foreign Policy and the Third World: Agenda 1983.* New York: Praeger.

Lim, L. Y. C. (1983). "Capitalism, Imperialism, and Patriarchy: The Dilemma of Third-World Women Workers in Multinational Factories." In J. Nash and M. P. Fernandez-Kelly (Eds.), *Women, Men, and the International Divison of Labor,* pp. 70-91. Albany, NY: State University of New York Press.

Lim, R. (1980). "Current Australian-ASEAN Relations." In *Southeast Asian Affairs.* Singapore: ISEAS.

Lim, R. (1985). "The Debate on the 'Political-Economy' of Australian-ASEAN Relations." In R. A. Higgott and R. Robison (Eds.), *Southeast Asia: Essays in the Political Economy of Structural Change.* London: Routledge and Kegan Paul.

Lindblom, C. (1977). *Politics and Markets.* New York: Basic Books.

Linz, J. (1979). "Europe's Southern Frontiers: Evolving Towards What?" *Daedulus,* 108(1):175-209.

Lipietz, A. (1982). "Toward Global Fordism?" *New Left Review,* (132) (March-April):33-47.

Locke, J. (1965). *Two Treatises of Government.* New York: New American Library.

Lorenz, C. (1981). "Why Technology Is a Matter of Strategy and Not Just Research." *Financial Times,* May 5, 1981.

Loveday, P. (1985). "Corporatist Trends in Australia." *Politics,* 19(1):46-51.

Macintosh, M. (1981). "Gender and Economics: The Sexual Division of Labour and the Subordination of Women." In K. Young (Ed.), *Of Marriage and the Market: Women's Subordination in International Perspective.* London: CSE Books.

Mackie, J. A. C. (1981). "Australia and Southeast Asia." In C. Bell (Ed.), *Agenda for the Eighties.* Canberra: Australian National University Press.

Madeuf, B., and C. Ominami. (1983). "Crise et investissement international." *Revue Economique,* 34(5):926-970.

Madigan, R. (1984). "Australia and Asia in the 1980s." In B. Catley (Ed.), *Australia and Asia: Towards New Horizons.* Adelaide: Australian Institute of International Affairs.

Magaziner, I., and R. Reich. (1982). *Minding America's Business.* New York: Harper and Row.

Mandel, E. (1962). *Marxist Economic Theory* (vols. 1 and 2). New York and London: Monthly Review Press.

Marshall, G. (1984). "On the Sociology of Women's Unemployment. Its Neglect and Significance." *The Sociological Review,* 32(2):234-259.

Marx, K. (1906). *Capital: A Critique of Political Economy* (Samuel Moore and Edward Aveling, Trans., from German 3rd ed.). New York: Modern Library.

Marx, K. (1955). *The Poverty of Philosophy.* Moscow: Progress.

Marx, K. (1963). *Theories of Surplus Value, Part I.* Moscow: Progress.

McAleese, D. (1977). *A Profile of Grant-Aided Industry in Ireland.* Dublin: Industrial Development Authority.

McCawley, P. (1983). "Australia's Miconceptions of ASEAN." In P. Dibb (Ed.), *Australia's External Relations in the 1980s: The Interaction of Economic, Political and Strategic Factors.* Canberra: Croom Helm.

McCormack, G. (1983). *Cold War, Hot War: An Australian Perspective on the Korean War.* Sydney: Hale and Iremouger.

McCracken, P., et al. (1977). *Towards Full Employment and Price Stability.* A report to the OECD by a group of independent experts. Paris: OECD.

McDermott, P. (1979). "Multinational Manufacturing and Regional Development." *Scottish Journal of Political Economy,* 26(2):287-306.

McMichael, P. (1981). "Redivisions of World Labour and Australian State Formation." Nathan: Griffith University, Conference on Economy Organization and Society. Mimeo.

McQueen, H. (1982). *Gone Tomorrow: Australia in the 1980s.* Sydney: Angus and Robertson.

Meek, R. L. (1956). *Studies in the Labor Theory of Value.* New York and London: Monthly Review Press.

Meenenm, J. (1972). *The Irish Economy Since 1922.* Liverpool: Liverpool University Press.

Merritt, G. (1982). *World Out of Work.* London: Collins Books.

Michalet, C. A. (1974). "France." In R. Vernon (Ed.), *Big Business and the State: Changing Relations in Western Europe.* Cambridge: Harvard University Press.

Michalet, C. A. (1976). "The International Transfer of Technology and the Multinational Enterprise." *Development and Change,* 7(2):157-174.

Michalet, C. A., M. Delapierre, B. Madeuf, and C. Ominami. (1983). *Nationalisations et internationalisations: strategies des multinationales françaises dans la crise.* Paris: Maspero.

Millar, T. B. (1977). *Australia in Peace and War.* Canberra: Australian National University Press.

Miller, J. D. B. (1980). "Economic Choices and Chances." In C. Bell (Ed.), *Agenda for the Eighties.* Canberra: Australian National University Press.

Miller, J. D. B. (1982). "The Politics Economics Nexus." In C. Bell (Ed.), *Academic Studies and International Politics.* Canberra: Canberra Studies in World Affairs, No. 6.

Ministerie van Economische Zaken. (1984). "Flexibele Productie-Automatiseringstechnologie. Japan zoekt toekomst in onbemande fabrieken." *Technieuws/Tokyo,* February 9.

Mollenkopf, J. (1983). *The Contested City.* Princeton: Princeton University Press.

Moore, B. (1972). *Reflections on the Causes of Human Misery.* Boston: Beacon Press.

Moran, T. (1974). *Multinational Corporations and the Politics of Dependence.* Princeton: Princeton University Press.

Moran, T. (1978). "Multinational Corporations and Dependency: A Dialogue for Dependentistas and Non-Dependentistas." *International Organization,* 32(1):79-100. Special issue edited by James A. Caporaso.

Mueller, D. C. (1979). *Public Choice.* Cambridge: Cambridge University Press.

Mulvey, C., and W. K. Norris. (1984). *Labour Market Efficiency in Australia.* Canberra: Bureau of Labour Market Research, Monograph No. 9, Australian Government Publishing Service.

Mytelka, L. K. (1978). "Technological Dependence in the Andean Group." *International Organization,* 32(1):101-140.

Mytelka, L. K. (1979). *Regional Development in a Global Economy: The Multinational Corporation, Technology and Andean Integration.* New Haven: Yale University Press.

Mytelka, L K. (1982). "In Search of a Partner: The State and the Textile Industry in France." In S. Cohen & P. A. Gourevitch (Eds.), *France in a Troubled World Economy,* pp. 132-150. United Kingdom: Butterworth.

Mytelka, L. K., and R. Mahon. (1983). "Industry, the State and the New Protectionism: Textiles in Canada and France." *International Organization,* 37(4):551-582.

Nasar, S. (1984). "Good News Ahead for Productivity." *Fortune,* December 10, pp. 30-41.

Nash, J. (1983). "The Impact of the Changing International Divison of Labor in Different Sectors of the Labor Force." In J. Nash and M. P. Fernandez-Kelly (Eds.), *Women, Men and the International Divison of Labor.* Albany, NY: State University of New York Press.

National Economic and Social Council (NESC, Ireland).

NESC. (1976). *Prelude to Planning.* #26 (October).

NESC. (1980). *Industrial Policy and Development.* #56 (December).

NESC. (1982). *A Review of Industrial Policy.* #64 (February).
National Science Foundation. (1981). *Science Indicators—1980.* Washington, DC: National Science Board, NSB-081-1.
Newfarmer, R. (1980). *Transnational Conglomerates and the Economics of Dependent Development: A Case Study of the International Electrical Oligopoly and Brazil's Electrical Industry.* Greenwich, CT: Jai Press.
Nicholas, R. (1983). "Misperception and Muddled Thinking in Australian-ASEAN Relations." *Contemporary Southeast Asia,* 5(2):153-71.
Noble, D. (1979). "Social Change In Machine Design: The Case of Automatically Controlled Machine Tools," in A. Zimbalist (ed.). *Case Studies in the Labour Process.* New York: Monthly Review.
Nora, S., and A. Minc. (1981). *The Computerisation of Society.* Cambridge: MIT Press. Press.
Nordhaus, W. (1974). "The Falling Share of Profits." *Brookings Papers On Economic Activity,* 1:169-208.
Oakley, A. (1981). *Subject Women.* New York: Pantheon Books.
Odell, J. (1982). *U.S. International Monetary Policy.* Princeton: Princeton University Press.
O'Donnell, G. (1973). *Modernization and Bureaucratic Authoritarianism: Studies in South American Politics.* Berkeley, CA: Institute of International Studies.
OECD. (1979). *Interfutures: Facing the Future.* Paris: Organization for Economic Cooperation and Development.
OECD. (1981). "Group of Experts on Economic Analysis of Information Activities and the Role of Electronics and Telecommunications Technologies: 5-Microelectronics, Productivity, and Employment." Paris: OECD.
OECD. (1983). *Industrial Robots. Their Role in Manufacturing Industry.* Paris.
OECD. (1984). *OECD Science and Technology Indicators. Resources Devoted to R and D.* Paris.
OECD. (1984). *Trade in High-Technology Products: The Semiconductor Industry: Industrial Structure and Government Policies* (2nd rev.). Paris: OECD, 9 May, DSTI/SPR/83.104.
Offe, C. (1984). In John Keane (Ed.), *Contradictions of the Welfare State.* Cambridge: MIT Press.
Ohlin, B. (1933). *Interregional and International Trade.* Cambridge: Harvard University Press.
Olson, M. (1965). *The Logic of Collective Action.* Cambridge: Harvard University Press.
Orridge, A. (1983). "The Blueshirts and the Economic War: A Study of Ireland in the Context of Dependency Theory." *Political Studies,* 31(3):351-369.
Pahl, R. E. (1984). *Divisions of Labour.* Oxford and New York: Basil Blackwell.
Parasothi, A. (1979). "India's Effort to Build an Autonomous Capacity in Science and Technology." *Development Dialogue,* 1:2.
Perkins, J. O. N. (1979). *Australia in the World Economic.* Melbourne: Sun Books.
Perlmutter, A. (1981). *Modern Authoritarianism: A Comparative Institutional Analysis.* New Haven and London: Yale University Press.
Ping, H. K. (n.d.). *The Implications of Export-Oriented Industrialisation for Southeast Asia.* Canberra. Mimeo.

Plaschke, H. (1975). "International Sub-contracting." *Instant Research on Peace and Violence,* 2:88-97.

Ploch, M. (1983). "Industry Invests in Research Centres." *High Technology,* (May):15-17.

Poynter, T., and A. Rugman. (1982). "World Product Mandates: How Will Multinationals Respond?" *Business Quarterly,* (Autumn):54-61.

Prebisch, R. (1971). *Latin America: A Problem in Development.* Austin, TX: University of Texas Press.

Przeworski, A. (1980). "Material Interests, Class Compromise, and the Transition to Socialism." *Politics and Society,* 10(2):125-154.

Putnam, R. D. (1976). *The Comparative Study of Political Elites.* NJ: Prentice-Hall.

Raasch, S. (1985). *Frauenarbeit in der Bekleidungsproduktion: Veränderungen der internationalen Arbeitsteilung durch Einsatz neuer Technologien?* Paper submitted at the seminar "Vom Verhältnis von Politik und Ökonomie im internationalen System" at the University of Osnabrück, 17/18 May.

Rada, J. (1981). "The Microelectronics Revolution: Implications for the Third World." *Development Dialogue,* 3:1.

Rada, J. (1985). "Information Technology and the Third World." In T. Forester (Ed.), *The Information Technology Revolution,* pp. 571-589. Oxford: Basil Blackwell, Ltd.

Ramsey, A. (1985). "The Cowards of Asia." *National Times,* February 1-7, p. 33.

Report of the Committee to Review Australia's Relations with the Third World. (1979). Canberra: Australian Government Publishing Service.

Report of the Committee to Review the Australian Overseas Aid Programme. (1984). Canberra: Australian Government Publishing Service.

Report of the Joint Committee on Foreign Affairs and Defence. (1984). *Australia and ASEAN: Challenges and Opportunities.* Parliament of the Commonwealth of Australia, Canberra: Australian Government Publishing Service.

Report of the Senate Standing Committee on Foreign Affairs and Defence. (1980). *The New International Economic Order: Implications for Australia.* Parliament of the Commonwealth of Australia, Canberra: Australian Government Publishing Service.

Resnick, S., J. Sinisi, and R. Wolff. (1985). "Class Analysis of International Relations." In Ladd Hollist and LaMond Tullis (Eds.), *An International Political Economy.* Boulder, CO: Westview Press.

Ricardo, D. (1973). *The Principles of Political Economy and Taxation.* London and Toronto: Everyman's Library.

Rix, A. (1982). "Australia and Japan." In P. J. Boyce and J. Angel (Eds.), *Independence and Alliance: Australia in World Affairs 1976-80.* Sydney: Allen and Unwin.

Robinson, J. (1979). *Aspects of Development and Underdevelopment.* Cambridge: Cambridge University Press.

Robison, R. (1985). "Class, Capital and the State in New Order Indonesia." In R. A. Higgott and R. Robison (Eds.), *Southeast Asia: Essays in the Political Economy of Structural Change.* London: Routledge and Kegan Paul.

Robison, R., and G. Rodan. (1983). "Restructuring Australian Industry: The Case for a More Active State Role." *Discussion Papers in Public Policy,* No. 2. Perth: Murdoch University.

Robison, W. (1985). "Imperialism, Dependency and Industrialisation: The Case of Japan in Indonesia." In R. A. Higgott and R. Robison (Eds.), *Southeast Asia: Essays in the Political Economy of Structural Change.* London: Routledge and Kegan Paul.

Rodan, G. (1985). "Industrialisation and the Singapore State in the Context of the New International Division of Labour." In R. A. Higgott and R. Robison (Eds.), *Southeast Asia: Essays in the Political Economy of Structural Change.* London: Routledge and Kegan Paul.

Rodan, G. (1985). *Singapore's "Second Industrial Revolution": State Intervention and Foreign Investment.* Canberra: ASEAN-Australia Economic Papers, No. 18.

Romeo, A. (1983). "Direct Foreign Investment and Technology Transfer." Paper presented to the SSRC Conference on International Technology Transfer: Concepts, Measures and Comparison. New York: SSRC, 2-3 June.

Roobeek, A. (1984). *Changes in the Structure of the Telecommunications Industry.* Amsterdam: University of Amsterdam, Department of Economics, Research Memorandum No. 8417, July.

Rosenberg, N. (1972). *Technology and American Economic Growth.* New York: M. E. Sharpe.

Rosenberg, N. (1976). *Perspectives on Technology.* Cambridge: Cambridge University Press.

Rosenberg, N. (1982). *Inside the Black Box: Technology and Economics.* Cambridge: Cambridge University Press.

Ross, R., and K. Trachte (1983). "Global Cities and Global Classes: The Peripheralization of Labor in New York City." *Review,* 6(3):393-431.

Samuelson, P. (1948). "International Trade and the Equalization of Factor Prices." *The Economic Journal,* LVIII(230):163-184.

Ruggie, J. G. (Ed.). (1983). *The Antinomies of Interdependence: National Welfare and the International Division of Labor.* New York: Columbia University Press.

Rumberger, R. W., and H. M. Levin. (1984). "Forecasting the Impact of New Job Technologies on the Future Job Market." Project Report No. 84-A4, School of Education, Stanford University, Stanford, CA.

Rutenberg, D. (1982). "International Operations Management: Global Product Mandating." In K. C. Dhawan, H. Etemad, and R. Wright (Eds.), *International Business: A Canadian Perspective,* pp. 588-598. Don Mills, Ont.: Addision-Wesley.

Sarvasy, W., and J. Van Allen. (1984). "Fighting the Feminization of Poverty: Socialist-Feminist Analysis and Strategy." *Review of Radical Political Economics,* 16(4):89-110.

Sassen-Koob, S. (1983). "Labor Migrations and the New International Divison of Labor." In J. Nash and M. P. Fernandez-Kelly (Eds.), *Women, Men, and the International Division of Labor,* pp. 175-204. Albany, NY: State University of New York Press.

Schultze, C. L. (1983). "Industrial Policy: A Dissent." *The Brookings Review,* 2 (Fall):3-12.

Schweizerischer Bankverein. (1983). "Ist der Zug abgefahren?" *Der Monat,* (11):21.

Science Council of Canada. (1980). *Multinationals and Industrial Strategy: The Role of World Product Mandates.* Ottawa: Minister of Supply and Services.

Scutt, J. (Ed.). (1985). *Poor Nation of the Pacific: Australia's Future?* Sydney: Allen and Unwin.

Secombe, W. (1974). "The Housewife and Her Labour Under Capitalism." *New Left Review,* (83):3-24.

Sekaly, R. (1981). *Transnationalization of the Automobile Industry.* Ottawa: University of Ottawa Press.

SEST. (1984). *Les Bonzai de l'industrie japonaise: elements de reflexion sur l'integration de la technologie dans la fonction strategique des entreprises japonaises.* Paris: SEST/CPE Ministère de la recherche et de l'industrie, mai.

Sharpston, M. (1975). "International Subcontracting." *Oxford Economic Papers,* (New Series) 27:94-135.

Shaw, T. M. (1982). "Beyond Neocolonialism: Varieties of Corporatism in Africa." *Journal of Modern African Studies,* 20(2):239-61.

Sirianni, C. J. (1984). "Justice and the Divison of Labour: A Reconsideration of Durkeim's *Division of Labour in Society.*" 32(3):449-470.

Smith, A. (1970). *The Wealth of Nations.* Middlesex, England: Penguin Books.

Smith, T. (1979). *The Pattern of Imperialism.* Cambridge: Cambridge University Press.

Sopiee, N. (1984). "Australia and ASEAN: Down the Road to Disengagement." Kuala Lumpur: Institute for Strategic and International Studies.

Souter, K. (1983). "Australia and the Third World." *Third World Quarterly,* 5(4):861-73.

Spero, J. (1985). *The Politics of International Economic Relations.* London: Allen and Unwin.

Staniland, M. (1985). *What is Political Economy?* New Haven: Yale University Press.

Statistics Canada. (1984). *Industrial Research and Development Statistics 1982.* Ottawa: Minister of Supply and Services. June Catalogue 88-2-2.

Steed, G. (1982). *Threshold Firms Backing Canada's Winners.* Ottawa: Science Council of Canada Background Study No. 48.

Stephens, E. H., and J. Stephens. (1983). "Democratic Socialism in Dependent Capitalism: An Analysis of the Manley Government in Jamaica." *Politics and Society,* 12(3):373-411.

Stewart, F., and J. James. (1982). *The Economics of New Technology in Developing Countries.* London: Frances Pinter.

Stockwin, J. A. A. (Ed.). (1972). *Japan and Australia in the Seventies.* Melbourne: Angus and Robertson.

Stohl, M. (1982). "The United States and the New International Economic Order: Domestic and International Interests and Consequences." Mimeo. West Lafayette, IN: Purdue University.

Stout, D. (1980). "The Impact of Technology on Economic Growth In the 1980s." *Daedelus,* 109(1):159-168.

Strange, S. (Ed.). (1985). *Paths to International Political Economy.* London: Allen and Unwin.

Sung-Joo, H. (1983). *Pacific Economic Co-operation: The Next Phase.* Jakarta: Centre for Strategic and International Studies.

Sunkel, O. (n.d.). "Dependence and Structural Heterogeneity." Sussex, England: Institute for Development Studies.

Sweeney, J. (1973). "Foreign Companies in Ireland." *Studies,* 62:267.

Technische Hilfen. (1983). *Technische Hilfen für industrielle Arbeitsplätze. Entwicklungen, Einsatzfälle, Auswirkungen.* Düsseldorf: VDI-Verlag.

Terkl, S. (1978). "The Shirt Off Your Back." Movie documentary. *Inside Europe*.

Tisdell, C. (1985). "Technological Change and Transfer in the Pacific: The Position of Australia and Japan." *Australian Outlook: The Australian Journal of International Affairs*, 39(1):39-43.

Todaro, M. P. (1977). *Economic Development in the Third World*. New York and London: Longman.

Todd, J. (1982). "The Politics of the Public Service: Some Implications of Recent Theories of the State for the Analysis of Administrative Systems." *European Journal of Political Research*, 10(4):353-366.

Uchida, T., et al. (1983). "Forecast of Growth Potential and Factors Influencing Asian Development." In T. Haseyama et al., *Two Decades of Asian Development and the Outlook for the 1980s*. Tokyo: Institute for Developing Economies.

UNCTAD. (1978). *Electronics in Developing Countries: Issues in Transfer and Development of Technology*. Geneva: UNCTAD, Doc. no. TD/B/C.6/34.

UNIDO. (1984). *International Industrial Restructuring and the International Division of Labour in the Automotive Industry*. Prepared by P. O'Brien and F. Lobo Aleu. Vienna: UNIDO, Doc. No. UNIDO/IS.472.

United Nations. (1983). *Annual Review of Engineering Industries and Automation 1981*. ECE/ENG.AUT/10. Geneva: Economic Commission for Europe.

United Nations. (1985). *Production and Use of Industrial Robots*. New York: Economic Commission for Europe.

U.S. Government Printing Office. (1981). *Economic Report of the President*. Washington, DC: U.S. Government Printing Office.

Vaitsos, C. (1974). *Intercountry Income Distribution and Transnational Enterprises*. Oxford: Clarendon Press.

Vaitsos, C. (1976). "The Revisions of the International Patent System." *World Development*, 4(2):85-102.

Vernon, R. (1966). "International Investment and International Trade in the Product Cycle." *Quarterly Journal of Economics*, 80:190-207.

Vilamil, J. (1978). "Puerto Rico 1948-76: The Limits of Dependent Growth." In Jose Vilamil (Ed.), *Transnational Capitalism and National Development*. New Jersey: Humanities Press.

Viorst, M. (1985). "Israel Faces Its Economic Woes." *The Nation*, 16 March, 4(10):300-306.

Vital, D. (1967). *The Inequality of States*. Oxford: Clarendon Press.

Wad, A. (1982). "Microelectronics: Implications and Strategies for the Third World." *Third World Quarterly*, IV(4) (October):677-697.

Wallerstein, I. (1974). *The Modern World System: Capitalist Agriculture and the Origins of the European World Economy in the Sixteenth Century*. New York: Academic Press.

Walzer, M. (1984). "Liberalism and the Art of Separation." *Political Theory*, 12(3):315-330.

Warr, P. G. (1983). "Structural Effects of Increasing Australia's Imports from LDCs." *Discussion Paper 72*. Canberra: Australian National University, Centre for Economic Policy Research.

Warren, Bill. (1982). *Imperialism: Pioneer of Capitalism*. London: New Left Books.

Weber, M. (1946). "Bureaucracy." In H. H. Gerth and C. W. Mills (Eds.), *From Max Weber: Essays in Sociology*. New York: Oxford University Press.

Weber, M. (1958). *The Protestant Ethic and the Spirit of Capitalism.* New York: Charles Scribner's Sons.

Whitlam, E. G. (1981). *A Pacific Community.* Cambridge: Harvard University Press.

Widl, G. (1982). "Situation am Markt." In T. Martin (Ed.), *Neuer Förderimpuls auf dem Gebiet Industrieroboter. Ergebnisse eines Fachgespräches.* Karlsruhe: Kernforschungszentrum Karlsruhe.

Willis, P. E. (1977). *Learning to Labour: How Working Class Kids Get Working Class Jobs.* England: Saxon House.

World Bank. (1984). *World Development Report.* New York: Oxford University Press.

Wright, E. O. (1979). *Class, Crisis, and the State.* London: New Left Books.

Yonemoto, K. (1982). "Robotisation in Japanese Industries." In *Microelectronics, Robotics and Jobs,* ICCP 7:235-245. Paris: OECD.

Zysman, J. (1977). *Political Strategies for Industrial Order.* Berkeley, CA: University of California Press.

Zysman, J. (1983). *Governments, Markets and Growth: Financial Systems and the Politics of Industrial Change.* Ithaca, NY: Cornell University Press.

Index